Baptists in Canada

 McMaster Divinity College Press
**McMaster Ministry Studies Series,
Volume 5**

Baptists in Canada

Their History and Polity

By
GORDON L. HEATH,
DALLAS FRIESEN,
AND
TAYLOR MURRAY

FOREWORD BY
MICHAEL A. G. HAYKIN

◕PICKWICK *Publications* · Eugene, Oregon

BAPTISTS IN CANADA
Their History and Polity

McMaster Ministry Studies Series, Volume 5
McMaster Divinity College Press

Copyright © 2020 Gordon L. Heath, Dallas Friesen, and Taylor Murray. All rights reserved. Except for brief quotations in critical publications or reviews, no part of this book may be reproduced in any manner without prior written permission from the publisher. Write: Permissions, Wipf and Stock Publishers, 199 W. 8th Ave., Suite 3, Eugene, OR 97401.

Pickwick Publications
An Imprint of Wipf and Stock Publishers
199 W. 8th Ave., Suite 3
Eugene, OR 97401

McMaster Divinity College Press
1280 Main Street West
Hamilton, Ontario, Canada
L8S 4K1

www.wipfandstock.com

PAPERBACK ISBN: 978-1-5326-8931-4
HARDCOVER ISBN: 978-1-5326-8932-1
EBOOK ISBN: 978-1-5326-8933-8

Cataloguing-in-Publication data:

Names: Heath, Gordon L., author. | Friesen, Dallas, author. | Murray, Taylor, author.

Title: Baptists in Canada : their history and polity / by Gordon L. Heath, Dallas Friesen, and Taylor Murray.

Description: Eugene, OR: Pickwick Publications, 2020. | McMaster Ministry Studies Series 5. | Includes bibliographical references and index.

Identifiers: ISBN 978-1-5326-8931-4 (paperback). | ISBN 978-1-5326-8932-1 (hardcover).| ISBN 978-1-5326-8933-8 (ebook).

Subjects: LCSH: Baptists--Canada--History. | Baptists--Canada--Polity. | Church history.

Classification: BX6251 M37 2020 (print). | BX6251 (ebook).

12/11/20

Contents

Foreword by Michael A. G. Haykin | vii
Introduction | ix

1 History of Baptists Around the World | 1
2 The Arrival and Growth of Baptists in Canada | 25
3 Baptists and Others: Cohesion, Divergence, and Distinctives | 81
4 Church Membership: A Believer's Church | 101
5 Church Ordinances: Baptism and Communion | 113
6 Church Governance and Issues of Authority | 130
7 Religious Liberty | 148
8 Baptists and the Future | 165

Appendix A: Baptist Landscape in Canada in 2020 | 177
Appendix B: Writing Your Local Church's History | 179
Appendix C: Baptist Distinctives in Canada Comparison | 184
Appendix D: Photographs | 186

Bibliography | 197
Index of Subjects | 217
Index of Names | 229

Foreword

WHAT STRUCK ME FORCEFULLY as I read through this account of Baptist history and polity as it has unfolded in the geographical context of Canada is the way in which the radical vision of the seventeenth-century English Baptists has shaped Canadian Baptist life down to the present day. The determination of the men and women of that distant world to create or, if you wish, to restore New Testament-like congregations that were free from the rule of the state so as to obey the radical call of the gospel of Jesus Christ has influenced profoundly the way Baptists have done church in Canada. Again and again, phoenix-like, Baptist thinking from that early period of the modern world has borne fruit in later Baptist history. And this is a key reason why a book like this needs to have been written: we Baptists need to both know our history and appreciate its ongoing impact on us.

Some forty-five years ago, when I first started attending Stanley Avenue Baptist church in Hamilton, Ontario—a daughter church of James Street Baptist Church—I asked one of the deacons of the church about the origins of the Baptists. "Where have Baptists come from?" I asked him. I have always loved history and wrongly assumed that he, as an office-bearer in the church, would have an answer for me. He did not, beyond assuring me that Baptists were Bible-people. As this book shows, such biblicism has indeed been an ever-recurring mark of Baptist life, but as this book also reveals, there is much more to Baptist history that this deacon could have told me. He needed this book! Our identity as modern-day Baptists is deeply bound up with the structures and thinking of past Baptists, which is a good thing in so many ways, even as Jesus

Foreword

assured his disciples in John 4:38: "others have labored, and you have benefited from their labor" (HCSB).

Yet, the other characteristic of Baptist life that this new study of the Canadian Baptist scene forcefully brings home is the way in which Baptists are far from being monochromatic. While they share common roots in the seventeenth-century English Baptist world, the development of the various Baptist communities in this nation has revealed a pattern as multi-coloured as Joseph's famous coat. Part of the freedom that comes with Baptist autonomy has been the freedom for Canadian Baptist congregations to be different from one another as they have sought to apply and interpret the scriptures in their varied contexts across this large geographical expanse. And, of course, this freedom has also carried with it a burden, even responsibility, to be different from the surrounding culture. Given current trends in Western culture to sideline, even reject, Christian thinking and ethics, this "courage to be a minority," as twentieth-century Baptist historian Jarold Zeman once put it so well, will need to be a vital part of Baptist life in the decades to come.

Michael A. G. Haykin

Introduction

VIRTUALLY EVERYONE THAT GOES through the process of ordination in a Canadian Baptist church has to read Harry Renfree's *Heritage and Horizon: The Baptist Story in Canada* at some stage of the process.[1] There are many good things about Renfree's work, and it has served as a valuable resource for ministry practitioners and researchers alike; however, it is now over thirty years old, and much has happened during that time! After some discussion a few years ago, we concluded that there was a need for fresh voices and an updated history. This book is the result of that conversation.

In this volume, we sought to avoid an old-school triumphalist, polemical, or parochial history and theology of Baptists in Canada. We recognize that Baptists are divided by region, ethnicity, history, and theology, yet we also recognize that, in spite of the differences, they do share a common tradition of holding to "Baptist distinctives." We also acknowledge that Baptists share a great deal with Christians from other traditions. With those realities in mind, our aim was to produce a volume that was up-to-date, fair, and charitable, yet also informative, insightful, and even challenging. Our desire is that it provides a sense of the ethos, pathos, and logos of the movement as it has grown and evolved in Canada, and perhaps even a sense of future possibilities for Baptists in the twenty-first century. You the reader will decide if we have accomplished that purpose.

Of course, there are other works to attend to for a more complete view of Baptist life and thought. There are a number of excellent

1. Renfree, *Heritage and Horizon*.

Introduction

collections of primary sources,² but at the moment, the second edition of William Brackney's *Baptist Life and Thought* (1998) is the only published source that includes Canadian Baptist material from across the country.³ The Baptist Heritage in Atlantic Canada series has published a number of other, regionally-specific primary sources, including early journals from pioneer Baptists and New Lights in the late-eighteenth- and early-nineteenth-century Maritime Provinces.⁴

In addition to these sources, there have been a few studies that trace the history of Baptists across the country. The first attempt at a national history was E. R. Fitch's *Baptists of Canada* (1911) and the second was the abovementioned Renfree's *Heritage and Horizon* (1988).⁵ Much more commonly, however, regional studies dealing with the different Baptist communities in their respective contexts have dominated the historiography for a long time. The twin difficulties of regionalism and divisions based on cultural and theological circumstances have, according to David Priestley, been partially to blame for leaving Baptist historiography in Canada "in search of cohesion for its story."⁶ While these regional studies are important and continue to find an audience, the last forty years have seen an impressive output of scholarly research related to Baptists in Canada that is intentionally national in scope and consciously engages the different Baptist communities across the country.⁷ Various conferences held throughout Canada from the 1970s to the 1990s supplemented this material,⁸ and the recent Canadian Baptist Historical Society series has

---

2. For instance, McBeth, *A Sourcebook for Baptist Heritage*; Parker, *Baptists in Europe*.

3. Brackney, ed., *Baptist Life and Thought*, 474–528.

4. Levy, ed., *The Diary of Joseph Dimock*; Bell, ed., *Newlight Baptist Journals of James Manning and James Innis*; and Robertson and Robertson, eds., *Memoir of Mrs. Eliza Ann Chipman*. The series also published important primary sources relating to the region's revivalist history, including Beverley and Moody, eds., *The Journal of Henry Alline*; Cuthbertson, ed., *The Journal of John Payzant*; Rawlyk, ed. *New Light Letters and Songs*; and Rawlyk, ed., *The Sermons of Henry Alline*. While most of the primary source material was from the late eighteenth and early nineteenth era, they also published a few works from the twentieth century, including Murray, ed., *"Through Him who Strengthens Me"*; and Zeman, ed., *Open Doors*.

5. Fitch, *The Baptists of Canada*; and Renfree, *Heritage and Horizon*.

6. Priestley, "Canadian Baptist Historiography," 76–77.

7. For lists of sources related to Baptist history and thought in Canada, see Griffin-Allwood, et al., *Baptists in Canada* and Murray, "Against 'Historical Amnesia,'" 77–113.

8. Zeman, ed., *Baptists in Canada*; Zeman, ed., *Costly Vision*; Ford, ed., *Canadian Baptist History and Polity*; Dekar and Ford, eds., *Celebrating the Baptist Heritage*;

Introduction

sought to continue this national conversation.[9] Other relatively recent studies have provided a national look at particular branches of the Baptist family in Canada, such as the Fellowship of Evangelical Baptist Churches in Canada[10] and the Canadian Baptist Federation (now Canadian Baptist Ministries).[11]

Finally, a number of recent works place Baptists in the larger context of the global movement. The trend started decades ago with H. Leon McBeth's *The Baptist Heritage* (1987), but more recently a number of excellent works have further developed this focus: David W. Bebbington's *Baptists Through the Centuries: A History of a Global People* (2010); Robert E. Johnson's *A Global Introduction to Baptist Churches* (2010), and Anthony L. Chute, Nathan A. Finn, and Michael A. G. Haykin's *The Baptist Story: From English Sect to Global Movement* (2015).[12]

This book functions in three sections. In the first, we look at the history of the Baptists (both on a global scale and in Canada), in the second we address issues of polity, and in the third we turn briefly to the future. It is intended as an introduction to each of these areas from a Baptist perspective in Canada. It should also be noted that there is no denominational imprimatur on this work. What we say is what *we* think, and what you find in these pages is not the "official" position of any denomination.

A note of thanks to David Bebbington, Callum Jones, Melody Maxwell, Pat Townsend, Paul R. Wilson, and Robert S. Wilson. All six were kind enough to read the manuscript and provide insightful comments and clarifications. Their collegial spirit and willingness to do so in the midst of their own obligations models the ideals of the academy. Of course, any mistakes or omissions in the text are ours alone. Thanks, also, to Michael A. G. Haykin for writing the foreword. His expertise on this subject is widely known, and a word from him is an honour.

Adam McCulloch, archivist at the Canadian Baptist Archives, and Pat Townsend, archivist at the Atlantic Baptist Archives, played key roles in finding sources and pictures. Adam Rudy and Dudley Brown,

---

Rawlyk, *Canadian Baptists and Christian Higher Education*; and Priestley, ed., *Memory and Hope*.

9. Heath and Wilson, eds., *Baptists in Public Life in Canada*; Heath and Haykin, eds., *Baptists and War*; Bowler, ed., *Canadian Baptist Women*.

10. Haykin and Lockey, eds. *A Glorious Fellowship of Churches*.

11. Bentall, *From Sea to Sea*.

12. McBeth, *The Baptist Heritage*; Bebbington, *Baptists Through the Centuries*; Johnson, *A Global Introduction to Baptist Churches*; Chute, et al, *The Baptist Story*.

xi

Introduction

Graduate Assistants at McMaster Divinity College, were also an invaluable help finding sources, formatting the manuscript, and compiling the indexes. David Fuller, Managing Editor of McMaster Divinity College Press, helpfully guided us through this process. Thanks to all for your assistance.

We say thank you to our families. Their support for our pursuit of this project is deeply appreciated.

Finally, we dedicate this volume to the "unknown Baptist minister":

> "Unknown, yet well known
> Poor, yet making many rich
> Having nothing, yet possessing all things"[13]

---

13. "The Unknown Baptist Minister" is the name of a sculpture at McMaster Divinity College (see the picture in Appendix D). The words quoted here hang alongside the sculpture and are from 2 Cor 6:9–10 (KJV).

1

History of Baptists Around the World

IT TOOK A SIGNIFICANT amount of courage to be a Baptist in the 1600s. One had to be willing, for example, to spend time in prison for one's convictions, for the first Baptists had a revolutionary, radical, and illegal vision for the church: they sought a church comprised of believers only. Baptists believed in baptizing adults who made a profession of faith, rather than baptizing infants who could not, and they believed that only such baptized believers were to be members of the church. They also rejected the Church of England's episcopal hierarchy and instead ran their churches on a congregational model of church governance that left all decisions in the hands of each local congregation. They were groundbreaking and outspoken advocates of religious freedom; while the state was necessary in civil matters, it was to have absolutely no say in the governance of the church. More specifically, it was not to enforce orthodoxy or conformity to the Church of England and it was to remain aloof from the local church's internal matters. It has sometimes been called a voluntary religion, for a person voluntarily seeks membership in a local church, a local church voluntarily associates with other Baptist churches, and members and churches voluntarily work together on various mission projects.[1] Baptist churches in geographical proximity chose to work with one another in an organization called associations, and, in subsequent centuries, a group of associations often formed a union, convention, or fellowship. A Baptist church did not have to join an association, but most did. They were not inherently pacifists like Anabaptists or Quakers, nor

---

1. Brackney, *The Baptists*, 71.

did they necessarily have qualms about trying to influence the laws of the land (e.g., Sabbath laws).[2]

THEORIES OF ORIGINS

But where did Baptists come from? Was it a brand-new movement birthed in the seventeenth century, or was it a more ancient tradition with roots going back to the early church founded by Christ and the apostles? These are not superfluous questions, for there have been a number of novelties in Christian history that were significant departures from apostolic teaching and tradition, and it is important to weigh any new movement carefully. In general, Baptists have been quite aware of the fact that their movement arose in the early 1600s, and have sought by various means and degrees of success to address the issue of origins. The following briefly outlines the three most common ways in which Baptists have sought to do just that.[3]

Unbroken Line to the Apostles (or Successionism)

A variety of attempts have been made to trace Baptist origins back to the New Testament by claiming kinship with an array of sectarian and persecuted groups such as Montanists, Waldensians, and Albigensians, maintaining that such groups were proto-Baptists of sorts. The oft-referenced booklet *The Trail of Blood* (1931) by James Milton Carroll is an example of one of the most popular attempts to trace this supposed ancient lineage; in it, a timeline chart with bright red dots through the centuries portraying a striking and continuous connection with the past, which shows readers that Baptists were indeed an ancient and legitimate—and superior—form of Christianity.[4] Another example of making links to the past through martyrs is visible in the front pages of Henry Vedder's *A Short History of the Baptists* (1907). One page in particular is dedicated to a beautiful colour image of the early church martyr Perpetua; of course,

---

2. Cross, "Baptists, Peace, and War," 1–31.

3. For helpful evaluations of theories of origins, see Leonard, *The Challenge of Being Baptist*, ch.2; Cross and Wood, eds. *Exploring Baptist Origins*.

4. The full title is *The Trail of Blood: Following the Christians Down through the Centuries—or, The History of Baptist Churches from the Time of Christ, Their Founder, to the Present Day.*

setting the stage for a narrative of Baptist continuity with a long illustrious pedigree of martyrs. The need for such links was to bolster the legitimacy of a relatively new movement, and to buttress claims of being the New Testament church. The weakness of such an argument was that the individuals and groups identified as "Baptist" had little, if anything, in common with seventeenth-century Baptists except for their being persecuted.

The Influence of Anabaptists

Others identify Baptist origins with the Anabaptists of the sixteenth century. In the maelstrom of the sixteenth-century Reformation(s) there arose a group of leaders quite unlike Lutheran, Calvinist, and Church of England reformers.[5] Those leaders believed that iconic figures such as Martin Luther, Ulrich Zwingli, John Calvin, and John Knox had done commendable work in purging the church of much of medieval Catholicism, but their criticism was that Protestantism had not gone far enough. Their call was for a further purging of the church of any remaining medieval corruptions. Two of the most significant reforms of Anabaptists were their calls to practice believers' baptism and pacifism, two convictions they deemed to be the position of Jesus and the earliest Christians. Anabaptists were called many things in their day, mostly derogatory. Walter Klaassen has stated that "By its enemies Anabaptism was regarded as a dangerous movement—a program for the violent destruction of Europe's religious and social institutions. Its practices were regarded as odd and anti-social, its beliefs as devil-inspired heresy."[6] Heinrich Bullinger called them "devilish enemies and destroyers of the church of God," and Calvin called them "fanatics," "deluded," "scatterbrains," "asses," "scoundrels," and "mad dogs."[7] More kindly, that trajectory of reform is often called the "Radical" stream of the Reformation, and the movement "Anabaptists."[8]

The pertinent question for researchers today is just how much or to what degree English Baptists drew upon Anabaptist theology and

---

5. Key Anabaptist leaders were Menno Simons (c. 1496–1561), Thomas Müntzer (c. 1490–1525), Balthasar Hubmaier (c. 1480–1528), Jacob Hutter (c. 1500–1536), Conrad Grebel (c. 1498–1526), and Felix Mantz (c. 1500–1527).

6. Klaassen, *Anabaptist*, 1.

7. George, *Theology of the Reformers*, 252.

8. The term "Anabaptist" means "rebaptizer." The movement was diverse, but a good starting point for Anabaptist theology is the *Schleitheim Confession* (1527).

polity—especially notions of baptism and church governance.[9] It is clear that Baptists rejected much of what the Anabaptists rejected, and embraced much of what they embraced. This alone has led some historians and theologians to emphasize the Baptists' Anabaptist roots. The issues are too complex to deal with here in such a short space,[10] but suffice it to say that actual personal contact between early Baptists and Anabaptists, as well as similarities in theology, suggest at minimum an Anabaptist influence on early Baptist thought. However, Baptists were not Anabaptists, for, among other things, they were neither pacifists nor were they adverse to serving as magistrates or soldiers. Also, unlike Anabaptists who were primarily from the continent, the first Baptists were Separatists from the Church of England, which has led many to conclude that the most significant factor in Baptist origins is to be found in England.

English Separatists

The basic argument of this position is that, besides the fact that the first Baptists were all English Separatists, virtually everything within seventeenth-century Baptist theology and polity can be found in English Separatism.[11] The Reformation in Britain was long and unsure, with the Protestant cause only made certain by the "Glorious Revolution" of 1688.[12] Many Anglicans had been disheartened by Queen Elizabeth's proposal of a *Via Media*, and wanted further reforms in the church to weed out any remaining vestiges of "Romish" doctrine and practice.[13] There were many who wanted to further purify the Church of England,

---

9. Richard J. Mouw calls debates between Baptists and Anabaptists "an intra-family argument." He goes on to say that "These disputes reach a high intensity because the differences between the two groups are of a more intimate character than are the arguments of either group with, say, the Lutherans or the Catholics." See Mouw, "Reflections on My Encounter with the Anabaptist-Mennonite Tradition."

10. For a helpful study on the Anabaptist links with Baptists, see Bebbington, *Baptists Through the Centuries*, chapter 3.

11. In this context, a Separatist was a person who wanted to separate from the Church of England.

12. Britain has had a Protestant monarch ever since.

13. The *Via Media* ("middle way"), or the Elizabethan Settlement, was a compromise to gain the support of the large middle, moderate, portion of the population.

and those who eventually separated from the Church of England were Separatists.[14]

Arguing Baptist origins from English Separatists rather than Anabaptists relies on a number of factors: early Baptists denied they were Anabaptists; Baptists rejected many aspects of Anabaptist life; almost all Baptists were Separatists before becoming Baptists; Baptist views were a logical outcome of Separatist thinking; and when John Smyth moved towards the Anabaptists he was rejected by the Baptist remnant that returned to England (under Thomas Helwys' leadership). To argue for Baptist origins from English Separatists is not to ignore similarities between Baptists and Anabaptists, for they seem obvious. It is, however, to argue that the Baptist movement was first and foremost a movement derived from English reformers' discontent with the pace of reform in the Church of England. And that is the position of the following brief survey of Baptist birth and growth.

BIRTH AND GROWTH IN THE ANGLOPHONE WORLD

Britain

The medieval world was crumbling in the sixteenth century, partly because of the religious revolution occurring in Western Christendom.[15] Early seventeenth-century England was still reeling from the impact of the Protestant Reformation that began in the previous century with the German monk and theologian Martin Luther. Various streams of reform took root in Germany, Scandinavia, Switzerland, Holland, as well as parts of eastern Europe and Britain. The Protestant cause in England had waxed and waned under the various monarchs: advancing under Henry VIII (1491–1547) and Edward VI (1547–1553), retreating under Mary (1553–1558), and then advancing again under the settlement made by Elizabeth (1558–1603). The arrangement with Elizabeth, however, left a number

---

14. There were many groups that sought to reform the Church of England in the late-sixteenth and early-seventeenth century: "Puritans and Laudians, Presbyterians and Independents, Latitudinarians and High Churchmen" being central to such activity. See Coffey, "Church and State, 1550–1750," chapter 4.

15. Generally speaking, the sixteenth century was when the medieval world transitioned to the early modern world. The birth of the Baptists occurred during this transition.

of reformers discontent, for they had wanted the Church of England to go even further in the reforms and completely eliminate any remaining vestiges of Roman Catholicism. A number of disgruntled members of the reform movements eventually separated from the state-sponsored established church (known as "Separatists"), the most well-known were the Puritans.[16] Facing persecution for their dissent, the ardent reform-minded groups had two options: flee to the continent or to the fledgling Thirteen Colonies, or remain in England to face persecution for trying to bring about the rebirth of what they considered to be the true church.

The origins of the first Baptist churches can be traced back to John Smyth (c. 1570–1612) and the Separatist movement.[17] Smyth has been called "the Baptist pathfinder" and the one who "stands at the fountainhead of consecutive Baptist history."[18] Those churches associated with his ministry are often referred to as General Baptists.[19] In 1586, Smyth entered Christ's College, Cambridge University, in order to prepare for ministry as an Anglican priest. After graduating in 1590, he was invited to stay and teach at Christ's College. He was ordained in 1594. During his time at Cambridge he was influenced by Francis Johnson, a Separatist who later led a Separatist congregation.

At first, Smyth was a moderate Puritan, but his views quickly became more radical. In fact, he spent some time in prison for his outspoken criticisms of the established church. Like others in his day, his language was harsh. He considered many Anglican priests to be "too papist," infant baptism was equated with spiritual adultery, and he was known to rebuke prominent sinners by name from the pulpit. There is not a great deal known about Smyth between 1600 and 1606, but it is certain that he continued to publish his criticisms of the state church.[20] In 1606, Smyth lived in Gainsborough, in Lincolnshire. Smyth was occasionally asked to preach in the church when the minister was away. When the church

16. Their name is derived from their aim to "purify" the church.

17. For further reading on British Baptist history, see Himbury, *British Baptists*; Payne, *The Baptist Union*; and Hayden, *English Baptist History and Heritage*.

18. McBeth, *The Baptist Heritage*, 32. See Lee, *The Theology of John Smyth*; Hayden, *English Baptist History and Heritage*.

19. General Baptist churches held to the Arminian version of the faith (Jacobus Arminius, 1560–1609). Unlike the Calvinists, General Baptists stressed human ability to choose to follow (or renounce) Christ and that no one was predestined to hell/heaven.

20. His two major works during this time were *The Bright Morning Starre* (1603) and *A Paterne of True Prayer* (1605).

authorities heard that he was preaching they decreed that the practice must stop. This was, as one historian notes, the "final straw" that caused Smyth to finally quit the Church of England and become associated with a group of Separatists in the area.[21]

The move to join a Separatist church was a dangerous one. King James I threatened to force such dissenters out of the land if they did not conform to the state church. The risk of detection and persecution increased as the church in Gainsborough grew, so the church divided into two smaller groups. Smyth joined with a well-to-do layperson named Thomas Helwys to provide leadership to one of the groups.[22] Both groups fled to Holland around the same time (1607). Through their study of the New Testament and the influence of Anabaptists, the Smyth-Helwys group adopted believer's baptism and became Baptists.[23] The other group left in 1620 on board the *Mayflower* to the nascent empire in America. In due course Smyth and Helwys (along with their followers) split over Smyth's affinity for the Mennonites. Smyth was never received into membership in the Mennonite Church (although his followers eventually would in 1615) and he died of illness on 20 August 1612 outside of any formal church.

In 1611, Helwys led his small band of followers back to Spitalfields, a section of London. This is considered to be the first Baptist Church on English soil. Once he was back in England, Helwys published his famous work *A Short Declaration of the Mystery of Iniquity* (1611/12), which was an attack on the Church of England and a defence of religious liberty that drew the government's attention. He was imprisoned and died in Newgate Prison in 1616. Upon Helwys' imprisonment, the leadership of the church passed into the hands of John Murton (or Morton). Murton also died in prison (1626), but the churches continued to grow. By 1624, there were at least five General Baptist churches in England; by 1650 there were at least forty-seven.[24]

---

21. McBeth, *The Baptist Heritage*, 33.

22. Kreitzer, *Thomas Helwys*.

23. Convinced that his infant baptism was not a real baptism, Smyth baptised himself—a practice called se-baptism—then subsequently baptized the others.

24. Baptists were not originally called "Baptists." Their opponents often called them "Anabaptists," but those now called Baptists preferred to be called "Brethren," the "Baptized Churches," or "Churches of the Baptized Way." By the 1640s some opponents were calling them "Baptists" and by the mid-1650s the group itself began to use the term. However, it was not until the 1700s that the term entered general usage. See McBeth, *The Baptist Heritage*, 48–49.

During the early-to-mid seventeenth century, another group of Baptists, known as the Particular Baptists, also took root in England. Whereas General Baptist churches held to an Arminian (or "General") view of atonement, Particular Baptist churches were Calvinist, and therefore believed in a particular atonement—that Christ died only for the elect. They also stressed how humanity could not respond or choose, but needed God's grace and election in order to do so.

One key figure to note in regard to Particular Baptist origins is Henry Jacob. While Smyth was becoming radicalized at Cambridge, Jacob developed a more moderate form of criticism at Oxford. Jacob called for reform in the Church of England but did not initially advocate separation. His relatively restrained *Reasons taken out of God's Word and the best humane Testimonies proving a necessitie of reforming our Chvrches in England* (1605) attracted the attention of the government and he was subsequently imprisoned. Upon his release, he fled to Holland like so many others. There, he served as a pastor of an independent church.

In 1616, Jacob returned to England and founded a church in the Southwark section of England. This is often called the JLJ church: its three pastors were Henry Jacob, John Lathrop, and Henry Jessey. This church would eventually give rise to the first Particular Baptist Church. In 1622, Jacob went to Virginia where he later died in 1624. Other Particular Baptist churches remained in London and, by 1644, seven churches in the London area issued a joint statement of faith, *The London Confession* (1644).

Baptists benefited from the sectarian environment that flourished during the Civil War,[25] but churches that carried out their ministry throughout the seventeenth century faced significant obstacles. The Toleration Act (1689) lifted some of the harsh conditions, but Baptists continued to face restrictions into the following century. As W. T. Whitley states, Baptists "were at liberty to live, be governed, pay taxes, think, print, preach, worship, on very simple conditions. But every avenue to civic and national life was blocked; some low post under the guardians, a halberd in the army, or warrant in the navy, was the limit of possibility."[26] However, the fortunes of Baptists changed significantly due to the evangelical revivals that occurred under figures such as John and Charles

---

25. See Hill, *The World Turned Upside Down*; Estep, *Revolution Within Revolution*; and Underwood, *History of English Baptists*, 64–65.

26. Whitley, *History of British Baptists*, 198.

Wesley and George Whitefield, and reported by Jonathan Edwards.[27] As a result of these mid-late eighteenth-century revivals their numbers rose substantially in Britain and America.

By the nineteenth century, Baptists had gained much in the way of enfranchisement, numbers, and organization. Baptists and other nonconformists benefited from the repeal of the Test and Corporations Acts in 1828, a law that had limited the rights of nonconformists. Baptist church membership in England, Wales, Scotland, and Ireland (England and Wales being by far the two largest contingents) in 1900 was around 362,000 with over 6,600 church buildings.[28] Nevertheless, Baptists in Britain remained a relatively small nonconformist denomination, for in the same year Church of England membership was close to 2,100,000, Scottish Presbyterians at 1,164,000, Roman Catholics at 2,000,000, and total nonconformists (including Baptists) just over 1,800,000.[29] Baptists had initially organized by association, but larger national unions followed. They formed the Particular Baptist Society for the Propagation of the Gospel Amongst the Heathen (later called the Baptist Missionary Society) in 1792 as a means to support and carry out overseas missions work primarily in areas controlled by the British Empire. Particular Baptists formed a Union in 1813, and, in 1832, reformed to allow a closer partnership with General Baptists. In 1891, the Baptist Union further evolved to allow for full membership of both General and Particular Baptists. The Baptist Union of Scotland was formed in 1869. These unions joined associations in common causes and provided necessary support for the local churches.

In spite of their small numbers within the larger religious landscape, Baptists were not an isolated sect disengaged from the wider culture—especially after the repeal of the Test and Corporation Acts opened up educational and public service opportunities. The ministry of the world-renowned late-Victorian Baptist preacher Charles Haddon Spurgeon contributed to the increased respectability of Baptists and global influence of Baptists in places as far away as Tasmania and New Zealand.

---

27. Roger Hayden claims that Edwards' reporting played a huge role in stoking revival fires among British Particular Baptists. He writes, "It is almost impossible to exaggerate Jonathan Edward's impact on eighteenth-century Particular Baptists." See Hayden, *English Baptist History and Heritage*, 120.

28. Currie et al., *Church and Churchgoers*, 163, 213.

29. Currie et al., *Church and Churchgoers*, 25.

The floodgates of British emigration opened after the revolutionary wars in America and France, with approximately 22.6 million people leaving the British Isles between 1815 and 1914.[30] Over half of those settlers went to the United States, while the remainder went primarily to the colonies of Canada, Australia, South Africa, and New Zealand. For those not heading to the US, Canada was the "favoured destination for British migrants" until around 1870, when the opening of the Suez Canal and technological improvements in ship design and communication made travel to Australia and New Zealand more appealing.[31] Included in those waves of settlers were Baptists, and many churches in the colonies were either birthed or bolstered by their arrival.[32]

The twentieth century has seen a contraction among British Baptists. Baptists have struggled to face the complex and changing social conditions of post-war, secularizing Britain, and, in spite of their efforts, they have lost roughly 50% of their membership.

United States

England's first permanent colonial settlement in North America was at Jamestown in 1607, with Plymouth (1620) and others following in the wake. Puritans departed for the New World during a time when it looked as though it was hopeless (or too dangerous) to further reform the Church of England. Consequently, in the 1620s and 1630s, over 20,000 Puritans fled England to the settle in the New World. Initially there were very few Baptists in early America, and the handful of them there were scattered and showed little promise.[33]

Roger Williams (c. 1603–1684) was the first key leader in America associated with the Baptist movement, albeit only briefly a Baptist.[34] Williams was born in London into a middle-class home. He graduated in

---

30. Bridge and Fedorowich, "Mapping the British World," 4.

31. Bridge and Fedorowich, "Mapping the British World," 4.

32. For the link between emigration, empire, and the spread of Baptists, see Heath, *The British Nation is Our Nation*.

33. For a detailed summary of early Baptist strength and diversity, see Gardner, *Baptists of Early America*. For general pattern of the arrival and development of Christianity, see Noll, *A History of Christianity in the United States and Canada*. For a history of Baptists in America, see Kidd and Hankins, *Baptists in America*; Brackney, *Baptists in North America*.

34. Barry, *Roger Williams*; Gaustad, *Liberty of Conscience*.

1627 with a Bachelor of Arts degree from Cambridge University, and shortly after was ordained in the Church of England. Over the next few years he became a rigid Separatist. Facing pressure to conform, he and his wife left England for New England in December 1630. In April 1631, he became a minister at a Separatist church in Salem, Massachusetts. There he preached, farmed, and traded with the indigenous population. He served as pastor (with a brief hiatus) until 1635. During those years his convictions about religious freedom continued to develop, and eventually became controversial enough that he was brought before the General Court in Boston. While his kind attitude towards Native Americans got him into trouble, what really upset the authorities was his view on church-state relations. More specifically, Williams argued that the civil authorities had no right to coerce people due to their religious views. He divided the Ten Commandments into two sections: the first table was to God, the second table to others. The civil authorities could punish in regard to the latter, but in no way could the civil authorities coerce in regard to the former. In late 1635, Williams was tried and found guilty, and was forced to leave the colony in 1636.

In March 1636, Williams and a few friends from Salem planted a church just outside the Massachusetts Bay colony jurisdiction. Convinced that their original baptism was not a true one, they re-baptized one another. This church, called Providence Church, was definitely a Separatist church, and is considered by some to be the first Baptist church in America (their baptisms were probably not by immersion, thus leading to questions as to whether or not it was truly a Baptist church). Over the next few years Williams worked towards developing a colony that practiced religious freedom. In 1643, he travelled to England to formalize Rhode Island's legal status, which was granted the following year. While in England he published his famous *Bloudy Tenent of Persecution for cause of conscience discussed* (1644). New England minister John Cotton sought to refute his arguments in his *Bloudy Tenent washed and made white in the Bloud of the Lamb* (1647), to which Williams responded with *Bloudy Tenent yet more Bloudy* (1652).[35] The Providence Church experienced turmoil in the following years, for not only did Williams leave the church and become a "seeker," never again joining a church, but also the church experienced splits over a variety of theological issues.

---

35. For some examples of the early persecution of Baptists, see Brackney, *Baptist Life and Thought*, 110–11.

The first officially self-identified Baptist Church in America was the church begun in Newport under the leadership of John Clarke, established in the 1640s. While those dates are after William's work in Providence, this church was the first committed exclusively to Baptist ideals. Other churches followed in their wake, moving southward and then westward into the frontier. The first association was the Philadelphia Association, established in 1707.

Those early Baptists faced persistent problems due to low numbers, theological diversity, deficient amount (and quality) of leaders, limited organizational structure uniting churches, rough frontier conditions, and lack of social status (and in the early years, legal restrictions). The turning point for American Baptists was the mid-later part of the eighteenth century. While other factors were at work, Baptists gained enthusiasm and numbers from the waves of revival coined as the First Great Awakening. Throughout much of the nineteenth century their growth continued, fueled by the Second Great Awakening and effective rural and urban revivalism, and successful missionary work among slaves. The growth in social respectability, organizational structures (e.g., local associations), mission societies, and educational institutions were not only signs of progress, but were also factors that contributed to yet even further growth. The arrival of waves of continental European Baptists further bolstered numbers. One blow to Baptist unity was the formation of the Southern Baptist Convention—a split from northern Baptists—over the issue of slavery (1845). By the early twentieth century, Baptists were well-established and the second largest Protestant denomination in the American religious landscape. They had also become the largest Baptist community in the world. So far, Baptists in America have been able to weather the storm of dramatic social and religious changes of the late twentieth century and early twenty-first century; however, time will tell if they will retain the same stability should American religious life begin to mirror the problems associated with secularization as seen in Europe.

Canada

The pattern of Baptist settlement in what would eventually be called Canada was from east to west.[36] The next chapter covers this topic in

---

36. Renfree, *Heritage and Horizon*; Ivison and Rosser, *The Baptists in Upper and Lower Canada before 1820*. For more details on Baptist history in Canada, see the

greater detail, so a simple sketch here will suffice. New England Baptists arrived in Nova Scotia in the mid-eighteenth century to take over land that had been vacated by the expulsion of the French-speaking Acadians. Other Baptists continued to arrive from the Thirteen Colonies (later the United States), and churches were planted in Nova Scotia and New Brunswick. Baptists benefited from the New Light revivals under Henry Alline (1748–1784) and by the end of the eighteenth century they formed the first Baptist association in modern-day Canada, which consisted of nine churches. They were particularly concentrated in the Annapolis Valley and South Shore in Nova Scotia, and the St. John River Valley in New Brunswick.

The ending of the American Revolutionary War in 1783 brought about yet another remarkable change in the religious composition of the British territory, for during and after the war over 50,000 United Empire Loyalists headed north to British-held territory (both the Maritimes and Upper and Lower Canada). Within the mix of Loyalists who arrived in the frontier land of Upper and Lower Canada were Anglicans, Presbyterians, Methodists, Lutherans, Mennonites, and Quakers, but few Baptists. After the flood of Loyalists came American settlers (including Baptists) to what would eventually be called Ontario. With the aid of American missionaries, and the arrival of Baptist British settlers, Baptist work continued to grow slowly in central Canada. Baptist work began much later in western Canada.

Baptists in Canada did not organize nationally in a Baptist Union, partly due to the size of the nation. Instead, Baptists organized as regional bodies, including the Baptist Convention of Ontario and Quebec in 1888, the United Baptist Convention of the Maritime Provinces in 1905–1906, and the Baptist Union of Western Canada in 1907/1909.[37] In 1944, the largest grouping of Baptists organized nationally under the banner of the Baptist Federation of Canada (now Canadian Baptist Ministries—CBM), although there are a number of Canadian Baptist denominations that are not a part of the CBM today.

---

following chapter.

37. The Canadian Baptist Federation was formed in 1944, but this was an umbrella organization wherein the regional conventions remained.

Australia

Australia was targeted for settlement by British authorities after the loss of the Revolutionary War with America. Settlement began in 1788 near Sydney Cove (narrowly beating the French who also had strategic designs on the region). Initially, the majority of those arriving were convicts, but over the following decades increasing numbers of settlers arrived (the last convict ship arrived in 1868).[38] Baptist settlers arrived in Australia from Britain in the early 1830s. The first worship service was organized in Sydney in 1831, and by the middle of the decade they had established a number of other congregations.[39] Baptist growth began in New South Wales and moved to the other states: Tasmania, Victoria, South Australia, Queensland, and Western Australia.

While Australian Baptist churches had a "fundamental British orientation,"[40] Australian Baptist life included a significant German presence, for Germans were the third largest immigrant group of European settlers (after British and Irish), and a number of them were Baptists.[41] Baptist associations formed within the various colonies of New South Wales, Victoria, Queensland, South Australia, Tasmania, and Western Australia. The formation of the new Federation in 1901 inspired Baptists to begin to work towards a national identity. They formed a national paper *The Australian Baptist* in 1913, and, in 1926, they formally organized on a national level with the birth of the Baptist Union of Australia.

Baptists in Australia faced a number of problems. Leon McBeth notes that the churches suffered from the irreligion of the earliest colonists (the continent being a dumping ground and penal colony for many of Britain's worst criminals), divisions among Baptists, neglect from Baptists in Britain, dependence upon lay preachers, and identification with the lower classes.[42] They were criticized for their Puritanism, and were divided on how to go about engaging social issues and modern theologies.[43] Nevertheless, Australian Baptists sought to engage in Australian public life and forge a particular Australian Baptist identity. Australian

---

38. Borrie, "'British' Immigration to Australia," 101–16.

39. Manley and Petras, *The First Australian Baptists*; Bollen, *Australian Baptist*; Hughes, *The Baptists in Australia*; Manley, *Woolloomooloo to 'Eternity'*, Vol. 1 & 2.

40. Manley, *Woolloomooloo to 'Eternity'*, Vol. 1, 108–9.

41. Manley, *Woolloomooloo to 'Eternity'*, Vol. 1, 168–76.

42. McBeth, *The Baptist Heritage*, 325–27.

43. Manley, *Woolloomooloo to 'Eternity'*, Vol. 1, chapter 7.

Baptists celebrated the birth of the Australian Commonwealth on 1 January 1901. The development of a national voice and identity, however, was limited by their minority status, reputation as "wowsers,"[44] and sectarian strife. In spite of such handicaps, by the end of the century they had restored a degree of optimism as the churches looked to the new century and the possibilities before them. Throughout the twentieth century Baptists managed to maintain a vibrant, but small, presence; however, like many other Christians in various Western nations, today they face the increasing difficulties of a post-Christendom context.

New Zealand

New Zealand formally became a colony of Britain in 1841, and the first Baptist settlers began arriving that same year. Initially, they often met for worship with other denominations due to a lack of pastors and churches. In 1851, the arrival of Decimus Dolamore, the first Baptist pastor in New Zealand, led to the formation of the first Baptist church in Nelson colony that same year. Baptists continued to arrive and the churches benefited from their arrival. Baptist strength was located around Auckland and Wellington on the North Island, and Christchurch and Dunedin on the South Island. However, Baptists remained a relatively small minority in the larger Christian community.

The organization of the churches began in 1873 with an association of six churches that came together to form the Canterbury Baptist Association. The Baptist Union of New Zealand, comprised of twenty-two churches, came into being in 1882, while the New Zealand Baptist Missionary Society formed in 1885. The churches were struck a blow in the 1880s when economic recession led numerous Baptists to leave for Australia or return to Britain. The number of church attendees declined during the economic depression years between 1882–1892.[45] While the 1890s were the "golden age" for New Zealand politics with regard to sweeping social reforms concerning land, labor and liberties, Baptists "were not much involved" in politics, for they were "numerically insignificant and were struggling to maintain their life and witness."[46]

---

44. A derisive term for those who sought to reform the morals of others.

45. McBeth, *The Baptist Heritage*, 332.

46. Clifford, *A Handful of Grain*, 57. For further details on New Zealand Baptist history, see Sutherland, *Conflict and Connection*; Sutherland and Guy, *An Unfolding*

Besides the struggle with declining numbers due to periods of emigration, Baptists in New Zealand faced similar problems that other settler Baptist communities in the white colonies faced, such as lack of leaders and resources, minority status, and theological conflicts that stifled growth. The "more confined environment" in New Zealand also often "exacerbated difficulty and differences"[47] for the struggling churches. More recently, like their co-religionists in Australia, Baptists in New Zealand face increasing difficulties in a post-Christendom context.

South Africa

The Baptist presence in South Africa was also a result of the expansion of the British Empire. There had been tensions between the Dutch settlers and the British authorities ever since the British annexation of the Boer territory during the Napoleonic Wars. The first English Baptists arrived with the earliest settlers in 1820 in the Cape Colony, and a number of German settlers in the 1850s added to the ranks of Baptists.[48] In fact, by the time the Baptist Union was formed in 1877, German Baptists slightly outnumbered the English Baptists. Baptist expansion among the Dutch settlers occurred, but was quite limited. Baptist growth was northwards, with aims of bringing the gospel to the hinterland and "natives." Limited resources meant that the churches had to rely on the arrival of settlers for infusions of people and finances. Theological controversy—whether dealing with the debate between Calvinism and Arminianism or the question of open versus closed communion—also hindered the church from further growth.

The formation of the Baptist Union was an important development in the life of the South African Baptists, although the number of Baptists in the newly-formed union was modest: six churches (four English and two German). By 1894, the union had over three thousand European members and close to two-hundred African members. Although this signaled significant growth, Baptists were still in no position to compete with the demographically dominant denominations such as the Anglicans and

---

Story.

47. Cupit, "Patterns of Development," 254.

48. Along with the English were also speakers of Welsh and Gaelic. This material on South Africa Baptist history taken from McBeth, *The Baptist Heritage*, 332–34; Hudson-Reed, ed., *Together for a Century*.

various Dutch Reformed churches. They also failed to make a noteworthy impact among indigenous groups whose numbers were significantly larger than all the white settlers combined. A part of the reason for lack of inroads among indigenous peoples was complicity in apartheid.[49] However, as the following section indicates, Baptist growth outside of the Anglophone white settler's world and into the African community would proceed apace in the twentieth century, leading to a thriving indigenous South African Baptist church by the twenty-first century.

GROWTH OF BAPTISTS IN THE NON-ANGLOPHONE WORLD

Up to this point in the telling of the Baptist story, the spotlight has been on Baptists in the Anglophone world. That focus reflects the reality that Baptists were predominately an English-speaking movement for the first few centuries of their existence. However, that English-speaking British orientation would begin to change in the nineteenth century as Baptists eventually spread into other parts of the world.[50] By the end of the nineteenth century, Baptists were in every habitable continent. In fact, the global community of Baptists is increasingly from the non-Anglophone world, reflecting the tremendous growth in general of the global church. The following is a brief survey of such expansion.

Europe

In 1815, there were relatively few (if any) Baptists on continental Europe, but by the end of the century there were close to a quarter of a million. Many European Baptists identified closely with the Anabaptists, and there was often cross-pollination of members in local churches. Certainly many of their critics saw them as a modern manifestation of the early Anabaptists (not necessarily a good thing, since they were seen as radicals and disruptive of the social order), and while the Methodist Revivals and Great Awakenings fueled Baptist growth in England and in America, it was the Pietist movement in central Europe that provided some initial

---

49. Hale, "The Baptist Union of Southern Africa and Apartheid," 753–77.

50. For helpful surveys of Baptist origins and growth around the world, see Bebbington, *Baptists Through the Centuries*; Johnson, *A Global Introduction to Baptist Churches*; Chute, et al., *The Baptist Story*; and McBeth, *The Baptist Heritage*.

impetus for Baptist growth, leading to "spontaneous spawning of Bible-study or prayer groups which were discovered or gathered together by travelling Baptists."[51]

Key pioneers played a significant role in founding and spreading Baptists throughout Europe, with the earliest being primarily German and Swedish. The "Father of Continental Baptists," Johann Gerhard Oncken, was baptized in 1834, and subsequently sought to plant churches throughout central Europe. His motto "Every Baptist a missionary" was embraced by countless others, thus contributing to the spread of the movement in villages, towns, and cities. Baptists eventually proliferated throughout much of central and eastern Europe, especially successful in Russia, Ukraine, and Rumania. Yet, Baptist work also suffered on the continent due to widespread and systematic persecution, which led one historian to claim that Baptists on the continent have faced "perhaps the longest Baptist persecution in history and some of the most severe."[52] With this in mind, the same author comes to the defence of European Baptists when he writes: "Perhaps outsiders who wonder that Continental Baptists are not more aggressive in proclaiming their faith do not realize what a victory it appears to some Baptists just to exist."[53]

In 1950, European Baptists agreed to work together under the banner of the European Baptist Fellowship (EBF). The EBF is comprised of more than 800,000 Baptists of 12,000 churches in fifty-one Unions stretching from Portugal to the far reaches of Russia. Included in this family are Baptists in Eurasia and the Middle and Near East. EBF leaders work continuously to help strengthen the relationships in these countries where, as of now, no formal union exists. The European Baptist Federation also serves as the European representative for the Baptist World Alliance.

Africa

Baptists were one of the first Protestant bodies in Africa. The oldest African Baptist congregation on the continent is the Regent Road Baptist

---

51. Parker, *Baptists in Europe*, 22. For further works on Baptists in Europe, see Jones and Randall, eds., *Counter-Cultural Communities*; and Randall, *Communities of Conviction*.

52. McBeth, *The Baptist Heritage*, 467.

53. McBeth, *The Baptist Heritage*, 468.

Church of Freetown, Sierra Leone, established in 1792 by David George (an ex-slave from the US, who ministered for a time in Nova Scotia), and is still in existence. Another early field in West Africa was Liberia, colonized by freed slaves from America. Lott Carey with six others, taking with them their church organization from Richmond, Virginia, and, after a stay in Sierra Leone, planted in 1822 the Providence Baptist Church in Monrovia.

The twentieth- and twenty-first-century growth of all traditions of Christianity in Sub-Saharan Africa has been astounding; growing from around 10,000,000 in 1900 to 500,000,000 in 2018. As Philip Jenkins notes, the center of Christianity has shifted southward, most certainly away from the Anglophone world of early Baptists:

> Over the past century . . . the center of gravity in the Christian world has shifted inexorably southward, to Africa, Asia, and Latin America. Already today, the largest Christian communities on the planet are to be found in Africa and Latin America. If we want to visualize a "typical" contemporary Christian, we should think of a woman living in a village in Nigeria in a Brazilian *favela*. As Kenyan scholar John Mbiti has observed, "the centers of the church's universality [are] no longer in Geneva, Rome, Athens, Paris, London, New York, but Kinshasa, Buenos Aires, Addis Ababa and Manila." Whatever Europeans or North Americans may believe, Christianity is doing very well indeed in the global south—not just surviving but expanding.[54]

Baptists both contributed to and benefited from this rapid growth, as well as been shaped by its Pentecostal convictions.[55] Baptists have a minimal presence in North Africa, where Islam dominates. However, Baptists are situated in thirty African countries, with concentrations in Nigeria, Uganda, and the Democratic Republic of Congo. One example of such growth is the Nigerian Baptist Convention, which claims 10,000 churches and 6.5 million worshippers.

Most Baptists on the continent belong to the All Africa Baptist Fellowship (AABF), which is one of the six regions of the Baptist World Alliance.[56] The AABF connects and coordinates the ministries of fifteen million church members, and is sub-divided into five regions: North Africa, East Africa, West Africa, Central Africa, and Southern Africa. The

---

54. Jenkins, *The Next Christendom*, 2.

55. Arnett, *Pentecostalization*.

56. www.aabfellowship.org.

future challenges for Baptists in Africa primarily revolve around carrying out the mission of the church in the midst of political and social tensions, and economic uncertainty. That being the case, African Baptist mission agencies are now sending missionaries not only to other African nations, but to once-sending nations such as Britain.

Latin America and Caribbean

Baptists are located in each of the countries and territories of Latin America, extending from Mexico to the southern tip of South America. In the mid-nineteenth century, there were no Baptists in Latin America. Fifty years later in 1904 there were over five thousand Baptists. Today there are over three million Baptists, with almost two million in Brazil alone.[57] The Portuguese-speaking country of Brazil has been the centre of Baptist expansion in South America, and is the only country on the continent where Baptists have experienced a mass movement. Baptist work in Spanish-speaking South America has been slower and more limited due to attempts by the powerful Roman Catholic Church (the vast majority of Latin America is Catholic) to suppress the movement, as well as political unrest and theological controversies. However, recent positive overtures between evangelicals and Catholics bode well for future relations. Most major Baptist bodies in Latin America are members of the Baptist World Alliance and also the Union of Baptists in Latin America, which is a regional organization of the Baptist World Alliance.

Canadian Baptists have a special history with South American Baptists. In 1898, Canadian Baptists sent Archibald Reekie to Bolivia, the second Protestant body to send a resident missionary to the country.[58] Canadian Norman Dabbs was a missionary martyr in Bolivia (1949).[59] In 1936, a Bolivian Baptist Union was formed with 345 members; today it numbers 25,000 in almost 250 churches. Brazilian Baptists began a mission in 1946; its work produced the Bolivian Baptist Convention which today has 3,000 members and forty churches. Several other Baptist missions also have small works in the country.

57. www.bwanet.org.

58. Brackney, ed., *Bridging Cultures and Hemispheres*; and Daniel, *Moving with the Times*.

59. Donaldson, "Who Killed Norman Dabbs?" 57–68.

History of Baptists Around the World

Asia

Baptist growth in Asia has been significant.[60] Whereas in 1904 there were 3.2 times more Baptists in Europe than Asia, by 2007 there were 6.7 times more Baptists in Asia than Europe.[61] William Carey's *An Enquiry into the Obligations of Christians to Use Means for Conversion of the Heathens* (1792) urged Baptist ministers to support a foreign mission enterprise. Those who heeded Carey's message founded the Baptist Missionary Society (BMS) in 1792, and, in the following year, William and Dorothy Carey and John Thomas sailed to India under its banner.[62] Canadian Baptist work began with the arrival of Richard and Leleah Burpee in Burma in 1846. Though faced with significant hardships, the Baptist work was very successful and an indigenous Baptist community took root. Nagaland, an Indian state in the northeast corner of the nation, was particularly receptive to the Baptist message. Nagaland is roughly ninety percent Christian, and up to eighty percent of those are Baptists.[63] Orissa was also an important center for Baptist growth, but Christians in that region have recently experienced persecution and face restrictions. The Asian countries with the most numerous numbers of Baptists are India, Myanmar, and South Korea. India contains the largest Baptist community, with over 2,000,000 members. Baptist growth has been primarily among the marginalized and disenfranchised.

Baptists have a minor presence in the Middle East. Growth in the twentieth century has been hampered by civil unrest, war, dislocation, and oppression, not to mention small numbers and limited resources. The loss of members to migration has also been crippling. There are roughly 100 Baptist churches in the Middle East with around 6,500 members. Due to their relatively small numbers, Baptist churches in the Middle East are clustered with the European Baptist Federation. One bright light for Middle Eastern Baptists is their seminary in Lebanon, the Arab Baptist Theological Seminary, a vibrant training ground for present and future leaders in the conflict-ridden region.

60. For further reading on Baptist history in Asia, see Choudhury, *Christianity in the North-East India*; Parker, *The Southern Baptist Mission in Japan, 1889-1989*; Gammell, *A History of American Baptist Missions in Asia, Africa, Europe and North America*; Stanley, *The History of the Baptist Missionary Society, 1792-1992*.

61. Johnson, *A Global Introduction*, 256.

62. Stanley, *History of the Baptist Missionary Society*.

63. Frykenberg, "Naga Baptists: A Brief Narrative of Their Genesis," 213–40; Ngursangzeli and Biehl, eds., *Witnessing to Christ in North East India*.

China was a target for Baptists missionaries in the 1830s.[64] A number of American and British missionaries sought to plant Baptist churches in the country; men and women such as Josiah Goddard, Timothy Richard, Cicero Washington Pruitt, and Charlotte Digges "Lottie" Moon committed decades of their lives to bring the gospel to China, facing innumerable hardships along the way. By the early-twentieth century they had been successful in planting local churches, mission centres, educational institutions, and hospitals. The twentieth century was particularly harsh due to the Boxer Rebellion, Japanese invasion, civil war, and communist takeover, and, due to their identity as "Westerners," many missionaries and their converts were targeted for violence. Actual numbers of Chinese Baptists are hard to confirm due to the lack of records and underground nature of the churches. Today most Baptists in China have been absorbed into the Three-Self Patriotic Movement (self-government, self-propagation, self-support—TSPM) or non-denominational underground house churches.[65] The TSPM works in conjunction with the China Christian Council, both of these are the only two legal Protestant bodies in China.

BAPTIST WORLD ALLIANCE

By the end of the twentieth century, Baptists had grown significantly from their roots as a small sect of English Separatists. At this juncture a few brief observations are in order as Baptists advance into the twenty-first century. First, Baptist have—though not without challenges—been remarkably adaptive to wildly different contexts; from urban England to frontier America, from the cold of the Russian Steppe to the heat of sub-Saharan Africa, Baptist have readily adapted to plant churches across the globe. Second, with few exceptions Baptists have remained on the margins of religious life, often persecuted as a result. While Baptists may have achieved significant numbers, social status, and political clout in the United States, elsewhere in the world limited Baptist numbers have kept them on the margins. Third, familiar patterns of theological controversy have plagued Baptists, often revolving around fundamentalism/liberalism, open/closed communion, Calvinism/Arminianism, and women in

---

64. For instance, see Hyatt, *Our Ordered Lives Confess*.

65. Leonard, *Baptist Ways*, 358. The TSPM was an attempt to eliminate external influences on the Chinese churches, and make them truly Chinese in leadership, content, and membership. Critics see it as a tool of the state to spy on and control churches.

ministry. Fourth, the Anglophone identity of Baptists is evolving as the church becomes increasingly global; and within the century the denomination will likely be more African and/or Asian than Anglophone.

One positive development in the twentieth century that arose out of the desire to coordinate this now global movement was the birth of the Baptist World Alliance (BWA).[66] There were a few antecedents to the formation of the BWA. In 1678, Thomas Grantham (a British Baptist) wished that "all congregations of Christians of the world that are baptized according to the appointment of Christ would make one consistory at least sometimes to consider matters of difference among them." A century later, John Rippon (a British Baptist preacher, hymn writer, and editor) urged that all the baptized ministers and people of the world arrange "a deputation from these climes [to] meet, probably in London, to consult the ecclesiastical good of the whole." In 1904, John Newton Prestridge, an American editor, called for a world gathering of Baptists in his publication *The Baptist Argus*. John Howard Shakespeare, editor of the *Baptist Times and Freeman*, London, quickly endorsed Prestridge's proposal. He and other leaders invited Baptists of the world to meet in London at Exeter Hall. The BWA was founded 11–18 July 1905 in London, England, by representatives from twenty-three nations. Prominent British Baptist pastor Alexander Maclaren was drafted to serve as provisional president. The BWA was meant to be a worldwide voluntary organization for fellowship, service, and cooperation. The founding constitution set forth the following objectives:

- to show the essential oneness of the Baptist people in the Lord Jesus Christ
- to impart inspiration to the brotherhood
- to promote the spirit of fellowship, service, and cooperation among its members

They made it clear from the outset that while the BWA was to promote fellowship and cooperation among Baptist worldwide, it was in no way to interfere with the independence of churches or assume administrative functions of existing organizations. The Baptist World Alliance has over 240 unions and conventions in over 125 countries, with church membership of over 47 million baptized believers.[67] This number represents

66. Pierard, ed., *Baptists Together in Christ, 1905–2005*. See also www.bwanet.org.
67. Estimates varying widely depending on how one counts. Counting Sunday

about half of all Baptists, for 50 million other Baptists around the globe do not affiliate with the BWA. The organizations of the BWA range widely, including ministries related to aid, relief, evangelism, education, religious liberty, youth, women, men, and advocacy.

CONCLUSION

Baptists have come a long way since their Separatist days at the end of the medieval world in the early 1600s, evolving from a tiny persecuted sect of English Separatists to become a global multi-ethnic movement of over 100,000,000. This chapter has provided a brief history of their birth and spread up to the twenty-first century, with only limited attention to Baptists in Canada. Since this book is primarily addressing Baptists in the Canadian context, the following chapter will zoom in on the Baptist experience in Canada, providing further details on its key people, events, ideas, and organizations.

---

morning worshippers gives one figure, counting official members another. Baptist World Alliance, *2019-2020 BWA Ministry Update*, 16.

2

The Arrival and Growth of Baptists in Canada

As demonstrated in the last chapter, the Baptist story in Canada traces its origins to the mid-eighteenth century, when settlers and refugees from the American colonies established churches in the modern-day Maritime Provinces. Since that time, Baptists have spread throughout the country through mission agencies and associations, ultimately forming a variety of different conventions, unions, and fellowships. Today, Baptists in Canada do not enjoy the same kind of religious hegemony as their counterparts in the United States, but throughout their history they have made many important contributions in shaping the religious and social landscape of the country. As of 2011, there were 635,840 Baptists across Canada, or roughly 2 percent of the total population.[1] Outside of New Brunswick (where Baptists are still the largest Protestant denomination) and Nova Scotia (where Baptists are the third largest Protestant denomination), Baptists have always been in the religious minority in each Canadian province.

In the two and a half centuries since Baptists began establishing churches in Canada, they have experienced both harmony and turbulence—they have formed unions and they have suffered schisms. This is due in large part to the fact that Baptists in Canada (much like their counterparts in other parts of the world) are not monochromatic. They have disagreed on matters ranging from the inerrancy of scripture to the colour of the carpet. Therefore, it is unsurprising that there are numerous Baptist groups in Canada. The largest of these are those connected with the Canadian Baptist Ministries (CBM, "Federation Baptists" before

---

1. *2011 National Household Survey.*

1995), sometimes referred to as the "mainstream" Canadian Baptists or "Convention Baptists," which include the Canadian Baptists of Atlantic Canada, the Canadian Baptists of Ontario and Quebec, the Canadian Baptists of Western Canada, and L'Union d'Églises Baptistes Francophones du Canada (the Union of French Baptist Churches in Canada); the second largest is the Fellowship of Evangelical Baptist Churches in Canada; the third largest is the Canadian National Baptist Convention; and the fourth largest is the Baptist General Conference. There are also a number of other, smaller Baptist denominations and independent congregations. Likewise, there are numerous nondenominational churches that reflect a Baptist polity, and various other denominations that have their roots in the Canadian Baptist tradition (such as the Atlantic District of the Wesleyan Church).

The purpose of this chapter is not to "airbrush" the Baptist narrative in Canada, but rather it is to trace both the good and bad developments in the Baptist story. What events or ideas have inspired them? What makes Baptist churches function the way they do? Why are there so many different kinds of Baptists? In order to address these questions, this chapter looks at each of the major Baptist bodies in Canada, from the foundations set in the earliest churches in rural Maritime communities up to the twenty-first century.[2]

CANADIAN BAPTIST ORIGINS

Eastern Baptists

The earliest Baptists in Canada arrived in the east in the mid-eighteenth century. Several waves of immigration changed the religious demographics of the region. The first wave took place in the 1760s, when a number of "planters" landed in the easternmost region in an effort to resettle the land left vacant from *le Grand Dérangement* (when the British authorities expelled the French-speaking inhabitants of Acadia, modern-day eastern Canada, during the French and Indian War). The second wave of immigration took place in the 1780s, when United Empire Loyalists

---

2. Presently there are two modern histories of Baptists in Canada. The first, published in 1911, is Fitch, *The Baptists of Canada*; and the second, published in 1988, is Renfree, *Heritage and Horizon*.

relocated to modern-day Canada after United States of America (formerly the thirteen southern British colonies) declared its independence and defeated the British authorities. It was in this evolving context that the Baptist story began in Canada. In 1761, Ebenezer Moulton—an ordained preacher from South Brimfield, Massachusetts—arrived in Nova Scotia, allegedly in an attempt to flee his creditors in New England.[3] His arrival marked an important moment in Baptist history in Canada, as he became the first-known ordained Baptist pastor in Canada. He began a new ministry in Nova Scotia as an itinerant preacher among the fishing villages on the south shore, and later throughout the Annapolis Valley.

This era also saw the formation of the first Baptist churches in Canada. Simultaneous to Moulton's ministry, in 1763, a group of thirteen settlers from Swansea, Massachusetts, under the leadership of pastor Nathan Mason, planted a six-principle (Arminian) Baptist church in Sackville in the Tantramar region that borders modern-day Nova Scotia and New Brunswick. The fertile ground cultivated by the Acadians looked promising; however, the settlers were not prepared for the region's harsh winters. As the wind and snow swept across the valley, it dissuaded many of them from remaining in the area and the majority returned to New England. The church fell out of visibility shortly thereafter, though some Baptists remained in the area.[4] Two years after the formation of the church in Sackville, in 1765, Moulton planted a Baptist church in the Horton Township (now Wolfville), Nova Scotia, which made it the first Baptist church organized on Canadian soil. Within a few years, however, much like the church in Sackville, the church in Horton disappeared. It was eventually reconstituted in 1778 with many of the same families, and has remained operational since then, which makes it the longest continuing Baptist church in the country. These two early churches—along with the important Baptist presence that has developed in the Maritime Provinces since—have garnered the region the appropriate title of the "heartland of Canadian Baptist churches."[5]

While these churches struggled for survival, ironically the most significant boon for Baptists in the region came in the form of a New Light Congregationalist spiritualist of planter stock named Henry Alline.[6] He

3. Stewart, "Moulton, Ebenezer."
4. Vickruck, "Middle Sackville Baptist Church," 27–28.
5. McCormick, *Faith, Freedom, and Democracy*, 5.
6. There are some differences of opinion over how to pronounce the name "Alline" (even among the authors of this book!). Various historians have called him "Allen,"

began his ministry in Nova Scotia in 1776 after a traumatic conversion experience that he described as being "ravished with a divine ecstasy" and "wrapped up in God."[7] He travelled throughout the colony (which at the time of his ministry included New Brunswick), especially across the Annapolis Valley and the south shore, and the St. John River Valley in modern-day New Brunswick. He denounced what he viewed as Calvinism's rigid legalism, and emphasized an emotion-driven religious experience. His services were fueled by the promise that one might actually meet God and experience his "boundless ocean of everlasting love."[8] Alline's unique ministry was the catalyst for Nova Scotia's First Great Awakening, which saw thousands of converts.[9] Although criticized by important religious leaders (including John Wesley, who called him "very far from being a man of sound understanding" and condemned him for preaching "such miserable jargon"[10]), his admirers identified him as "Nova Scotia's George Whitefield" and his grave marker memorialized him as "the apostle of Nova Scotia."[11]

When Alline died at the age of 35 in 1784, his followers moved in multiple directions. The experiential nature of his approach led many to adopt antinomianism. Now saved, they claimed that they were under a "New Dispensation," which meant that they could no longer sin. This plateaued with several high-profile incidents. In 1796, controversy erupted in Liverpool, Nova Scotia when the unmarried New Light preacher Harris Harding announced that he had impregnated a teenager. In another bizarre incident, in 1805, a man in Shediac, New Brunswick murdered his

---

"Al-line," or "Al-leen." For an extended discussion on this discrepancy, see Moody and Beverley, eds., *The Journal of Henry Alline*, note 1.

7. Alline, *Life and Journal*, 63. Much of Alline's theology was rooted in this conversion experience. See Flatt, "Theological Innovation," 285–300.

8. Alline, "Sermon Preached," 55. On the egalitarian nature of these services, see Rawlyk, *Wrapped up in God*, 51–52; Coops, "That Still Small Voice," 113–31.

9. Rawlyk, *Wrapped up in God*, 28–31.

10. Letter from John Wesley to William Black, 13 July 1783, in Wesley, *The Letters*, 7:182.

11. Historians have used the designation, "Whitefield of Nova Scotia," consistently since Alline's death. For examples, see Bourinot, *Builders of Nova Scotia*, 52 and Saunders, *History of the Baptists*, 15. For more recent examples, see Rawlyk, *Ravished by the Spirit*, 3 and Rawlyk, *Wrapped up in God*, 1–31. One modern historian went as far as to identify him as "the greatest 'Canadian' of the eighteenth century, the greatest Maritimer of any age and the most significant religious figure this country has yet produced." See Bell, "Preface," xiii.

daughter over a prophetic message that she had preached that forecasted the return of Jesus Christ.[12] Although Baptists had existed in the Maritimes prior to these events, the antinomian debacle shepherded several important New Light leaders into the Baptist fold. In the early 1790s, notable figures, such as the beleaguered Harding and the preacher-brothers Edward Manning and James Manning, renounced the New Dispensation and instead turned to believer's baptism as a way to cleanse themselves from past mistakes. At the same time, others sought believer's baptism out of a "desire for additional post-conversion religious experiences," which eventually gave Baptists their prominent position in the region.[13]

These baptized believers came together in 1798 to form a partnership with others who remained (non-antinomian) New Lights, including Alline's own brother-in-law, John Payzant. In 1800, however, the emerging Baptist cohort severed its ties with the un-immersed New Lights and instead formed the Nova Scotia Baptist Association, which included nine Regular (Calvinist) Baptist congregations in both Nova Scotia and New Brunswick. Among the most influential figures in this early generation of Baptist leadership were those whom historians have identified as the "Fathers" of the Maritime Baptists.[14] They included Thomas Handley Chipman, Joseph Crandall, Joseph Dimock, Thomas Ansley, and Theodore Seth Harding, as well as the aforementioned Manning brothers and Harding. Another important individual was David George, a freed slave from Virginia, who established several black and mixed-race congregations in Nova Scotia before relocating to Sierra Leone.[15] George's work inaugurated the important black Baptist work in the Maritime Provinces,[16] and therefore it may be appropriate to retrospectively count him among the "Fathers"—albeit an unsung one. (As an aside, there is a lacuna when it comes to black Baptist history in Canada, something that needs to

12. Goodwin, *Into Deep Waters*, 22.

13. Goodwin, *Into Deep Waters*, 18; Goodwin, "Footprints," 193–94.

14. E.g., Renfree, *Heritage and Horizon*, 30–39. To date the best study on the "Fathers" is Goodwin, *Into Deep Waters*.

15. Gordon, *From Freedom*.

16. Terms used to describe a people are often contested, and some are outright offensive. The terms Africadians, Afro-Canucks, Africanadians, and African Canadians have been used in the Canadian context, however, we have opted to use black Canadians or black Baptists. Every term is problematic, this one included; however, in the Canadian context "black" is widely used by advocacy groups, governments, and scholars. Its usage also avoids the debate between those Canadians who stress their African origin versus those who stress their Caribbean origin.

be remedied.)[17] Significantly, as William H. Brackney has noted, "The 'Fathers' form a constant point of reference for understanding Maritime Baptist identity."[18]

Although they had their roots in the Allinite revivals, the emerging Baptists departed from Alline in several key areas. The Allinite revivals had famously included women, who were well known to exhort and prophesy, and even plead with men and children to convert, during gatherings.[19] The New Dispensation debacle, however, had convinced many Baptist leaders of the need to reform the New Light tradition. They believed Baptist order would be achieved by "reining in Newlight disorder," which in part required "reining in assertive women."[20] Moreover, in spite of Alline's strident Arminianism and his attempts to unseat the established church's Calvinism, the significant majority of his spiritual heirs simply fell back to the region's overwhelmingly Calvinistic posture. Similarly, in a move that would have disturbed Alline, in 1808, the association adopted closed communion. The strong feelings on this matter were reflected in the case of Harris Harding—who, in spite of his checkered past, had become one of the most prominent preachers in the Maritimes for his leading role in Nova Scotia's Second Great Awakening. Even though he had demonstrated himself as a gifted preacher and leader, the association's move toward a closed table effectively expelled him (and his church in Yarmouth) from their fellowship because he allowed for an open table. He remained disassociated from his friends until 1828, when he reluctantly accepted the closed position.[21] What they did retain, however, was Alline's unique emphasis on personal spiritual

---

17. Winks, *The Blacks in Canada*; Bertley, *Canada and Its People of African Descent*; Walker, *Racial Discrimination in Canada*; Sealey, *Colored Zion*; Oliver, *A Brief History of the Colored Baptists of Nova Scotia*. Black Baptists have played an important role in Canada. William A. White, for example, was a military chaplain during the First World War and a prominent Baptist preacher in Nova Scotia. One later historian went as far as to identify him as "the universally recognized leader of the province's Negroes [sic] regardless of faith or heritage." Winks, *The Blacks in Canada*, 350. Another important black Baptist was Viola Desmond, often called the "Rosa Parks of Canada" for refusing to leave a "whites-only" section of a movie theatre in Nova Scotia in 1945, who has been on the ten-dollar bill since 2018.

18. Brackney, *A Genetic History*, 474.

19. Goodwin, *Into Deep Waters*, 181.

20. Bell, "Allowed Irregularities," 23. Bell credits Rawlyk, *Canada Fire*, 95–96, 129–30.

21. Goodwin, *Into Deep Waters*, 43.

transformation, which, according to George Rawlyk, later manifested in a kind of "accommodating theology" that helped insulate them from various theological controversies.[22]

While the revivalist origins of Baptists in Nova Scotia and New Brunswick allowed them to retain a significant presence in those provinces, the experience in Prince Edward Island was notably different. Less affected by the enthusiasm of the Allinite revivals, originally Baptists on Prince Edward Island were comprised almost exclusively of Scottish Baptists who had immigrated to the region. The earliest Baptist preacher in the area was Alexander Crawford, an immigrant to Nova Scotia in 1810, whose penchant for order led him to distance himself from what he viewed as the radical spiritualism of Baptists in Nova Scotia and New Brunswick. Instead, he settled on the Island province in 1815 and began preaching with great success to his own countrymen because of his "more relational less emotional brand of evangelicalism [that] struck a responsive chord among the Scots settlers."[23] The success of his labours eventually resulted in the formation of bodies in Bedeque, Tryon, and East Point—each of which, beginning with Bedeque in 1826, formally affiliated with the Baptists in Nova Scotia and New Brunswick.

Central Baptists

Unlike the relatively localized development of the Baptists in the Maritimes, central Baptists benefitted more substantially from their counterparts south of the border. Much like the situation in the east, the arrival of the United Empire Loyalists significantly changed the religious demographics of the region, but because the majority of Baptists in the United States had supported the American War for Independence, there were very few (if any) Baptists counted among the loyalists that immigrated north after the conflict. The Constitutional Act of 1791 saw the division of the former colony of Quebec into the provinces of Upper Canada and Lower Canada. Settlers could obtain a parcel of land for a nominal expense, which resulted in a wave of post-loyalist homesteaders to the central region, especially in Upper Canada (modern-day Ontario). Various Baptist missionary groups in New England and New York mobilized

---

22. Rawlyk, "J. M. Cramp," 119–34 and Rawlyk, *Champions of the Truth*, 3–38, 70–74. See also Coops, "Shelter," 214–15.

23. Goodwin, "Footprints," 196.

in an effort to reach these previously-untouched areas, including: the Woodstock Baptist Association of Vermont; the Shaftsbury Baptist Association (Vermont); the Massachusetts Baptist Missionary Society; the Lake Baptist Missionary Society (New York); the New York Baptist Missionary Society; and the Black River Baptist Association (New York).[24]

While it is true that "most of the [Baptist] missionary activity [in the Canadas] occurred after 1800," there were a number of important and formative missionary excursions in the late-eighteenth century.[25] The first on record took place in summer 1793, when John Hebberd and Ariel Kendrick, two missionaries working for the Woodstock Baptist Association, visited Caldwell's Manor in Lower Canada and preached to a group of settlers from Connecticut. Although no baptisms resulted from these efforts at the time, the following January, a group of believers at Caldwell's Manor called for a pastor from the Woodstock Association to baptize them.[26] Elisha Andrews, a minister in Fairfax, Vermont, responded to the invitation. As he later recorded:

> we met at 9 o'clock in the morning and spent the whole day in examining candidates for baptism; we heard and received thirty of all ages from 10 to 50 years . . . The next day we repaired to the Lake, cut a whole in the ice, and fifteen of those happy and devoted disciples were, in the name of the Father, Son and Holy Ghost, immersed agreeably to the command of the divine Saviour. The baptism of the remaining fifteen was deferred until the next Monday.[27]

This body of baptized believers formed the nucleus of the first Baptist church in Lower Canada.

There is some ambiguity with regard to which church was the earliest Baptist church in Upper Canada.[28] What is clear is that by the

---

24. For an overview of the latter five groups, see Ivison and Rosser, *The Baptists*, 9–16.

25. Renfree, *Heritage and Horizon*, 44.

26. Ivison and Rosser, *The Baptists*, 156.

27. As cited by Ivison and Rosser, *The Baptists*, 156. Unfortunately, Ivison and Rosser do not provide bibliographic details for this quote, except to note that it was later printed in *The Christian Watchman* and reprinted in the *Triennial Baptist Register* (see *The Baptists*, 158).

28. Popular memory suggests that the first was formed in present-day Beamsville in 1776; however, historical evidence to that effect is scarce and unverifiable. This claim is noted in popular histories, such as Fitch, *The Baptists of Canada*, 102.

middle of the 1790s, congregations had grown in Hallowell, Thurlow, and Beamsville.[29] At the turn of the century, Joseph Cornell, a missionary who operated under the auspices of the Massachusetts Baptist Missionary Society, reported that he had heard "the Macedonia cries [for help] . . . from Canada,"[30] which led him to begin making regular trips to Upper Canada. Because of the strong Baptist emphasis on the independence of the local congregation, after the missionaries planted a church as a baptized body of believers they would leave the job of securing a minister to the infant church. Most churches simply selected one of their own congregants (typically one who was self-sufficient) to lead them, who would then serve in a part-time capacity. Many of these new preachers would then "comb the surrounding townships for converts," and would even plant other churches.[31] While these early missionaries played a significant role in the development of the Baptist community in central Canada, it is important to note other external influences, such as at the first Baptist church in York (what would become Toronto), which was a black Baptist church founded in 1826 by fugitive slaves who had fled north to freedom.[32]

The various published reports from the American missionaries contain significant details for understanding the region's religious context. As was customary for his era, Cornell routinely recorded a bleak image of what he found when he visited the area. In one of his earliest reports, he recorded travelling to Cataraqui (Kingston), where he found "the people in general . . . to be very loose in their morals," and, in a nearby community, he found Christians who were "most entangled with the doctrine of the Pharisees."[33] One of his co-workers, Peter Root, noted about the same area: "some of the few of other denominations, who bear the name of ministers, are said to be immoral characters, given to wine, card-playing, etc." He concluded: "How much worse are such preachers than none at all!"[34] Yet, their reports also contained flashes of hope, as the

29. Renfree, *Heritage and Horizon*, 45–47.

30. Joseph Cornell, "To the Massachusetts Baptist Missionary Society," *The Massachusetts Missionary Magazine*, September 1803, 16.

31. Grant, *A Profusion of Spires*, 44–45.

32. According to its website, First Baptist Church in Toronto is the oldest black institution in Toronto.

33. Joseph Cornell, "To the Massachusetts Baptist Missionary Society," *The Massachusetts Missionary Magazine*, September 1803, 13.

34. Peter Root, "Extracts from Rev. Mr. Root's Letters," *The Massachusetts*

missionaries witnessed the birth and significant growth of a number of Baptist churches. In 1802, three churches located near the Bay of Quinte came together to form the Thurlow Baptist Association, named after the location of the group's first meeting. In addition to Thurlow, the other two congregations were in Hallowell and Cramahe-Haldimand. Cornell celebrated the association's formation by writing that "pools of water have broken out in the desert, and it begins to look like a garden."[35] Upon learning of Cornell's assessment, Baptists from the region responded: "Amen, Lord, even so let it be."[36]

Outreach from the United States also resulted in the first Baptist ministry to the indigenous populations of Canada. Under the auspices of the New York Missionary Society, Elkanah Holmes ministered to the Tuscaroras people on both sides of the border in the Great Lakes region. According to David Elliott, by the first decade of the nineteenth century, Holmes' fellow missionaries from other societies recognized him as "the senior missionary among native Canadians."[37] The war of 1812, however, ended Holmes' involvement in Canada, and he returned to the United States. Baptist work among the indigenous populations does not appear to have been restarted for at least two decades, when another New York missionary, John Miner, began outreach to the Six Nations Reserve around 1835. Furthermore, it was during this time that a group of Baptist natives emigrated from New York. Barred from holding services in the local Anglican Church, the growing body of converts decided to form their own church, and on 6 March 1842, they formed the Tuscarora Baptist Church (Ohsweken Baptist Church since 1964), which became the mother church to a number of "branch churches" on the reserve and as far as London.[38]

The American origins of many of the Baptist churches in central Canada meant that "Baptist associations of New York and New England exercised a determining influence on [central] Canadian Baptist polity."[39] They were generally Calvinistic in orientation, they restricted

---

Missionary Magazine, September 1805, 153.

35. Joseph Cornell, "Extract from the Rev. Joseph Cornell's Letter to the Society," *The Massachusetts Baptist Missionary Magazine*, September 1804, 67.

36. "Extract from the Minutes of the Thurlow Baptist Association in Upper Canada," *The Massachusetts Baptist Missionary Magazine*, September 1804, 72.

37. Elliott, "Canadian Baptists and Native Ministry," 150.

38. Elliott, "Canadian Baptists and Native Ministry," 152.

39. Ivison and Rosser, *The Baptists*, 16.

communion to immersed believers, and they strongly emphasized the role of the local congregation—sometimes, unfortunately, while minimizing the larger association.

CANADIAN BAPTIST GROWTH

Eastern Baptists

In the eastern provinces, size and the attendant difficulties of keeping fellowship over the region led the Nova Scotia Baptist Association (renamed the Nova Scotia and New Brunswick Baptist Association) to form sister groups, the New Brunswick Baptist Association (1821) and the Prince Edward Island Baptist Association (1856). Unique to the area, in 1854, the former slave Richard Preston carried on David George's legacy when he formed the African Baptist Association of Nova Scotia, which, unlike the other associations that were based on geographic location, was based on race and comprised of historically black congregations scattered throughout the region. In 1846, the Baptist associations in the Maritimes came together under the umbrella of the Baptist Convention of Nova Scotia, New Brunswick, and Prince Edward Island (known as the Baptist Convention of the Maritime Provinces after 1878, and sometimes known colloquially as the Maritime Baptist Convention). Though they were comprised of Regular (Calvinist) Baptists, most identified them simply as "Baptists."

Through these associations—and later the convention—Baptists remained in close contact with one another, which they used as a launching pad for a variety of shared ministries. They launched the *Baptist Missionary Magazine of Nova Scotia and New Brunswick* in 1827—making it the oldest religious periodical in Canada—which became the *Christian Messenger* a decade later in 1837.[40] Among the earliest of these was the Home Mission Board, which they formed in Chester, Nova Scotia in 1814 as a way to support both the itinerant preaching of the "Fathers" and to

---

40. For a good overview of the newspaper and its successors, see Robert S. Wilson, "Saying Goodbye to an old Friend: The Final Edition of the Atlantic Baptist," *Atlantic Baptist*, May-June 2005, 8–11. In 1849, Baptists in New Brunswick formed their own newspaper, *The Christian Visitor*, which combined with the *Christian Messenger* in 1884 to form *The Messenger and Visitor*. At the same time, from 1853, the Free Christian Baptists operated their own, separate newspaper, *The Religious Intelligencer*.

generate funds for the "poor heathen" abroad.[41] Eventually they divided this work between a Home Mission Board and a Foreign Mission Board. Domestically, much of their missionary zeal was directed toward reaching the east coast's predominantly Anglo-Saxon population, and they did not even sincerely see the indigenous peoples as a mission field until at least 1830. Indeed, much of their effort in reaching the native Canadians was concentrated in the person of Silas Tertius Rand, a Baptist layperson "with an exceptional gift for languages," who translated the Bible into Mi'kmaq in the 1850s. While he is remembered as the "pioneer" Baptist missionary to indigenous peoples, he received very little actual support from the Baptist community, who on several occasions even tried to interfere with his efforts, including trying to convince him to translate "baptize" as "immerse."[42]

The same year that saw the creation of the Maritime Baptist Convention, they began sending foreign missionaries. Following the example of their American Baptist counterparts, they identified Burma as their mission field. The newly-formed Baptist body commissioned the first Canadian Baptist foreign missionaries when they sent Richard and Laleah Burpee to Burma in 1846, where they remained until 1853.[43] Following the Burpees was A. R. R. Crawley, an Acadia-educated preacher, who served in Burma from 1853 to 1876. The Maritime Baptists' missionary agenda changed in the mid-1870s, when they partnered closer with their counterparts in Ontario and agreed to change their area of focus from Burma to India in 1875.[44]

As the Baptists developed their missionary program, women took a central role. John Webster Grant has observed that in the nineteenth century, "church women undoubtedly came to know and care more about distant countries than any other class of Canadians."[45] In addition to raising money to support foreign missions, women began traveling overseas—first as part of a husband-wife team (as demonstrated by the Burpees) and later as single missionaries. The first single female

---

41. Gibson, *Along the King's Highway*, 6.

42. Elliott, "Canadian Baptists and Native Ministry," 146–48. For a biography of Rand, see Lovesey, *To be a Pilgrim*.

43. The Burpees did not use the double-e spelling (opting instead for "Burpe"), but the "Burpee" spelling has been used since the late nineteenth century. It is used here for consistency.

44. Ross, "Sharing a Vision," 81.

45. Grant, *Church in the Canadian Era*, 57.

Baptist missionary from the Maritimes (and from Canada) was Minnie B. DeWolfe, who travelled to Burma in 1867. Due to a lack of funds in the Maritime Baptists' Foreign Mission Board, she had to travel under the auspices of the American Baptists. Hannah Maria Norris (later Armstrong) followed DeWolfe in 1870. Unlike DeWolfe, however, she did not turn to the American Baptists for support, but rather to her "sisters" across the Maritime Provinces, which resulted in the creation of dozens of women's mission aid societies across the Maritime Provinces, with central boards located in Saint John (for New Brunswick) and Halifax (for Nova Scotia and Prince Edward Island). These bodies later combined to form the Woman's Baptist Missionary Union in 1884.[46] Upon her death, one newspaper eulogized Norris by writing: "Among Canadian Baptist pioneer missionaries there has been no more honoured name than that of Mrs. Armstrong [Norris]."[47]

Although they were content with allowing women to serve abroad, the question of women in the ministry serving domestically remained a sensitive issue. Reinforcing their past experiences and what appeared to be a clear biblical mandate not "to teach or to assume authority over a man" (1 Tim 2:12), Victorian gender roles emphasized the woman's domestic responsibilities and generally relegated them to the private sphere, which meant discussions of women in the public life of the church raised both theological and cultural questions. In the 1840s, Joseph Dimock, one of the Baptist patriarchs, went as far as to note that the Apostle Paul's letters that forbade women to speak in the church meant they could not do *anything* that might "usurp the authority over the man," which, from his perspective, even included voting in churches. As he reasoned, it was problematic because women often made up the majority of congregants in any given church, which meant if they voted they would be able to make decisions for men.[48] On the other hand, other prominent Baptist leaders, such as Charles Tupper, father of the future Prime Minister of the same name, "did not believe that the passage forbade women to exhort the congregation to holy living," and instead encouraged this practice.[49] Likewise, one Baptist preacher in New Brunswick during this era reflected on one prayer meeting, wherein eleven women either prayed or

---

46. Ross, "Sharing a Vision," 81.
47. "Mrs. H. M. N. Armstrong," *Canadian Missionary Link*, November 1919, 1.
48. Lane, "Women and Public Prayer," 8.
49. Goodwin, *Into Deep Waters*, 181.

addressed the attendants, by observing that their piety and ability served as "A deth Blow to All those that did not Believe that Females Should take A Part In Prayer metings."[50]

In spite of the general air of debate, the nineteenth century saw the emergence of several important female Baptist leaders. Among the most significant was Mary Narraway Bond, an Anglican-turned-Baptist who had led services, along with her husband, in an independent chapel near Saint John Harbour in New Brunswick since the early 1820s. According to David Bell, "several accounts leave no doubt that it was she rather than her husband who exercised the gift of spiritual teaching."[51] The two had received believers' baptism in the 1830s, and their chapel officially joined the Baptists in 1854. Significantly, her obituary in the Baptist press—written by prominent Baptist leader, I. E. Bill—made no mention of the fact that she had preached for more than thirty years. Bell has rectified this rather shocking omission by lauding her as "the most successful woman preacher in the entire history of the Maritimes."[52]

While the Regular Baptists were the largest group of Baptists, they were not the only numerically significant Baptists in the region. Free Christian Baptists had existed in the region since at least the early-nineteenth century, including a mixed Free Christian Baptist and New Light congregation in Barrington, Nova Scotia. While they differed from the Regular Baptists in a number of theological ways, such as their retention of Alline's Arminian theology, perhaps their primary difference was their emphasis on open communion. In the 1830s, several significant "Free" groups emerged in the Maritimes. In 1832, in Carleton County, New Brunswick, seven churches combined to form the Free Christian Conference. This eventually became the Free Christian Baptist Conference, before ultimately becoming the Free Baptist Conference of New Brunswick in 1898. While they were the spiritual cousins to the Free Will Baptists in New England, the evidence suggests their heritage is traceable directly to

---

50. As quoted by Griffin-Allwood, "'The Sucksess of the Baptist denomenatsion In New Brunswick,'" 43. The errors are consistent with how the quote appears in the source.

51. Bell, "Allowed Irregularities," 15.

52. Bell, "Allowed Irregularities," 13, 16. Moreover, significantly, in Bill's influential denominational history, published in 1880, he does not mention her a single time. See Bill, *Fifty Years with the Baptist Ministers and Churches of the Maritime Provinces of Canada*.

The Arrival and Growth of Baptists in Canada

Alline's "New Light" revivals.[53] In 1837, a similar group named the Free Christian Baptist Conference emerged in Nova Scotia, and in 1867, they became the Free Baptist Conference of Nova Scotia. These groups sought to retain Alline's simplistic approach to the ministry. They did not meet in churches, they met in "meeting houses," and they did not have pastors, they had elders, who were usually responsible for several churches at a time. Quite contrary to the Regular Baptists, a distinctive of the early Free Baptists "was the comparatively prominent role females assumed in exhortation and public prayer."[54] This was further evidence of their commitment to Allinite theological heritage, as they were initially able to avoid the Regular Baptists' subordination of "disorderly" and "assertive women."

In spite of their emphasis on simplicity, the Free Baptists (particularly those in New Brunswick) suffered two schisms that birthed two competing Baptist groups in the region. In 1874, George Whitfield Orser charged the Free Baptists with departing from Allinite minimalism. Approximately forty churches of "Orserites," as they became known, separated and formed the Primitive Baptists (who, in 1981, joined the Free Will Baptists based in Tennessee). Over a decade later, in 1888, there was a second schism, this time over the topic of entire sanctification. That year, 433 individuals departed to form the Reformed Baptists (who, in 1966, joined the Wesleyan Church USA, and became the Atlantic District of the Wesleyan Church).[55] By the turn of the century, between the various groups—Regular, Free, Primitive, and Reformed—Baptists occupied approximately 19 percent of the population of the Maritime Provinces.[56]

It was during the nineteenth century that Baptists in the Maritimes stepped into the field of higher education. Baptists in Nova Scotia formed Horton Academy in 1828 and Acadia College (originally "Queen's College" until 1841) in 1838, both in Horton (Wolfville).[57] In New Brunswick, Baptists formed the New Brunswick Baptist Seminary in 1836, located in the capital city of Fredericton, which, after debilitating financial woes, relocated to Saint John and then St. Martins. When it arrived

---

53. For example, see Bell, "Yankee Preachers," 93–112.

54. Bell, "Allowed Irregularities," 24

55. On both the Primitive and Reformed Baptists, see Rawlyk, "The Holiness Movement," 293–316.

56. *The Fourth Census of Canada, 1901*, 144–45.

57. On Acadia, see Moody, "The Maritime Baptists," 88–102. Horton Academy eventually became a part of Acadia in 1959.

in the latter location, it became a joint effort between the Regular and the Free Baptists, and was renamed "Union Baptist Seminary" in 1884, which significantly predated the eventual union of these groups by more than twenty years (see below).[58] While Acadia thrived and became a central part of Baptist life, eventually reaching University status in 1891, Union was unable to weather its mounting financial difficulties and closed in 1895.

Central Baptists

Although Baptists in central Canada experienced similar growth, it was not nearly on the same scale as in the Maritimes. Unlike the "grass-roots evangelical impulse" felt in the Maritimes that gave Baptists their prominence and allowed them to engage and influence the culture, Baptists in central Canada had "no such common foundational ethos . . . , which left them divided and without a gospel that could effectively penetrate the culture."[59] Although the War of 1812 frustrated ties to American missionary agencies,[60] modest Baptist growth during these years and afterwards continued through waves of immigration from England and Scotland. These new sources, particularly those influenced by the English tradition, brought different emphases to the churches in the region. Among the most significant differences was their adherence to open communion, which, unlike the common American Baptist position, stipulated that any believer could partake in the Lord's Supper, regardless of denominational background. Where the English and Scottish differed from each other was in their view of the ordained ministry: while many of the Scottish settlers, influenced by the European revivals of James and Robert Haldane, had a relaxed view of church leadership, the English settlers emphasized the importance of a trained, professional clergy.[61] In spite of their differences, together they introduced a different flavour of Baptist identity into the region.

The scattered nature described above is perhaps most evident in several unsuccessful attempts to form larger denominational bodies from

---

58. Trites, "New Brunswick Baptist Seminary," 103–23.
59. Goodwin, "Footprints," 191–92.
60. Heath, "Ontario Baptists and the War of 1812," 49–50.
61. Goodwin, "Footprints," 197.

The Arrival and Growth of Baptists in Canada

1833 to 1851.[62] One Baptist observer credited these difficulties to the "fear on the part of some churches that co-operation would undermine the independence of the local congregation, and partly because of differences of opinion on the ordinance of Communion."[63] These included the Baptist Missionary Convention of Upper Canada (1833); the Upper Canada Baptist Mission Society (1836); the Canada Baptist Missionary Society (1837); the Canada Baptist Union (1844); and the Regular Baptist Missionary Union of Canada (1848). Many of these bodies were comprised of smaller association bodies, though the majority failed to have any lasting success.

Among the most active during this period was the Canada Baptist Missionary Society, as they began publishing a monthly newsletter, *The Canada Baptist Magazine and Missionary Register*, in 1837; and formed the Canadian Baptist College in Montreal "for the purpose of training up pious and promising young men among ourselves for the Christian ministry" in 1838.[64] Even these ambitious efforts, however, could not permanently unite the Baptists, as the newsletter discontinued publication in the early 1840s, and the college closed in 1849 when its geographic location and controversial stance on open communion led many to lose interest in it.[65] Although central Baptists clearly exhibited a desire for some kind of working relationship, the churches simply were unable to overcome the communion question or find a balance between independence and interdependence.

One body worth noting that formed during this era was the Amherstburg Regular Missionary Baptist Association. In 1836, an escaped slave named Anthony Binga formed the Amherstburg First Baptist Church close to the border, south of Windsor, Ontario. The church's proximity to the border was no accident, as it functioned as a safe haven for those who had travelled the Underground Railroad. As the black Baptist community grew, several other churches were established in the region, and in 1841, they formed Amherstburg Regular Missionary Baptist Association, unfortunately in part because of the racism they encountered on each side of the border.

---

62. This timeframe is adopted from Renfree, *Heritage and Horizon*, 96.

63. McKay, "The Story," 32.

64. "Announcement," *The Canadian Baptist Magazine and Missionary Register*, June 1837, 1.

65. Wilson, "British Influence," 26.

Although Baptists in central Canada experienced turbulence in the mid-nineteenth century, many continued to work toward unity. Some held to a wider ecumenical vision,[66] but most Baptists interested in union at the time focused on uniting denominational bodies. Although Upper and Lower Canada became Canada West and Canada East—two parts of the newly-formed Province of Canada—in 1841, attempts at Baptist union during this era remained largely restricted to the traditional regional divisions. In 1851, Baptists gathered in Hamilton and formed the Regular Baptist Missionary Convention of Canada West, whose purpose it was "to promote the preaching of the Gospel [sic] and to disseminate the Word of God in the Province of Canada."[67] As a counterpart to this body, in 1858 another group of Baptists formed the Canada Baptist Missionary Convention East. Each of these bodies sought "to assist struggling churches, educate the laity, provide a Baptist voice in provincial affairs, and employ evangelists to plant churches."[68]

A related ministry was the Canadian Baptist Foreign Missionary Society, which they formed in Ontario in 1874. Much like the Baptists in the east, from early on central Baptists were interested in foreign missions. Perhaps in a conscious effort to follow in the footsteps of William Carey, in 1867, Baptists in Ontario and Quebec identified India as their primary foreign mission field and that year commissioned Americus and Jane Timpany for service in that region. Six years later, in 1873, John and Mary Bates McLaurin joined them. Of course, the Baptists in central Canada were not limited to India, and in 1898 commissioned Archibald Reekie to serve in Bolivia—a field that he had personally identified.[69]

As with the eastern Baptists, women were deeply involved in the missionary enterprise in central Canada. A few years into their missionary service in India, the Timpanys returned to Canada on furlough seeking "help for women from women." As a response, a group of interested women formed the Women's Baptist Foreign Mission Society of

---

66. "Religious State of Canada," *The Canadian Baptist Magazine and Missionary Register*, February 1838, 194; and "On the Probable Causes of Disunion in Churches, and the Means by Which love and Harmony may be Effectually Secured," *The Canadian Baptist Magazine and Missionary Register*, December 1839, 126–30.

67. "The Constitution of the Regular Baptist Missionary Convention of Canada West," as cited in Fitch, *The Baptists*, 132.

68. "The Constitution of the Regular Baptist Missionary Convention of Canada West," as cited in Fitch, *The Baptists*, 132.

69. Brackney, "A Good Knight in a New Crusade," 32–33.

Eastern Canada (later of Eastern Ontario and Quebec) in Montreal in 1876.[70] Shortly thereafter similar circumstances saw the formation of the Women's Baptist Foreign Missionary Society of Ontario (West) and in 1882, they sponsored their first missionary, Mary Jane Frith, to minister directly to the women in India. (The two women's missionary societies combined in 1953 to form the Baptist Women's Missionary Society of Ontario and Quebec.)[71] One fascinating example of an early female missionary from central Canada is that of Isabel Crawford, a missionary to the Kiowa peoples in Oklahoma and daughter of prominent Canadian Baptist leader Jonathan Crawford. Her recent biographer has supplied an assessment of her life that might equally apply to some of the larger trends on Canadian Baptists and women in the missionary enterprise as those who "crossed many boundaries . . . of nation, [and] of gender roles."[72]

The Baptists in central Canada turned also to the indigenous population. Although American missionary societies had started the work among the native Canadians at the beginning of the nineteenth century, it was not until after confederation that central Baptists took interest. To serve the Six Nations Reserve, they sponsored two indigenous missionaries, Joseph Longfish and Seth Claus, and two white missionaries, J. Burke and Alexander Stewart. In 1874, a frustrated Stewart wrote to the convention: "I am afraid that the Baptists of Ontario have been somewhat indifferent in the past to the work which God requires them to do among the Indians."[73] Stewart's plea resulted in an increase of support from the central Baptists and the growth of the Baptist community on the reserve; however, by the end of the nineteenth century, the central Baptists' involvement with the indigenous peoples had again stagnated, especially as they diverted their resources to expanding westward.

The historiography surrounding the sudden impulse toward union (over and above previous theological roadblocks) is surprisingly underdeveloped, although Daniel Goodwin has suggested that it came out of the quest for denominational respectability in Canadian society.[74] If Goodwin is correct, then perhaps no Baptist in central Canada from that

70. Barnes, *Our Heritage Becomes our Challenge*, 14.

71. Renfree, *Heritage and Horizon*, 322–23.

72. Whiteley, "Crossing Boundaries," 113. See also Whiteley, *More than I Asked For*.

73. As quoted in Elliott, "Canadian Baptist Native Ministry," 152.

74. Goodwin, "Footprints," 200–1.

era represents the desire for respectability more that Robert Alexander Fyfe.[75] A graduate of Canadian Baptist College, Fyfe had a high view of education and believed it was time for Baptists in the Province of Canada to again enter the field of higher education. He admitted later that at the time he "found but two or three men who had any confidence that the Canadian Baptists could be again induced to lay hold of this [higher education] work." Learning a lesson from the feeling of isolation that had ruined Canadian Baptist College, Fyfe observed that any new school should be in a location much more central to Baptist work, which he estimated was somewhere between London and St. Catharines, with the significant stipulation that the area "should have a good Baptist Church, out of which an executive committee could be chosen."[76] Ultimately they selected Woodstock, and in 1857 formed the Canadian Literary Institute. In 1860, Fyfe became the first principal. In many ways it had the earmarks of a "Canadian Baptist" institution of higher education, as it did not restrict students based on denomination and it did not accept financial support from the government.

In an effort to further establish a degree of denominational respectability, Baptists in Ontario sought to form a reputable Baptist university in the province's capital of Toronto.[77] In 1879, with financial assistance from Senator William McMaster, a wealthy banker, businessman, and Baptist layperson, they relocated the Canadian Literary Institute's theology department to Toronto to form Toronto Baptist College. Baptists in central Canada appealed to their counterparts in other parts of the country to do likewise and transfer their theology departments to Toronto in order to have one centralized Canadian Baptist training centre. Acadia agreed, and in the 1880s, temporarily discontinued its theological education in favour of this united vision (they retained a reduced version of that department, until they reoffered a full theological training until 1923). Central Baptists reconstituted Toronto Baptist College as McMaster University in 1887 after receiving a generous endowment from McMaster upon his death. As a university, it developed competent Arts and Science programs, as well as its theological disciplines. According to Rawlyk, the 1887 Act of Incorporation suggested that "while McMaster

---

75. For a biography of Fyfe, see Gibson, *Robert Alexander Fyfe*.

76. From an untitled history written by Fyfe in 1878, as published in Wells, *Life and Labors*, 291–93.

77. Rawlyk, "A. L. McCrimmon," 31–32.

University was to be a Christian institution, only its seminary was to be explicitly Baptist."[78]

French Baptists

Until the 1830s, the vast majority of Baptist ministries in British North America had been directed toward the English-speakers in the region. In 1834, Henri Olivier, a Reformed missionary from Switzerland, arrived in Montreal with the intention of travelling southward to minister to the aboriginal peoples. Instead, believing Lower Canada to be a mission field unto itself, the Oliviers remained in Montreal and invited Henrietta Feller, a shrewd young widow from their church in Switzerland, to join them.[79] In 1835, under the auspices of the nondenominational Commission of the Churches of Switzerland Associated for Evangelism, Feller travelled with Louis Roussy, a young theologically-educated Swiss evangelist, to Lower Canada to minister to the French Canadians. The Oliviers remained in Lower Canada for only one more year before returning to Switzerland, thus leaving the work entirely to Feller and Roussy.

For the Swiss missionaries, the region's religious climate proved to be a significant obstacle. While the Constitutional Act of 1791 gave the Church of England preferential treatment (in the form of the Clergy Reserves) in Upper Canada, it allowed Lower Canada to retain the religious customs enshrined in the earlier Quebec Act of 1774, which had effectively institutionalized the Roman Catholic Church as the state church. After a string of unsuccessful attempts to crack the Roman Catholic hegemony in Montreal, Feller and Roussy moved to the much smaller Saint-Jean-sur-Richelieu, where again they struggled to establish a foothold. Finally, they relocated again to La Grande Ligne, where an early convert, Mary Lore, gave them use of what Harry Renfree characterized generously as "her unpretentious cabin,"[80] where in 1836 Feller and Roussy formed La Grande Ligne Mission. From this base of operations, Roussy evangelized in the surrounding villages and towns, while Feller taught children during the day and held daily prayer meetings for adults during the evening.[81] In January of the following year, the mission held

---

78. Rawlyk, "A. L. McCrimmon," 41.
79. Griffin-Allwood, "Mere Henrietta Feller," 90.
80. Renfree, *Heritage and Horizon*, 135.
81. Renfree, *Heritage and Horizon*, 135.

a service that included four baptisms. According to Sharon Bowler, Lore's influence was more than that of a generous supporter and in fact the mission's real momentum should be traced to her, because her testimony functioned as an important evangelistic tool to inspire a number of others in the province to make a similar decision.[82]

Although not originally a "Baptist" ministry, it received generous support from the Baptists in the region. In 1838, the Canadian Baptist Missionary Society reported that they viewed "the mission to the French Canadians as at present the most important of its missionary operations."[83] These connections strained relationships with Feller and Roussy's nondenominational commissioning body, which in turn frustrated the degree of Baptist support. This changed, ultimately, when Feller and Roussy each received believer's baptism in 1847. La Grande Ligne became a Baptist mission in 1849,[84] and later came under the auspices of the Baptists in Ontario and Quebec. Feller's school became known as the Feller Institute and remained an important part of Baptist work in Quebec until the second half of the twentieth century. By 1855, the mission had grown to include twenty preaching locations and had more than three thousand converts.[85]

Western Baptists

As Baptists spread throughout the central region, they looked also to a new field: western Canada. Manitoba and the Northwest Territories (which included modern-day Saskatchewan and Alberta until 1905) joined confederation in 1870; and British Columbia joined in 1871. With the promise of a nation-wide railway, the west was opened in new and exciting ways; however, the sparsely-populated nature of the region also guaranteed a unique set of challenges. Believing they were duty-bound to serve the western region, in 1868 Baptists in Ontario commissioned two of their pastors, Thomas Davidson and Thomas Baldwin, "to visit and explore the North West Territory, with a view to the commencement

---

82. Bowler, "Madame Mary Lore," 41–67.

83. "Report of the Committee of the Canadian Baptist Missionary Society," *The Canadian Baptist Magazine and Missionary Register*, August 1838, 54.

84. Goodwin, "Footprints," 199.

85. Wilson, "Union d'Églises Baptistes Françaises au Canada," 2950–51.

of future missionary operations therein."[86] After three months they returned and reported that they were unable to locate any Baptists, but believed that the convention should sponsor a missionary to begin work throughout the region to ensure that the forecasted influx of immigrants was met with a Baptist presence. (Of note in their initial assessment is that Davidson and Baldwin appear not to have considered the indigenous population as a potential mission field.)[87] Perhaps unaware of the history of their own denomination's reliance on missionaries—or else otherwise blind to the irony—the convention determined initially:

> it is our opinion . . . that the conditional appointment of a missionary, providing a colony of Baptist families would unite, move and settle together, in the great North-West would be a means of spreading Baptist principles in that far off country faster than by any other way within our reach . . . [but] *We would not recommend the Convention to send a missionary for the sake of the present inhabitants.*[88]

Among the determining influencers responsible for ultimately changing this decision was Fyfe, whose enthusiasm for the task landed him in a leading role on an advisory committee for western missions in 1871.[89] Within a year they had generated enough support and financial assistance to sponsor a missionary for three years.

The committee selected Alexander McDonald to serve as the convention's missionary to the western region. Born in Osgoode, Ontario, McDonald was a graduate of Fyfe's Canadian Literary Institute. He travelled to Winnipeg on 30 May 1873. Popular memory records that when asked why he would seek to labour in an area with so few Baptists, it is reported that he replied: "I have come to make Baptists." On 7 February 1875, he founded First Baptist Church of Winnipeg, the first Baptist church in western Canada, with a total of fourteen members. They reportedly celebrated their formal organization by reading the *New Hampshire Confession of Faith* and taking communion.[90] With this new "mother" church, Baptists expanded throughout the region, eventually planting

---

86. As cited by Gibson, *Robert Alexander Fyfe*, 316.

87. Elliott, "Canadian Baptists and Native Ministry," 154.

88. Extract from "Report of Deputation of the North West Territories," n.d., as cited by McLeod, "To Bestir Themselves," n.p. Emphasis added.

89. Gibson, *Robert Alexander Fyfe*, 316.

90. Harris, *The Baptist Union*, 8.

churches in Emerson (1876), Stonewall (1878), and Shoal Lake (1880), which, with McDonald's help and influence, all came together to form the Red River Association in 1880. Much like their sponsoring body in central Canada, they reflected a Calvinistic orientation. Only four years later, in 1884, Baptists had expanded throughout the region and formed the Regular Baptist Missionary Convention of Manitoba and the North-West. For his contributions to the Baptist cause in the region, McDonald is remembered as the "Pioneer."

Harry Renfree has astutely observed that in spite of "the tardiness of Baptist development in western Canada, the women in that region were right on the heels of their central and eastern sisters in organizing missionary societies."[91] Lucinda McDonald, Pioneer McDonald's wife, launched the first such attempt in 1878, based out of the Baptist church in Winnipeg. They focused primarily on domestic needs, such as helping the disenfranchised in their own region.[92] This circle of support eventually lost steam and was not replaced until 1887, when they formed the Baptist Women's Home and Foreign Missionary Society, and in 1889, they commissioned their first missionary, Lucy Booker, who travelled to India with the central Baptists.

In spite of the sizable indigenous population in the west, as already noted, ministering to them was not an immediate concern for the Baptists. It was not until William Henry Prince, the son of a native chief in Manitoba and a teacher at an Anglican-operated residential school, met Alexander Grant, the pastor of First Baptist in Winnipeg, that the western Baptists even entertained the idea. Grant did not mince words when it came to his dislike of what he saw as the inherently racist "reserve" system, which in 1891 he had linked to being "corralled like cattle, and quarantined like lepers until they fester and grow mad, then we shoot them down."[93] Prince joined Grant's congregation and, under the auspices of the Manitoba and North-West Convention, in 1892 became a missionary to the indigenous peoples.[94] He operated out of St. Peter's Reserve, north of Winnipeg, from which he traveled (by boat in summer and by sled in winter) to a number of other reserves in the area. The fruits of his labours were made visible in January 1894, when twenty-nine individuals that he

---

91. Renfree, *Heritage and Horizon*, 318.

92. Harris, *The Baptist Union of Western Canada*, 196.

93. *Northwest Baptist*, 1 February 1891, 2, as cited in Goertz, "Alexander Grant," endnote 56.

94. Elliott, "Canadian Baptists and Native Ministry," 155.

had shepherded into First Baptist Church of Winnipeg withdrew to form a Baptist church on St. Peter's Reserve.[95] Due to changing demographics, however, many departed from St. Peter's Reserve, which caused the church to lose visibility after 1914.

Compared to the development of the Baptist community on the Prairies, the establishment of the Baptist cause in British Columbia was much more "grassroots" in origin. Unlike the commissioned missionaries and pastors that began the outreach in Manitoba, laypersons were responsible for beginning Baptist work in the region. Black Baptists who had emigrated from California had lived in Victoria since as early as 1858, but there is no evidence of a Baptist church being planted until nearly twenty years later. In March 1875, in Victoria, Alexander Clyde, a recent-transplant from Stratford, Ontario and a Baptist, published a notice in the local newspaper that read: "All the Baptists in and round [sic] Victoria are requested to meet at the house of A. Clyde . . . on Friday, April 2d at 7 p.m. for the purpose of making arrangements toward organizing a Baptist Church. Come one, come all."[96] Those who responded to the advertisement formed a multiracial Baptist fellowship, and formally organized as First Baptist Church of Victoria in May 1876. In January of the following year they dedicated their new $6,000 building, which the press lauded as "very creditable to the Baptists of Victoria," before adding, "Their congregations [congregants?] are increasing, and the outlook appears hopeful both for minister and people."[97] In spite of this appraisal, the following years were ones of disunity for the church, primarily (and unfortunately) over issues of race relations. This tension plateaued when half the membership withdrew when the church voted to leave "the entire business and management of the church" to the white members in 1881, which eventually led to the church's closure in 1883.[98] After almost exactly a year, the Baptist community in Victoria reorganized as Calvary Baptist Church in June 1884 and, determined to learn from the lessons of the previous decade, this time they enshrined a statement against discrimination on the basis of race in their new covenant.[99]

---

95. Harris, *The Baptist Union of Western Canada*, 175–76.

96. "Notice," *The British Colonist*, 31 March 1875, 2.

97. "Opening of the Baptist Church Edifice," *The British Colonist*, 26 January 1877, 3.

98. Richards, "Baptists in British Columbia," 54–57.

99. Richards, "Baptists in British Columbia," 58.

As Baptists in Victoria were sorting out their situation, several other churches emerged throughout the province. The second Baptist church in the province (and first on the mainland) was Olivet Baptist Church in New Westminster, which they formed in 1878. Following this church were first churches in Vancouver (1887), Kamloops, (1888), Nanaimo (1889), and Nelson (1889); and second churches in Vancouver (1891) and Victoria (1892).[100] In 1897, they formed the British Columbia Baptist Convention. Of particular note, "there were no known attempts ever made by the Baptists to evangelize the natives" in British Columbia.[101] So far removed from their Baptist counterparts in the rest of the country, Baptists in the province relied almost exclusively on aid from Baptists in the United States for at least the first twenty-five years.[102]

As Baptists in the most western province were planting churches, their counterparts only slightly to the east in Manitoba were developing their program of higher education for the region. Sensing that the region might become a significant location for Baptist expansions, John Crawford, an Irish-born Baptist preacher then-working as a professor of New Testament at the Canadian Literary Institute, relocated to Rapid City, Manitoba and established Prairie College, which opened in March 1880. His vision for the school was essentially a transplanted version of the Canadian Literary Institute, as a seminary that focused on literary and theological topics. The promise of the transcontinental railway suggested that Rapid City was set for a massive expansion; however, those dreams were dashed when the Canadian Pacific Railway determined ultimately to change the proposed route to bypass the area entirely.[103] Coupled with their inability to resist or compete with the plan to centralize Baptist theological education in Toronto, the College filed for bankruptcy and closed in 1883.[104] Baptist education in the area continued in a much-reduced form at the Rapid City Academy, which opened in 1884 and focused specifically on literary studies. The key player in this instance was S. J. McKee, one of Crawford's peers, who had arrived in the region with the expectation of establishing a Baptist school. Fearing that they might experience the same fate as Prairie College, after the 1888–1889 school

---

100. Harris, *The Baptist Union*, 24.
101. Elliott, "Canadian Baptists and Native Ministry," 156.
102. Harris, *The Baptist Union*, 15.
103. McLeod, "McKee of Brandon College."
104. On Prairie College's short history, see Whiteley, "Prairie College," 85–97.

The Arrival and Growth of Baptists in Canada

year the Academy relocated southward to the growing city of Brandon, where it became the Brandon Academy. Yet there remained a need for a Baptist centre of higher education in the west, as students who travelled to central Canada for their education tended not to return to their home communities, where Baptist pastors were desperately needed. Sensing this reality, in 1898 the convention approved a motion to expand the Academy's offerings to include an Arts faculty affiliated with the University of Manitoba and a Theology faculty affiliated with McMaster University. The following year, on 2 October 1899, the newly minted Brandon College opened its doors.[105]

German and Swedish Baptists

Baptist growth during the nineteenth century was not limited only to these Baptist bodies, as a number of recently-arrived immigrants formed the nucleuses of long-lasting and significant Baptist communities. The mid-nineteenth century saw a flood of approximately fifty thousand German immigrants to Upper Canada, especially in the Waterloo County, where they settled in Berlin (modern-day Kitchener) and the surrounding area. In 1847, August Rauschenbusch—a German-born Lutheran-turned-Baptist preacher—travelled to the region under the auspices of the American Tract Society.[106] He returned in 1851, when he took a three-month leave of absence to lead services, which led to the formation of the Bridgeport Baptist Church, the first German Baptist church in Canada. In the subsequent years, the sizeable Baptist population in the region facilitated the planting of at least three other churches in the area.

In western Canada, similar waves of German immigration provided a fertile bed for Baptist growth. As the frontier sprawled westward, among those who travelled with it were German Baptists from Waterloo County. In Winnipeg, while attending First Baptist Church, J. B. Eschelmann, a German immigrant who had come by way of Waterloo County, began hosting a German-language Bible study, and formed German Baptist Church (today known as McDermot Avenue Baptist Church) on

---

105. Ellis, "What the Times Demand," 63–87. Since 1877, the University of Manitoba had the exclusive right to grant degrees in that provinces, which necessitated that the Baptists affiliate with them.

106. August Rauschenbusch was the father of Walter Rauschenbusch, a famous advocate of the social gospel in the early twentieth century. See below.

31 December 1889.[107] Reports of German Baptists in Alberta date from 1889 in Rabbit Hill, south of Edmonton; however, they did not form a church for three years, when they organized Heimthal Baptist Church (today known as Rabbit Hill Baptist Church) in 1892.[108] They called F. A. Mueller, a German Baptist missionary, as their pastor the following year. "He began his work visiting the people and preaching in the miserable huts called homes," recorded one report from 1896, before adding, "The blessing of the Lord has rested abundantly on his labors."[109]

Similarly, the late-nineteenth century was also when the Swedish Baptist Conference of America began its outreach to Canada. The first recorded Swedish Baptists arrived in western Canada from Michigan in 1874, only one year after Pioneer McDonald. It was not until 1894, however, when Martin Bergh, a Norwegian-born preacher then-living in North Dakota, visited Winnipeg and began holding revival meetings, where he found particular success among the Swedish immigrants. On 1 May 1894, he formed the First Scandinavian Baptist Church of Winnipeg (today known as Grant Memorial Baptist Church)—often recognized as the longest continuing Swedish Baptist church in Canada.[110] As Swedes continued to immigrate to western Canada, the Swedish Baptist community continued to see growth. By 1905, this number increased to roughly 10 churches throughout the region; and by 1914 they had 27.[111]

CANADIAN BAPTIST UNIONS AND DIVISIONS

Baptist Unions

The turn of the twentieth century saw significant unions in each of the three regional, English-speaking Baptist bodies. As other denominational bodies in Canada deliberated over organic union (such as the Methodists,

---

107. "McDermot Ave. Baptist Church, Winnipeg, Manitoba, Canada," *Heritage Horizons*, Fall 2014, 2.

108. On German Baptists in Alberta, see Priestley, "Ethnicity and Piety," 143–63.

109. G. A. Schulte, "A Tour Among the Germans in the Northwest," *The Home Mission Monthly*, November 1896, 371.

110. The earliest Swedish Baptist church in Canada was formed in Waterville, Quebec in 1892, but it lasted only one year.

111. Funk, *Our Story*, 19.

The Arrival and Growth of Baptists in Canada

Congregationalists, and Presbyterians, who would later form the United Church of Canada in 1925), Baptists in each region began considering the benefits of consolidating. The first to arrive at this decision were the Baptists in central Canada. In 1888, the Regular Baptist Missionary Convention and the Canada Baptist Missionary Conference, together with the Canadian Baptist Foreign Missionary Society of Ontario and Quebec, came together to form the Baptist Convention of Ontario and Quebec (BCOQ). While the question of open-closed communion was never fully resolved, as discussed above, by the time of union it was simply a non-issue, and the benefits of uniting eclipsed any previous debate over the matter. By the year 1900, the BCOQ consisted of 464 churches and approximately 44,000 members.[112]

Next was the union between the Regular Baptists and the Free Baptists in the Maritime Provinces. In 1905–1906, the Maritime (Regular) Baptists joined with the Free Baptist conferences in New Brunswick and Nova Scotia to create the United Baptist Convention of the Maritime Provinces. These groups relegated theological differences—including thorny topics such as election and the sovereignty of God—to the fringe of their discussion, and it was ultimately their regional identity and common heritage in the previous century's revivalist culture that united them into one body.[113] Because many routinely identified the Regular Baptists as *the* Baptists, it was necessary for this new union to develop an entirely new identity. It was for this purpose that they chose the name "United Baptist" in an effort to signal that this was a new, unified body. In 1906, they claimed 589 churches and 64,189 members.[114]

Unlike their central and eastern counterparts, Baptists in the west did not have as much of the theological baggage that had hampered attempts at union in the past; rather, their biggest challenge was in bridging the expansive geographic region and the Rocky Mountains. The appointment of W. T. Stackhouse—a Maritime-born pastor then-serving in Vancouver—to the position of superintendent of the Home Mission Board for the Baptist Convention of Manitoba and the North-West in 1901 proved to be a unifying factor. Universally respected by Baptists in western Canada, in 1906 he agreed to serve joint appointments with both

---

112. Renfree, *Heritage and Horizon*, 202–3.
113. Goodwin, "The Meaning of 'Baptist Union,'" 153–74.
114. Renfree, *Heritage and Horizon*, 210.

western conventions.[115] Ultimately encouraged by this arrangement, the two conventions entered into talks toward union and formed the Baptist Convention of Western Canada in 1907; however, they changed the name to the Baptist Union of Western Canada (BUWC) in 1909 to emphasize each constituent body's regional autonomy. Callum Jones describes their structure as "a union of virtually-autonomous regional conventions with a centralised executive and reduced local representation."[116] At the time of union, they had 201 churches and approximately 11,000 members.[117]

Baptist Opportunities and Actions

Throughout the mid- and late-nineteenth century, Canada's changing social climate provided a fresh set of challenges for these new Baptist groups. Immigration increased dramatically, and those who arrived usually settled in Canada's larger urban centres. In turn, industrial advances created unsafe or otherwise problematic working conditions. Rapid technological changes, such as the construction of railways, and the concomitant social changes, led to pressures on once well-established practices such as Sabbath observance. As Chris Crocker notes, Regular Baptists in Upper Canada "viewed the observance and celebration of the Lord's Day as vital and of paramount significance in the quest for social reform and religious piety." It was deemed a critical target for reform, for its "observation strengthened personal holiness and the family unit, its desecration was harmful to society, and . . . its observance would bring a blessing to the nation."[118] That impulse to shape a distinctly Christian nation through legal enforcement was a departure from Baptist aversion to coercion.

Baptists in Canada often looked to their counterparts south of the border for answers on how to confront alarming changes, and their answer often came in the form of the social gospel movement and in the likes of Walter Rauschenbusch—a professor at Rochester Theological Seminary in New York and son of August Rauschenbusch (who had earlier planted the first German Baptist church in Canada in the mid-nineteenth

---

115. Harris, *The Baptist Union*, 55.
116. Jones, "The Canadian Baptists of Western Canada," 3.
117. Renfree, *Heritage and Horizon*, 212.
118. Crocker, "A Worthy Cause," iv.

century).[119] Underlying the social gospel was the idea that Christianity could speak into various societal ills and could in fact lead to social reform, ultimately with the hope of ushering in the kingdom of God.[120]

Each Baptist group in Canada was influenced by the social gospel in different ways. In the west, a number of prominent BUWC leaders had trained under Rauschenbusch at Rochester, including D. R. Sharpe, his later biographer.[121] Callum Jones has observed that during the early twentieth century, "The social gospel was ingrained in Western Baptist thought; at Union assemblies it received significant attention and went unchallenged."[122] At the forefront for many western Baptists was the topic of alcohol consumption, which they contended should be prohibited or at least more strictly regulated. Indeed, they traced many of society's problems, including gambling and corruption, back to alcohol abuse. Even seemingly pressing topics, such as "unemployment, poverty, atrocious working conditions, inadequate housing, and militarism" were considered secondary to temperance.[123]

Both the BCOQ and the United Baptists responded to the social climate by issuing detailed social platforms. These documents articulated their respective stances on a number of issues contemporary to the time, such as the labour laws and temperance. Among the twenty-one planks in the BCOQ's platform (1913) were: "the abolition of child labour"; better regulations for "the conditions of toil for women"; "the protection of the individual and society from the social, moral, and economic waste of the liquor traffic"; "suitable provision for the old age of workers . . . those incapacitated by injury, and for the needy widows"; and for "a release from employment . . . on the Christian Sabbath."[124] Although the first

119. William H. Brackney has recently published a three-volume set of Rauschenbusch's work. See Brackney, *Walter Rauschenbusch*.

120. Nancy Christie and Michael Gauvreau have maintained that "Canadian progressive [Christian] leaders cannot be properly called social gospellers, as all but a handful believed that individual salvation must be the antecedent of the larger project of Christianizing the social." See Christie and Gauvreau, *Christian Churches and their Peoples*, 148.

121. Sharpe, *Walter Rauschenbusch*. For a list of important western Baptists that studied under Rauschenbusch, see Jones, "The Canadian Baptists of Western Canada," 52 and Scott, "D. R. Sharpe and A. A. Shaw," 197–99.

122. Jones, "The Canadian Baptists of Western Canada," 53.

123. Scott, "D. R. Sharpe and A. A. Shaw," 206–7.

124. M. C. MacLean, "Social Service: An Announcement and a Platform," *Canadian Baptist*, 10 April 1913, 4.

sixteen planks were taken directly from the Federal Council of American Churches of Christ, George Rawlyk has characterized their platform as "perhaps the most radical general socio-economic statement ever put forward by Central Canadian Baptists."[125]

In a similar way, the United Baptists had what Rawlyk identified as an "Evangelical social gospel consensus."[126] Their social platform (1921) had nineteen planks, but also included lengthy discussions on temperance, child welfare, and domestic relations.[127] Among other things, they sought "a more rigid and impartial enforcement of the Prohibitionary laws" and stronger protections for children, as "Every child has the right to play and be a child." They added, also, that they believed that divorce was acceptable only upon one's infidelity or if the life of one of the partners was "in absolute danger."[128] The social concern felt by Baptists across Canada is captured by one preacher's sermon given in Fredericton, New Brunswick in 1918: "no man can be a true disciple of Jesus Christ and ignore the physical needs of his fellow men."[129]

Baptist Divisions

The early-twentieth century was also a time of turbulence for Baptists in Canada, as the fundamentalist-modernist controversy threatened to overshadow any gains of union. Some evangelicals believed that the ideas introduced during the intellectual awakening, such as higher criticism and evolution, inappropriately questioned the authority of the Bible. They saw themselves as the bulwark to this rising tide of liberalism/modernism. Determined to defend the fundamentals of the faith, they adopted a militant attitude. By the early 1920s, they were known as "fundamentalists."[130]

---

125. Rawlyk, "Champions of the Oppressed?" 111.

126. Rawlyk, *Champions of the Truth*, 36.

127. For a good study on the United Baptists' platform, see Feltmate, "The Help Should be Greatest Where the Need is Most."

128. Beals, ed., *The United Baptist Year Book of the Maritime Provinces, 1920–1921*, 112–14.

129. Milton Addison, "The Divine Commission and the Time Limit: A Sermon Preached in the George Street United Baptist Church," *Maritime Baptist*, 6 February 1918, 2, as quoted in Feltmate, "The Help Should be Greatest Where the Need is Most," 51–52.

130. Curtis Lee Laws, "Convention Light Sides," *The Watchman Examiner*, 1 July 1920, 834. For an important study on fundamentalism, see Marsden, *Fundamentalism*

The seeming pervasiveness of the social gospel throughout the Baptist communities in Canada spurred additional questions, as it was often associated with theological liberalism.[131] A number of prominent Canadian Baptists, especially from the central region, joined the fundamentalist cause in its early stages, such as Elmore Harris, a missionary and the founder of what is today known as Tyndale University; and E. J. Stobo, who authored a chapter for the series that eventually lent its name to the movement, *The Fundamentals*.

The militancy of these individuals was soon dwarfed by that of T. T. Shields, the British-born pastor of Jarvis Street Baptist Church (JSBC) in Toronto.[132] As Shields and other fundamentalists mobilized, they looked to the growing use of modernist curriculum in the classroom. As a sitting member of McMaster's Board of Governors, initially he believed that if the school were to retain the evangelical principles upon which it was founded, it might serve as a fortification against the emerging modernist trend.[133] As the 1920s unfolded, however, Shields became unconvinced of McMaster's ability to remain sufficiently evangelical. In 1924, the school's waning evangelical identity became abundantly clear to Shields when it

and American Culture.

131. While the fundamentalists responded in part to the supposed liberal underpinnings of the social gospel movement, they shared some of their concerns as well, namely those related to the various perceived evils in society. When T. T. Shields preached his famous "The Christian Attitude Towards Amusements" sermon in 1921, in which he lambasted those who participated in "worldly" pastimes (such as going to the movies), he had ironic resonance with the United Baptists' social platform (issued the same year), which noted: "We recommend sending out a warning to parents against indiscriminate patronage of 'the movies' by their children." Beals, ed., *The United Baptist Year Book of the Maritime Provinces, 1920-1921*, 113. They likewise shared various positions against liquor and working on the Sabbath. For a copy of Shields' sermon, see T. T. Shields, "The Christian Attitude Toward Amusements," *The Gospel Witness*, 16 April 1931. This sermon was printed and reprinted in Shields' *Gospel Witness* on several occasions, but it was preached originally on 13 February 1921.

132. On Shields' development as a fundamentalist, see Adams, "The Call to Arms," 115-47. On McMaster's modernism during this period, see Pinnock, "The Modernist Impulse at McMaster University, 1887-1927," 196.

133. T. T. Shields, "McMaster Urgently Needs Money," *The Gospel Witness*, 5 October 1922, 3; T. T. Shields, "A Great Opportunity," *The Gospel Witness*, 3 June 1922, 2-3; and T. T. Shields, "Baptists and Education," *The Gospel Witness*, 21 September 1922, 3-4. Only a decade earlier, in 1910, Shields had defended McMaster from fellow Toronto-based pastor, Elmore Harris, who criticized the school for its perceived compliance with modernism. In 1894, Harris had opened the Toronto Bible Training School (now Tyndale University) as a missionary training ground and something of an alternative to McMaster.

announced its decision to give William H. P. Faunce, the President at Brown University and a purported modernist, an honorary Doctorate. The fundamentalists saw this act as an endorsement of Brown's modernism and a betrayal of their evangelical heritage, but for Shields, it was especially insulting, for he had received this same honour only six years earlier. He demanded that the university reconfigure the process by which they conferred honorary degrees in order to ensure that the honoree was actually an evangelical—a request with which the university reluctantly complied. Only one year after the Faunce controversy, the university appointed L. H. Marshall, also a purported modernist, to the Chair of Pastoral Theology. Shields was outraged. Using his prestige and position, he rallied a sizable fundamentalist unit in the BCOQ.

In October 1926, the BCOQ gathered for its annual meeting, with the larger purpose of discussing issues that Shields had raised about McMaster's modernism. In order to get ahead of the conversation, Shields hired courtroom stenographers to document the proceedings at convention. As each session closed, Shields sent the typed reports back to JSBC in order to prepare them for publication in his newspaper, *The Gospel Witness*. As a result, only two weeks after the convention, Shields published a mammoth 176-page edition of the newspaper (which usually ran for only eight pages). On the cover page, famously he declared: "Ichabod! McMaster's new name."[134] The impressive turn around on the convention proceedings gave his allies updates practically in real time, but it did not endear him to his opponents. Moreover, in his approach he often resorted to personal character attacks, which limited the support he received from those who shared his theological convictions. In early 1927, Shields opened Toronto Baptist Seminary and launched the Regular Baptist Missionary and Education Society of Canada. In late 1927, the BCOQ introduced a Private Bill in the Provincial Parliament to amend their constitution to allow them to remove churches from their fellowship. Once officially approved, the BCOQ immediately expelled thirteen churches, including JSBC. Those churches formed the Union of Regular Baptist Churches of Ontario and Quebec and, by the end of the year, seventy-seven additional churches separated from the BCOQ and joined them. Robert S. Wilson has called the 1927 schism "probably the most discussed incident in Canadian Baptist history."[135]

---

134. *The Gospel Witness*, 4 November 1926, 1.
135. Wilson, "Baptist Convention of Ontario and Quebec," 288.

The Arrival and Growth of Baptists in Canada

Much like the Baptists in central Canada, western Baptists were significantly affected by the fundamentalist-modernist controversy. In the early 1920s, Baptists in western Canada targeted Brandon College in the same way that Shields had targeted McMaster. Among the earliest protestors was W. Arnold Bennett, the pastor of Emmanuel Baptist Church in Vancouver and a recent Brandon graduate. At a meeting in 1920, he informed the Baptist Ministerial Association of Greater Vancouver that his former professor, Harris MacNeill, head of Brandon's department of theology, was a modernist and had revealed to him in a private conversation that he did not find "verbal inspiration and infallibility of the Bible . . . tenable in the light of modern knowledge and research."[136]

The scandal of these views soon reverberated throughout the entire union. As early as 1921, William "Bible Bill" Aberhart, the lay-leader of Westbourne Baptist Church in Calgary and future premier of Alberta, convinced his church to unofficially distance itself from the BUWC in part over modernism[137]—making it one of the earliest churches to do so. While this may have been the first church to depart from the union, the most concentrated fundamentalist cohort in the BUWC was in British Columbia. In early 1922, Bennett self-published a pamphlet entitled, "Facts Concerning Brandon College."[138] In it he again targeted MacNeill, this time using his recollections from his time as a student and supplementing them with those of his classmates. Other pastors joined his protests, including James B. Rowell, the pastor of First Baptist Kamloops and later founding-pastor of Central Baptist in Victoria. Moreover, several pamphlets written by "interested laymen" circulated the BUWC that highlighted the union's precarious financial situation and blamed it solely on Brandon's modernism.[139] In response to these various charges, in 1926, fundamentalists in the westernmost province formed the British Columbia Missionary Council, and the following year, on 6 July 1927, 16 churches separated from the union to form the Convention of Regular Baptist Churches of British Columbia. In Alberta, Westbourne joined one other congregation, Benalto Baptist Church, to form the Regular Baptist Missionary Society.

---

136. As quoted in Burkinshaw, *Pilgrims in Lotus Land*, 77–78.

137. Aberhart's appointment had already strained relations with the BUWC.

138. Bennett, "Facts Concerning Brandon College."

139. Interested Laymen, *A Further Message*; and Interested Laymen, *The Dangerous Peril of Religious Education*.

Out of each of the three regional Baptist bodies, the United Baptists were the least affected by the fundamentalist-modernist controversy. Largely preoccupied with the events elsewhere in the country, Shields had left the fundamentalist efforts to the locals, J. J. Sidey and J. B. Daggett, who targeted Acadia in the same way that he had targeted McMaster and their western counterparts had targeted Brandon. The differences between how these protests were received is perhaps best demonstrated in Acadia's 1928 decision to confer an honorary Doctorate on Shirley Jackson Case, who served as Professor of New Testament at the University of Chicago. Both a New Brunswicker and a graduate of Acadia, Case was also a leading modernist in North America. Rather than stir controversy—as had been the case with the Faunce incident in central Canada—this event passed without a sigh of opposition from the general constituency. The contrast is made even more pungent when one recognizes that this took place only one year after the BCOQ ejected Shields from their fellowship. The fundamentalist campaign ultimately faded away without any sizable lasting effects. Rawlyk has observed that their inability to split the convention stemmed not simply from their lack of clout in the convention, but also from fundamentalism's incompatibility with the region's religious climate.[140]

CANADIAN BAPTISTS IN NATIONAL PERSPECTIVE

Federation Baptists

While the fundamentalist-modernist controversy had lasting effects across the country, it did not dampen the Baptists' impulse toward union. Talks of forming an "all-Canada" body had dated to the early-twentieth century, culminating in a meeting in Winnipeg in 1900. Ultimately, regionalism discouraged these talks from producing fruit for many years. In spite of their inability to form a united body, in 1911 they did combine their foreign mission efforts to form the Canadian Baptist Foreign

---

140. Rawlyk, *Champions*, 34–37, 70–74; and Rawlyk, "J. M. Cramp," 119–34. On the fundamentalist movement in Nova Scotia, see also Murray, "From Exodus to Exile," 282–303. The small fundamentalist offshoot founded the Kingston Bible College in 1930 and an academy in 1935. They chose to identify as "undenominational," which ultimately caused an internal schism in 1939 from which they never fully recovered. Murray, "Exodus to Exile," 296–99.

Mission Board (later renamed the Canadian Baptist Overseas Missions Board in 1970 and then the Canadian Baptist International Mission in 1991). This remained their most tangible evidence of cross-pollinated ministries until the three regional Baptist bodies—the BCOQ, BUWC, and the United Baptists—met at a joint convention gathering on 7 December 1944 in Saint John, New Brunswick and came together under the banner of the Baptist Federation of Canada, later renamed the Canadian Baptist Federation in 1982. At the time of their formation, they celebrated being "the first Canada-wide Baptist fellowship with a common mind and voice reaching from coast to coast."[141] Each constituent body within the Federation remained wholly autonomous, but the Federation provided a mechanism through which to fellowship. The purpose of this national body was to combine their efforts in domestic evangelism and to speak with one voice on various social or theological issues, such as the peace process and abortion.

The Federation served also as a forum for Canadian Baptists to speak into ecumenical discussions. They participated in the Canadian Council of Churches, and played a formative role in the early stages of the Inter-Church Committee on Protestant-Roman Catholic Relations, which functioned from 1945 to 1972.[142] By the mid-twentieth century, however, these ecumenical connections had become problematic, as a number of Baptists began revaluating their partnership with Roman Catholics and with Protestants who were more liberal than them, such as the United Church. Questions on the efficacy of ecumenism soon populated the denominational press, as they asked: "can evangelicals travel the new ecumenical road?" and "ecumenism—right or wrong?"[143] As John Webster Grant has highlighted, this was part of a general trend toward the theological right that took place in numerous denominational bodies in Canada during the post-war period.[144] For many Canadian Baptists,

---

141. Adiel J. Moncrief, Jr., "Canada Baptists Join," *The Christian Century*, 19 July 1944, 863.

142. Reilly, "Baptists and Organized Opposition," 189.

143. David Kucharshy, "Can Evangelicals Travel the New Ecumenical Road?" *The Atlantic Baptist*, 1 April 1970, 1; and Thomas B. McDormand, "Ecumenism—Right or Wrong?" *The Atlantic Baptist*, 15 May 1970, 5. These examples are from the Atlantic region, but Baptists across the country printed similar ones. For examples, see Rudy, "The Ecumenical Movement, is it of God?" (including the one Rudy employs as his title).

144. Grant, *The Church in the Canadian Era*, 160–63.

the ecumenical discussion was the proving ground for their evangelical *bona fides*.

This was perhaps most pronounced in the eastern region, where they had not experienced a fundamentalist schism on par with their counterparts in central and western Canada. A group of conservative pastors formed the Concerned Pastors group in the 1960s to engage what they saw as the convention's drift toward modernism.[145] In 1971, they succeeded in passing two motions at the convention assembly that illustrate the United Baptists' new conservative identity—that all future delegates to the annual assembly needed to have received believer's baptism by immersion, which passed 359 to 115; and that they would cease all contributions to the Canadian Council of Churches, whether directly or indirectly (through the Federation), which passed 242 to 181.[146] Through this latter change they effectively disassociated themselves from the Canadian Council of Churches. In response to these changes, a group of progressive pastors formed the Atlantic Baptist Fellowship, later renamed the Canadian Association for Baptist Freedoms, which prioritized ecumenical dialogue. Robert S. Wilson has identified this period as "the closest that the Convention [ever] came to divisive fundamentalism."[147] Ultimately, in response to the growing polarization between these two ends of the theological spectrum, a group of moderate and conservative pastors gathered and developed a diplomatic statement of faith known as the "Wentworth Statement," in which they summed what would become the prevailing United Baptist attitude:

> Recognizing both the liberty conferred and the discipline imposed by the authority of Holy Scripture, we shall accept as brothers in Christ and in our denomination those whose views are different from ours, and we shall expect the same acceptance from them, as a necessary application of our belief that Baptist unity does not require uniformity.[148]

---

145. Their agenda had four major pillars: first, to implement designated giving as a way to boycott ministries with which they did not agree; second, to demand future ordinands to supply statements on the inerrancy of scripture and the virgin birth; third, to reprimand *The Atlantic Baptist* newspaper for its universally favorable coverage of the ecumenical movement; and fourth, to withdraw from the Canadian Council of Churches. See Wilson, "Atlantic Baptist Confront the Turbulent Sixties," 165.

146. Hobson, ed., *Year Book of the United Baptist Convention of the Atlantic Provinces, 1971*, 21a–22a, and 24a.

147. Wilson, "Atlantic Baptist Confront the Turbulent Sixties," 168.

148. Harlow, et al, "The Wentworth Statement," United Baptist Convention of the

The attitude captured by the Wentworth Statement demonstrated an appealing and irenic perspective for many Baptists across the theological spectrum and it came to typify United Baptist identity in the latter half of the twentieth century.

Simultaneously a similar conversation was occurring among western Baptists. In the 1960s, a growing cadre of conservative voices "suspected the Ecumenical Movement of seeking to create a global super-church . . . [and] feared that participation created only superficial unity and would compromise Baptist convictions."[149] Much like the eastern Baptists, in 1980, they pulled their support from the Canadian Council of Churches (ultimately rejoining in 2011). They likewise terminated many of their on-going partnerships with the increasingly-liberal United Church. They solidified their evangelical identity in 1986, when they formally affiliated with the Evangelical Fellowship of Canada.[150]

The 1960s were much less decisive for the central Baptists than they were for their counterparts elsewhere in the country. Although the other Federation Baptists eventually settled on a thoroughgoing evangelical identities, the BCOQ remained more inclusive into the second-half of the twentieth century—effectively striking a balance between both ecumenical and evangelical perspectives, and affirming both to a degree.[151] By 1980, for example, as already noted, the BCOQ found itself as the only Federation Baptist body still affiliated with the Canadian Council of Churches. Of course, labeling the BCOQ as "progressive" can only be understood in a relative sense (to the other Federation Baptists), as they too occupied a place largely on the conservative end of the theological spectrum.

Throughout the twentieth century, Canadian Baptists have been active in public life. As already noted, the Federation provided an opportunity for Baptists to speak into various social concerns of the era, but others—while remaining active in the larger Baptist community—forged their own paths. Among the most significant was Thomas Clement "Tommy" Douglas, Premier of Saskatchewan from 1944 to 1961 and federal leader of the New Democratic Party from 1961 to 1971, who helped introduce a single-payer, universal healthcare program into

---

Atlantic Provinces, signed 15 November 1971. Copy in the possession of the author.

149. Jones, "The Canadian Baptists of Western Canada," 330.

150. To date the best study on western Baptist identity is Jones, "The Canadian Baptists of Western Canada."

151. Rudy, "The Ecumenical Movement, is it of God?" 153–54.

Canada. Reared in the social gospel-rich atmosphere of Brandon College, he imbibed a progressivism that he would carry with him for his whole life. As his recent spiritual biographer, Sandra Beardsall, has written, he was not deterred by the social gospel's apparent optimism and he did not find "its expectation that humanity could reach for the Kingdom of God unrealistic or hubristic."[152] Another example is Watson Kirkconnell, the president of Acadia University from 1948 to 1964, sometimes called the "father of Canadian multiculturalism." "In contrast to most discussions of immigrants in Canadian society [in the 1930s]," writes Robert R. Smale, "Kirkconnell sought to promote tolerance towards ethnic minorities through a sympathetic portrayal of their cultural backgrounds, their countries of origin and by demonstrating the cultural creativity of these minorities through translating and publishing their writing."[153] During the post-9/11 tensions, Ken Bellous, executive minister of the BCOQ, joined with other denominational leaders to urge the government to carry out a restrained, circumspect, and responsible military response in line with a United Nations mandate.[154] Even more recently, the actions of Chief Marcia Brown, a Baptist Sunday School teacher as well as Beaverhouse First Nation Chief, have compelled the government to admit and make recompense for its abysmal mistreatment of First Nation children and families. As these representative examples demonstrate, Baptists remain engaged in civil affairs, seeking justice and the betterment of life for all Canadians.

Fellowship Baptists

The Federation Baptists were not the only Baptists in Canada that experienced important growth during the mid-to-late twentieth century, as those Baptist bodies that emerged from the fundamentalist-modernist controversy had a national vision and eventually became one of the largest Baptist groups in the country today: the Fellowship of Evangelical Baptist Churches in Canada. During the 1930s and 1940s, the Union of Regular Baptists experienced two significant internal schisms that eventually shaped their movement. The first occurred in 1931, over the direction of two of their ministries, the Women's Missionary Society and

---

152. Beardsall, "One Here Will Constant Be," 161.
153. Smale, "For Whose Kingdom?" 226
154. Project Ploughshares, "Canadian Churches say 'No' to Iraq War."

the Fundamentalist Baptist Young People's Association. Shields criticized the former with working in areas that had "no relation to the work the churches are trying to do," and the latter with influencing its young members "to return poisoned at heart against their church and the Union."[155] He withdrew his support from each of these ministries and expelled nine pastors (and their churches) from the Union. They were joined by a number of other churches that were more sympathetic to them than they were to Shields, which reduced the number of churches in the Union to only 60.[156] Those expelled formed the Fellowship of Independent Baptist Churches of Canada in 1933. Quite unlike Shields, who was an outspoken critic of dispensationalism and tended toward amillennialism, the Independent Fellowship enshrined a premillennialist stance into their basis of formation.

The second major schism occurred in 1948–1949, when Shields dismissed the dean of Toronto Baptist Seminary, W. Gordon Brown over the institution's direction. In response, on 4 January 1949, Brown rallied together with pastors from the Union and the Independent Fellowship to form the Canadian Baptist Seminary, which they renamed Central Baptist Seminary in April of that year. Interested pastors and laypersons from either group soon rushed to support this enterprise. Churches pulled support from the Toronto Baptist Seminary and redirected it to benefit Brown's new seminary, and the majority of students likewise exited the former in order to join the latter.[157] The schism at Toronto Baptist Seminary soon spilled into the Union, and at the gathering of October 1949, the delegates did not re-elect Shields to the position of President. Shields slowly detached JSBC from the Union, before officially departing to form the Conservative Baptist Association of Canada with several ally churches in 1951, which they later renamed the Association of Regular Baptist Churches in 1953.[158]

No longer under Shields' direction, Union members sought to reconnect with their one-time co-workers in the Independent Fellowship. As one active participant later reflected: "For too long the outside world had recognized our splits and divisions and hopefully now they would

---

155. "The Woodstock FBYPA Convention," *The Gospel Witness*, 4 June 1931, 10–11.

156. Watt, *The Fellowship Story*, 34.

157. The best and most thorough analysis of these events is found in Wilson, "Torn Asunder," 48–65.

158. Wilson, "Torn Asunder," 65–70.

soon see a reversal of this trend and be forced to acknowledge a new spirit among us."[159] On 21 October 1953, under the influential leadership of Norman W. Pipe, the moderator of the Independent Fellowship, and W. H. MacBain, the president of the Union, these two estranged groups reunited as the Fellowship of Evangelical Baptist Churches in Canada.[160] Paul Wilson has identified this moment as a "turning-point in Canadian Baptist history," because "The Shields variant of militant fundamentalism was rejected in favor of a less strident, more cooperative, more inclusive and less tightly organized expression of conservative evangelicalism."[161] Yet, as early commentary indicates, inclusion could only go so far. Commenting on the formation of the new body, Pipe wrote:

> There are evangelicals who are not Baptists, and there are Baptists who are not evangelicals. The modernists of our day who cling to the name "Baptist," yet deny His Word, are no more "Baptist" than many who cling to the name "Christian" and have never been "born again." . . . This newly formed body is not a fellowship which countenances the "inclusivist policy" . . . The churches and pastors of The Fellowship of Evangelical Baptist Churches in Canada, could not and would not endorse the modernism of McMaster University, or of certain churches and pastors in the [BCOQ]. . . . The formation of this new fellowship will enable us to present an increasingly effective testimony to our historic Baptist convictions, and to maintain a more effective protest against modernism.[162]

The new body elected MacBain to fill the role of president, who articulated his desire to see *all* evangelical Baptist churches in Canada under the Fellowship banner and noted, "How far are we going? Geographically, we have no limitations in Canada."[163] They had a national vision and, as explored below, soon expanded throughout the country.

---

159. Watt, *The Fellowship Story*, 45.

160. For a good overview of key theological beliefs in the Fellowship, see Lockey and Haykin, "Polemic, Polity, and Piety," 145–73.

161. Wilson, "Torn Asunder," 72.

162. Norman Pipe, "This Fellowship Whence?" *The Fellowship Baptist*, November 1953, 5, as reprinted in Brackney, ed., *Baptist Life and Thought*, 518—19.

163. W. H. MacBain, "Inaugural Address," 23 October 1953, as reprinted in Haykin and Lockey, *A Glorious Fellowship*, 143.

The Arrival and Growth of Baptists in Canada
German and Swedish Baptists

The twentieth century was a period of change for several other significant Baptist bodies as well, including the German and Swedish Baptists. In the late-nineteenth and early-twentieth century, the BUWC financially supported both of the burgeoning foreign Baptist communities with the hope that if either were to become an English-speaking body, they would join one of the regional Baptist bodies. By the time either was ready to join a larger body, however, both the Germans and Swedes looked to their counterparts in the United States.

The Germans were the first to do so and officially joined their southern counterparts in fellowship in 1919. In spite of their new wider family, these early years proved to be difficult ones for them. They had always relied on immigration for growth; however, international tensions had effectively frustrated the once-steady stream of German immigrants. These tensions climaxed ultimately with the dawn of the First World War, when Germans in Canada suddenly found that their Anglo-Saxon neighbours viewed them with suspicion simply because of their heritage. While they experienced some growth from modest German immigration during the interwar years, they again faced a similar problem during the Second World War. Each of these conflicts contributed to the eventual Anglicization of the German Baptist community, as they made every effort to prove their loyalty to Canada. Many churches began conducting services in English—first evening and then eventually morning services—and some churches even Anglicized their names.[164] In 1944, they became the North American Baptist Conference. They opened a training institute in Edmonton in 1940, which later expanded to become an undergraduate training centre, the North American Baptist College in 1967. They again expanded this institution to include a divinity school, the North American Baptist Divinity School, in 1980, which they renamed Edmonton Baptist Seminary in 1990. Combining their college and seminary under one banner, they selected Taylor University College and Seminary in 2002, named after the prolific missionary J. Hudson Taylor. They closed the University College in 2008, and decided instead to focus on seminary education.

The Swedish Baptists joined with the Baptist General Conference of America (formerly the Swedish Baptist Conference of America) in 1948. This was, at least in part, because they believed that "some Canadian

---

164. Link, "North American (German) Baptists," 92–99.

Baptist churches and their schools" had departed from "their historic evangelical positions,"[165] which was a clear remnant of the fundamentalist-modernist controversy. The 72 Canadian churches met in 1977 and again in 1979 to discuss the formation of an autonomous Canadian body; and in 1981 they voted nearly unanimously to form the Baptist General Conference of Canada. Among their ongoing ministries is the Canadian Baptist Seminary in Langley, British Columbia, which they formed in 1988.

Southern Baptists

Among the most recent and significant transplants to Canada has been the Southern Baptist Convention, which has come to occupy a prominent place in Canadian life. As will be discussed further below, by the early 1950s, they made significant inroads into the Regular Baptist Convention of British Columbia, which they used as a base of operations to spread throughout the country. While they were initially based in western Canada, they had a national vision from their earliest days, as they set their sights as far as the easternmost province, Newfoundland. In 1954, Baptists in central Canada criticized the Southern Baptists' sudden interest in the north as a "Southern Baptist Invasion."[166] G. Richard Blackaby has written that the arrival of Southern Baptists in Canada was not an "invasion," per se, but that it "exemplifie[d] the historic Canadian struggle to provide an unattained Baptist witness amidst overwhelming demographic and ecumenical pressures." While Federation Baptists grappled with the ecumenical question, the Southern Baptists entered with a distinct and unwavering Baptist perspective that according to Blackaby "could never be sacrificed on the altar of ecumenical or national expediency."[167]

Over the next forty years the Southern Baptists spread throughout the country. They became the Canadian Southern Baptist Conference in 1957 and then the Canadian Convention of Southern Baptists in 1985, before finally adopting the name the Canadian National Baptist

---

165. Funk, *Our Story*, 47.

166. As cited by Jones, "Western Canadian Baptists and the Southern Baptist 'Invasion,'" 413.

167. Blackaby, "The Establishment of the Canadian Convention of Southern Baptists," 108–9.

The Arrival and Growth of Baptists in Canada

Convention in 2008. In 1986, they opened the Canadian Southern Baptist Seminary and College in Cochrane, Alberta.

EXPANSIONS AND CHANGES

Federation Baptists

The mid-to-late twentieth century was also a time of expansion for the Federation Baptists. Beginning in 1956, every three years the Federation adopted a "Triennial Project," which usually involved expanding existing ministries or launching new ones. From 1956 to 1962, these were focused largely on their efforts to Newfoundland.[168] Prior to the mid-twentieth century, the Baptist presence in Newfoundland was nonexistent, but when it became Canada's tenth province in 1949 it soon entered discussions. Early in the century, the island colony/dominion had large populations of Roman Catholics, Methodists (United after 1925), Salvation Army, Anglicans, and Pentecostals, but very few (if any) Baptists. Indeed, it was not until the post-Second World War period that Baptist missions began in Newfoundland in earnest. According to Canadian Baptist leader Thomas B. McDormand, there were three motivating factors for beginning work in the region: first, to reach the remaining United States troops stationed there from the war; second, to establish a work before the independent Baptists; and third, to establish a work before the Southern Baptists.[169] After labouring in the province for approximately two years, the Canadian Baptists planted their first church on "the rock" in St. John's in 1955. In 1960, Baptists in central Canada looked to these developments and celebrated:

> within five years, we [Federation Baptists] have built four Baptist Churches in Newfoundland and now have four resident Baptist ministers in Canada's youngest province. No one who was associated with the initiation of our work in Newfoundland envisaged such remarkable progress in such a brief period of time.[170]

---

168. Bentall, *From Sea to Sea*, 173.

169. McDormand, *A Diversified Ministry*, 53–55.

170. Gregory, ed., *Year Book 1960–1961 of the Baptist Convention of Ontario and Quebec*, 142.

The United Baptists took a leading role in the new initiative and invited the Newfoundland churches to join the convention. In 1963 they changed their name to the United Baptist Convention of the *Atlantic* Provinces to reflect their new geographical makeup.

Other projects that the Federation sponsored during these early years involved outreach to the indigenous community. Of note, in 1963, the Federation agreed to support the Tuscarosa Baptist Church on the Six Nations Reserve and, in particular, pledged to construct a new church building for the native Baptists. David Elliott has observed the Federation's involvement quite derisively by suggesting that their intention was to build "a new sanctuary . . . according to white standards."[171] Naturally, the Federation records give a very different reason, apparently owing to the fact that the existing building had been condemned. Moreover, they believed that "with a new building and proper equipment for religious education . . . our work on the reserve would take on new life and new importance."[172] Upon the completion of the building in 1964, the congregation moved to its new location and became the Ohsweken Baptist Church.

Other projects also revolved around the evolution of the work among French Baptists, as La Grande Ligne became L'Union d'Églises Baptistes Francophones du Canada in 1969 and joined the Federation as the fourth member body the following year. By virtue of La Grande Ligne's affiliation with Baptists in central Canada, it became an association within the larger BCOQ in 1888. With its strong enrolment figures, the Feller Institute remained the centerpiece of the Baptist work in French Canada well into the twentieth century.[173] The rest of La Grande Ligne, however, was facing a steady decline in numbers. In 1949, La Grande Ligne saw a net loss of 68 members—a drop from 940 to 872.[174] While the fate of the Feller Institute unfolded a little differently, it was not entirely saved from these difficulties. It had seen relative success in the first half of the century and held steady enrollment figures until 1943, when the Second World War forced its temporary closure and the government converted its facilities into a prisoner-of-war compound. It reopened in 1948, but

---

171. Elliott, "Canadian Baptists and Native Ministry," 153.

172. *Proceedings and Minutes of the Assembly of the Baptist Federation of Canada* (1962), 51–52.

173. In 1902, for example, they had 139 students. Renfree, *Heritage and Horizon*, 268.

174. Renfree, *Heritage and Horizon*, 273.

The Arrival and Growth of Baptists in Canada

never fully recovered and closed permanently in 1967. Outside of Quebec, French Baptist work began in Moncton, New Brunswick in 1934 under the leadership of Henri Lanctin with tent meetings in predominantly Roman Catholic areas. He called his ministry La Bonne Nouvelle, and founded a bookstore, a summer children's camp, and a radio ministry. Various French-speaking Baptist congregations began to populate the eastern province, beginning with L'Église Baptiste Francaise in Moncton (1935). Although they operated under the auspices of the United Baptists eventually they affiliated also with La Grande Ligne.

In both Quebec and New Brunswick, the French Baptist churches' associations with English-speaking mother bodies was problematic. In particular, many Quebecois believed the Baptist work was an instrument to subvert French nationalism. It did not help that beginning in 1910 La Grande Ligne had moved away from strictly French work and instead developed various bilingual ministries.[175] By the mid-twentieth century they had realized that the bilingual experiment had failed and that it was necessary to again form a strictly French Baptist body. In 1966, Albert Lefrancois, a French-speaking pastor, motioned that they convert their association into a union.[176] As they reported:

> The people the Mission seeks to serve are French Canadians, therefore the need is for a French Canadian Baptist organization... The transformation of the "French Association" into the "Union of French Baptist Churches in Canada" was the answer to the need for a totally French Canadian structure.[177]

In 1969, they incorporated as L'Union d'Églises Baptistes Francophones du Canada; and in 1970, they became the fourth member of the Federation. In 1980, they founded La Faculté de Théologie Évangélique in Montreal, which is affiliated also with Acadia University, who officially confers the degrees.

Not all changes were geographic in nature, as Federation Baptists increasingly raised questions that were more theological—including *who* could be a pastor, and more specifically if one's gender could preclude them from serving in a church and eventually becoming ordained. As noted earlier, this was not a new issue for Canadian Baptists, as they had wrestled with it since their earliest days. The question of women

---

175. Thomson, "Witness in French Canada," 54.
176. Thomson, "Witness in French Canada," 54.
177. As quoted in Thomson, "Witness in French Canada," 54.

in ministry leadership has been a thorny one for many Baptists, but surprisingly the tradition of ordained women serving in Baptist circles in Canada dates back to the early-twentieth century to Ella Hadassah Kinney Sanders, a Reformed Baptist and missionary from New Brunswick. For two years she laboured as an evangelist with another female preacher, Mary Everett, and shared the gospel throughout the region. In 1901, she and her husband were commissioned to serve as missionaries to South Africa. As Sanders later reflected: "Because we cannot organize a church without two or more ordained ministers, I was ordained in Saint John the night before we sailed so I could help my husband when we would organize our African Churches."[178] Thus on 5 September 1901, the Reformed Baptists ordained her in Saint John, New Brunswick, which, significantly, made her the "First woman in the Dominion of Canada to be ordained."[179] Another important early ordained woman was Jennie Johnson, a black Baptist preacher from Chatham Township in Ontario.[180] Born in 1868, she underwent a conversion experience at the age of sixteen and dedicated her life to the ministry. With dreams of becoming a missionary, she enrolled at Wilberforce University, a historically black institution, in Xenia, Ohio. Instead of travelling abroad, after two years at school, she returned to her hometown and helped form a circle of believers in the Prince Albert district. Because her own denomination did not ordain women, she looked across the border, to the Michigan Association of Free Will Baptists, who ordained her in October 1909. She provided pastoral leadership in her area of southern Ontario for several years, and even after she relocated to Michigan, she remained in contact with her friends and co-labourers in the BCOQ.

While Sanders' and Johnson's stories are important ones in Baptist history in Canada, it was not until the middle of the century that the Federation Baptist bodies themselves began accepting women as candidates for ordination. Each of the major Canadian Baptist bodies had debated the issue in the past. For example, in 1930, a special committee in the BCOQ issued a report on the ordination of women that concluded that they did not feel "that there is either demand or need, especially at the present time, for beginning a practice which is entirely new to us

---

178. As quoted in Mullen, *"I Believe in the Communion of Saints,"* 340.

179. Mullen, *"I Believe in the Communion of Saints,"* 338. We are indebted to Pat Townsend for bringing Sanders to our attention.

180. For a recent study on Jennie Johnson, see Reid-Maroney, *The Reverend Jennie Johnson*.

The Arrival and Growth of Baptists in Canada

as a people."[181] An amendment to the report that added that the BCOQ "express its approval of the ordination of women on equal terms with men" was defeated and the report passed as written.[182] It was not for another seventeen years that the BCOQ passed a motion to begin ordaining women, and in 1947 ordained Muriel Spurgeon Carter. Following suit, the United Baptists ordained Josephine Moore in 1954, and the BUWC ordained Mae Benedict in 1959. A statement from a Baptist pastor and scholar named William Elgee at the time of Moore's ordination sums up the moment: "Ladies and gentlemen, do you realize that this is an historic moment in the life of our convention?"[183] In spite of this cataclysmic change in these Baptist communities, the matter was far from settled theologically, and continued to be a talking point moving forward, as complementarians and egalitarians coexist in each community.[184]

Another significant change in Federation Baptist life during the latter half of the twentieth century relates to higher education. In 1957, McMaster University became a public institution, and the BCOQ instead chartered the McMaster Divinity College as a separate yet affiliated institution that effectively functioned as the university's faculty of theology.[185] In general, Baptists in central Canada were quite satisfied with this arrangement. No doubt the sheer size of the institution had become daunting to many Baptists, but it is likely that others were ambivalent toward its devolution because they still remained suspicious of it since the schism of 1927. Since the mid-twentieth century, the Divinity College has worked to reverse its historical designation as a modernist institution. One of the first major shifts was in the appointment of Clark H. Pinnock, a well-known evangelical scholar, as Professor of Systematic Theology in

---

181. MacLeod, ed., *Baptist Year Book, 1930*, 252.

182. MacLeod, ed., *Baptist Year Book, 1930*, 42–43.

183. As quoted in Hugh McNally, "Let's Keep Ordaining Women," *Atlantic Baptist*, April 1987.

184. For a good example of the on-going conversation, in April 1987, the United Baptists dedicated a special edition of their newspaper, *The Atlantic Baptist*, to discussing the topic of women in ministry. They styled it as a forum for voices on either end of the debate to come together and discuss the topic in a civilized way. Historian Robert S. Wilson describes it as "one of the few occasions in the Baptist world where key leaders on both sides of the issue made their views known in convincing and thoughtful manner in the same publication." Robert S. Wilson, "Saying Goodbye to an Old Friend," *Atlantic Baptist*, May-June 2005, 10.

185. On this transition, see Brackney, *Congregation and Campus*, 329–30.

1977.[186] This trend continued into the late-twentieth century, especially with the appointment of William H. Brackney, a distinguished Baptist historian and theologian from the United States, as the principal in 1989. Early in Brackney's tenure, one journalist identified the significant changes as "The Unlikely Transformation of McMaster Divinity College."[187] That trajectory continued into the twenty-first century under the tenure of principal Stanley E. Porter.

Baptist higher education underwent similar changes on the east coast. In 1949, they formed the United Baptist Bible Training School (UBBTS) as a "conservative, but not contentious" alternative to fundamentalist and modernist options in the region.[188] It was initially a high school with a lay-bible training program, but by the early 1950s began offering courses that could be transferred for college credit. As it offered an increased number of courses at a college level, it soon became apparent that the two convention-operated institutions, UBBTS and Acadia, would be fighting for enrolments and finances. Yet, another issue that had lain dormant for many years came to the forefront of the discussion: Acadia's purportedly modernist curriculum. As suspicion of the traditional Baptist training ground grew, it further limited the amount of financial support they received from churches. Feeling that the Baptists had taken Acadia as far as they could, in 1966, the Associated Alumni had a bill introduced into Nova Scotia's Legislative Assembly that effectively limited Baptist control to the faculty of theology, which they reformed in 1968 as Acadia Divinity College. This institution would later employ a number of well-known Baptist scholars, such as Jarold K. Zeman, Allison Trites, and Craig Evans. Additionally, in 2019, when Anna Robbins became president of the college, she also became the first female president of a Baptist seminary in Canada. Yet, in spite of Acadia's academic pedigree and its legacy, the United Baptists were not content to be limited to seminary education and immediately sought to regain what they had lost. In 1968, they voted to turn UBBTS into a "College of Arts and Bible," which they

---

186. Pinnock's later career stirred some controversy, beginning with his evolving view on inspiration in *The Scripture Principle* (1984), and later with his views on open theism, as published in "Systematic Theology" (1994) and *Most Moved Mover* (2001).

187. Doug Koop, "The Unlikely Transformation of McMaster Divinity College," *Christian Week*, 17 December 1991, 7–8. For a conversation on this "transformation," see Rawlyk, *Is Jesus your Personal Saviour?* 46; and Brackney, *A Genetic History*, 472–73n8.

188. Wilson, "Conservative, but not Contentious."

renamed to Atlantic Baptist College in 1971. They later renamed it the Atlantic Baptist University in 1996, and then Crandall University (after the New Brunswick Baptist patriarch, Joseph Crandall) in 2009. In its new role it filled the role that Acadia always had as their undergraduate institution.

In the west, the BUWC also looked to the field of higher education. Unlike the situations at McMaster and Acadia, at Brandon the mounting fundamentalist criticisms caused support for the college to wane, which created an increasingly dire financial situation. Finally, when the Great Depression hit in 1929, it was Brandon's deathblow. Brandon's finances could not recover and, in 1938, the college affiliated with the University of Manitoba and became Brandon University, after which the BUWC relinquished itself from its responsibility to the institution.[189] A decade later, in 1949, the BUWC formed the Baptist Leadership Training School in Calgary, which, like UBBTS, focused on training people for Christian ministry. Yet, this was only a one-year program and did not necessarily prepare its students for full-time pastoral ministry. They turned again to developing a robust theological program. Along with several other Christian denominations in the region, earlier in the century the BUWC received a plot of land from the University of British Columbia under the condition that they construct a theological college. In 1959, they established Carey Hall, which opened the following summer as a residence for men studying at the university. They introduced various theological courses in the 1970s and formally affiliated with nearby Regent College, a transdenominational evangelical seminary, in 1980 to offer a graduate education.[190] Although they are no longer affiliated with Regent, they continue to operate as the western Baptists' denominational seminary. Since 1991, the educational arm of the institution has been known as Carey Theological College. Carey has played an important role in western Baptist life, as demonstrated in the position of Pioneer McDonald Chair of Baptist Studies, a position that has historically functioned as "the denominational theologian and consultant" for the BUWC.[191] A number of important Baptist leaders have occupied this chair, including Samuel J. Mikolaski and Stanley J. Grenz.

---

189. On Brandon, see Ellis, "What the Times Demand," 63–88.

190. For a brief overview of the history of Carey Hall, see Jones, "The Canadian Baptists of Western Canada," 289–93.

191. Carey Theological College, "Grenz Returns to Carey," n.d.

The four member bodies of the Federation remained closely associated for the remainder of the century and into the present. In the second half of the century, Federation Baptists participated in ecumenical relations that were much more palatable to the majority—by the early twenty-first century, each member group had affiliated with the Evangelical Fellowship of Canada; and, under historian Jarold Zeman's influential leadership, they began courting closer relationships with the believers' church movement.[192] In 1995, the Federation combined with the Canadian Baptist International Ministries to create the Canadian Baptist Ministries (CBM). While the CBM remains active in Canada today, it does not take as prominent of a role in the life of each regional body as the Federation had earlier in the century.

Fellowship Baptists

Although the Fellowship began in the English-speaking central region, they did not remain isolated to that area and soon set their sights beyond their own traditional geographic location by expanding previous initiatives and developing new ones across the country. In 1953, the Fellowship had six pastors working among the French Canadians in Quebec, mostly in the Abitibi area. The Toronto Baptist Seminary had made studying French compulsory in order to ensure that would-be Union pastors were able to reach a sizable portion of the population that they believed remained relatively untapped.[193] The Fellowship inherited this method. The founding of the Séminaire Baptiste Évangelique Du Québec on 12 January 1974 was a defining moment, as it signalled their new emphasis on training home-grown leaders. Paul Wilson has further traced this evolving ministry, as they reoriented their focus from rural areas in the 1930s to urban ones by the 1980s, and increasingly found "new methods such as radio, television, camps and crusades" for their outreach.[194] They went from six churches in the province in 1950 to 63 in 1990.[195]

The Fellowship made inroads into the Maritime Provinces as well, but it was on a much smaller scale. The first two churches to affiliate

---

192. For example of how the Baptists received the believers' church movement, see Jones, "The Canadian Baptists of Western Canada," 333.
193. Keefe, et al., "Fellowship Baptist Churches," 61–62.
194. Wilson, "A Mission Transformed," 204.
195. Keefe, et al., "Fellowship Baptist Churches," 97.

were in Nova Scotia: Faith Baptist Church (Sydney) joined in 1957 and Melvern Square Independent Baptist Church joined in 1969.[196] While these churches were independent churches, others came out of the United Baptist Convention, such as Main Street Baptist Church in Sackville, New Brunswick who voted to leave the convention in the 1970s over the United Baptists' perceived waffling over the question of biblical inerrancy.[197] The Fellowship's presence in eastern Canada has remained relatively minor.

The Fellowship's expansion to the west was quite different. Regular Baptists in British Columbia had initially turned their attention southwards instead of eastwards. From 1945 to 1955, they attempted two separate courtships with significant Baptist bodies in the United States, first with the General Association of Regular Baptist Churches (1945) and then with the Washington-Oregon Convention of the Southern Baptist Convention (1952).[198] While some elected to remain affiliated with the latter group, neither experiment proved successful on a large scale.[199] The British Columbians' choice not to unite permanently with either body signaled that a possible Canadian union was on the horizon. They had experienced positive relations with their counterparts in Alberta in the past, which manifested in the 1945 formation of the Northwest Baptist Bible College in British Columbia—but would it be possible to unite on a larger, more permanent scale? Kenneth Davis has outlined the motivating factors in the west as "their disillusionment with southward . . . associations and a concern to strengthen the sense of Baptistic identity . . . [which] tended to combine to create a desire for a Canadian Baptist identity."[200] In 1963, the Alberta churches joined the Fellowship; and in 1965 the British Columbia churches joined on the stipulation that they could remain a regionally organized convention, ultimately under the larger auspices of the Fellowship.[201] With this final arrangement, the Fellowship became a truly national body. The Fellowship has seen rapid expansion in recent years. Today they are among the largest single Baptist denominational bodies in Canada.

196. Lockey, "Fishing for Men," 45–46, 49.

197. Lockey, "Fishing for Men," 56–57.

198. Davis, "The Struggle," 239.

199. Jones, "Western Canadian Baptists and the Southern Baptist 'Invasion,'" 421; and Davis, "The Struggle," 239–40.

200. Davis, "The Struggle," 245.

201. Davis, "The Struggle," 248–58.

The Fellowship has been very active in higher education. When the western Regular Baptists joined the Fellowship, the national body inherited the Northwest Baptist Bible College, which eventually became the Northwest Baptist Theological College, and then finally the Northwest Baptist Seminary. In 1976, they opened the London Baptist Bible College and Seminary. This new institution emphasized a more premillennial dispensational position (reflecting their Independent Fellowship roots), and thus became known as "the Dallas of the North," referring to the historically fundamentalist and thoroughly premillennialist Dallas Theological Seminary in Texas.[202] In 1993, it combined with Central to become Heritage College and Seminary, located in Cambridge, Ontario. Heritage has employed significant Baptist leaders, such as Michael A. G. Haykin and Stanley K. Fowler.

BAPTISTS IN TWENTY-FIRST CENTURY

In the early twenty-first century, each of the three English-speaking regional Baptist bodies took steps to foster closer relations with one another through symbolic means—changing their names. In 2007, the BUWC became the Canadian Baptists of Western Canada; in 2008, the BCOQ became the Canadian Baptists of Ontario and Quebec; and in 2016 the United Baptists became the Canadian Baptists of Atlantic Canada (after a brief window as the Convention of Atlantic Baptist Churches since 2001). Opting to use the "Canadian Baptist" descriptor signalled several realities: "This new identity designation will enable us to highlight our strength and national unity as a family of Baptist Christians operating as four regional groups, but in partnership for mission and ministry. Further, it will help us to differentiate our unique status as the first and largest Baptist group in the country."[203] Moreover, significantly, as one member body observed: "While we have strength of numbers (almost 1200 churches across Canada) our identity seems to have weakened in the past number of years."[204] Using the "Canadian Baptist" designation was one way to reclaim that identity.

202. Wilson, "Patterns of Canadian Baptist Life," 48.

203. "Rationale and Notice of Motion Re: Change of Name from the Convention of Atlantic Baptist Churches to Canadian Baptists of Atlantic Canada," (February 2016), 2. Accessible online at www.baptist-atlantic.ca.

204. "Frequently Asked Questions re: Proposed Name Change," (February 2016), 2. Accessible online at www.baptist-atlantic.ca.

Significantly, relations between the Fellowship and the Canadian Baptists have been slowly improving for the last number of years. This is a far cry from the controversies of nearly a century ago. One clear example of the dramatic changes occurred in 2015—almost 90 years after the 1927 schism—when the Fellowship invited Tim McCoy, the Executive Minister of the Canadian Baptists of Ontario and Quebec, to open their annual assembly in prayer. There remain various theological differences between these groups; however, many have been encouraged by the recent progress.

Since the beginning of the twenty-first century, Baptists in Canada have been much more aware of the need to recognize and acknowledge indigenous peoples' struggles in Canada, and therefore to work toward reconciliation. In 2016, Terry Smith, the Executive Director of the CBM, issued an apology to Canada's indigenous population for past injustices inflicted by the church in general. He observed that while Baptists in Canada were not directly involved in the development of Residential School system, "we failed our Indigenous brothers and sisters by not speaking out against it, when your language, culture, religion and values were being assaulted and harm was being inflicted on your children. We sinned when we were not the voice of the oppressed." In his conclusion, he committed:

> Practically speaking, Canadian Baptist Ministries commits itself to working with local bands to identify and assist Indigenous women and girls at-risk and cooperating with local churches to participate in the healing of broken communities. We recognize that the path ahead will not be easy. Unjust systems are always difficult to dismantle, but we commit ourselves to doing all we can.[205]

This recognition and apology is an important marker highlighting how Baptists have come a long way since the days of a national vision marked by a distinctly Anglo-Saxon imperial identity.[206]

---

205. Smith, "An Apology in the Making."

206. For Baptist conceptions of an imperial Anglo-Saxon national identity, see Heath, *A War with a Silver Lining*.

CONCLUSION

This chapter has surveyed the various Baptist groups in Canada—from the earliest in the eighteenth century, up to those in the present. It is impossible to capture every nuance, event, or change that occurred in Canadian Baptist life in such a short space, but this chapter has endeavoured to highlight some of the most significant features.

It has shown that Baptists in Canada have a history both of union and division, of celebration and mourning. It is clear from this study that Baptists are not monochromatic. Today the majority of Baptists in Canada are on the conservative end of the theological spectrum, and each of the largest Baptist bodies in the country profess to be thoroughly evangelical,[207] but there is still significant diversity. Counted among their ranks are Calvinists and Arminians; premillennialists and amillennialists; open communionists and closed communionists; fundamentalists and liberals. The arrival of immigrant communities has also led to the growth of ethnic churches in major urban centres, providing renewal and a fresh outlook on church life. Much in the same way that Canada is a cultural mosaic, so too are the Baptists that live there. What does this mean for those who search for a Baptist identity in Canada—*is* there such a thing? With this chapter as a foundation, the remainder of the book partially approaches this question by exploring the historically prominent distinctives that have both differentiated and connected Baptists and other Christians, and shows how they remain relevant today.

---

207. Wilson, "Patterns of Canadian Baptist Life," 29.

3

Baptists and Others

Cohesion, Divergence, and Distinctives

THIS CHAPTER MARKS A shift away from telling the story of Baptist history to examining Baptist theology and polity. This particular chapter looks at Baptists in the larger Christian world: what they share with other Christian groups, how and why they have often clashed with other denominations, and with what larger trajectories they resonate and often identify. It also seeks to cast an ecumenical vision for Baptist relationships with other Christian communions, all the while identifying Baptist distinctives. Subsequent chapters will then explore a number of Baptists distinctives, and will identify key Baptist convictions related to their particular vision of a believers' church.

A HISTORY OF HOSTILITY

Sadly, the history of Baptists has been often marred by harsh attitudes towards Christians from other theological camps, even those with whom they share commonalities. In spite of Christ's prayer that his followers might "be one" (John 17:21), and Paul's admonition that out of the trio of faith, hope, and love the "greatest" was love (1 Cor 13:13), and even with such statements as "[Baptists] have always claimed to be part of the one catholic Church of our Lord Jesus Christ,"[1] the history of Baptists has been tarnished by painful conflicts and schisms, not to mention

---

1. Statement in 1948 by Baptist Union, as quoted in McBeth, ed., *A Sourcebook for Baptist Heritage*, 369.

mean-spirited behaviour and outright violence. The most antagonistic posture has been to Roman Catholics. Baptists were born in the unrest and tumult of the Reformation, a period when both Protestants and Catholics often used vicious rhetoric in their debates. The strength and nature of those polemics "reflected prevailing social, political, and religious conditions,"[2] but at the core of Protestant arguments was the view that the Pope was the antichrist and the church he led was, to a large extent, a corrupted shell of the true church.

Protestantism had "a significant impact on the religious, social, and cultural fabric of the British Empire,"[3] and with the triumph of Protestantism in Britain the view developed that Britain and its empire were uniquely Protestant entities with divine blessing.[4] Early evangelicals—including Baptists—continued the legacy of often-rabid anti-Catholicism. John Wolffe argues that "anti-Catholicism was, on both sides of the Atlantic, very much the essence of evangelicalism."[5] For instance, consider the words in one of George Whitefield's sermons, given at a time of British victory over the rise of Catholicism in England: "How soon would our pulpits every where [sic] have been filled with these old antichristian doctrines, free-will, meriting by works, transubstantiation, purgatory, works of supererogation, passive-obedience, non-resistance, and all the other abominations of the whore of Babylon."[6] As Wolffe notes, "anti-Catholicism was very deeply rooted in evangelical identity and ideology. It was not a mere negative prejudice but an impulse at the heart of the movement's spiritual aspirations and religious activity."[7]

Protestant-Catholic tensions were transplanted into the New World, and played out differently in different contexts. In Canada, with a large French-Catholic population, tensions were often palpable between Protestants and Catholics, with both sides jostling to protect and expand their demographic position and power. Organizations in Canada such as the Orangemen and Protestant Protective Association formalized and mobilized prejudices,[8] and Baptist preachers such as T. T. Shields reinforced

2. Wolffe, *The Protestant Crusade in Great Britain*, 9.
3. Wolffe, "Anti-Catholicism and the British Empire," 58.
4. McLeod, "Protestantism and British National Identity," 50.
5. As quoted in Wolffe, "Anti-Catholicism and the British Empire," 179.
6. As quoted in Noll, *American Evangelical Christianity*, 119.
7. Wolffe, "Anti-Catholicism and Evangelical Identity,"184.
8. See Houston and Smith, *The Sash Canada Wore*; Watt, "Anti-Catholic Nativism in Canada," 45–58.

such views.[9] American Baptists, along with other Protestants, sought to keep Catholics marginalized from mainstream political life, seeking to ensure the light shining from the "city on the hill" was not dimmed by Catholic corruption. And a relatively tiny Baptist community in South America sought to survive in an often-hostile social context.

Baptists have also experienced difficulty in their relations with Eastern Orthodoxy. Baptist attitudes to the Orthodox have been shaped by three key realities: the likeness (in Baptist opinion) of Orthodoxy to Catholicism, the limited exposure to Orthodoxy in the West, and the repressive response of Orthodoxy to Baptists in Eastern Europe. While Protestants may have shared with the Orthodox a common dislike of the Pope—rooted in a rejection of papal claims of primacy over the church— that "mutual dislike of the Papacy . . . was hardly a sufficient bond."[10] The theological differences with Orthodoxy often led to animosity, harsh rhetoric, and in certain cases, repression of Baptists in traditionally Orthodox lands.[11] As a result of such mistreatment, Baptists have often struggled in their relationships with the Orthodox. The recent closure of the Baptist Union's Moscow Theological Seminary illustrates that such tensions still exist in some contexts.

Baptists also displayed hostile attitudes to other Protestant denominations, although not with the same degree of vitriol as directed to Catholics. Early Baptists in North America faced severe censure and repression from other Protestants, a situation that lent itself to Baptists condemning their Protestant oppressors. For instance, in 1651, one Baptist referred to infant Baptism among Congregationalists as a sin and "a badge of the whore" and "they who stayed while a child was baptized do worship the devil."[12] Even after being freed from legal disenfranchisements, Baptists could still look askance at other Protestants. For instance, Landmarkists in the United States were convinced that they alone were the New Testament Church: "Baptist churches are the churches of Christ, they *alone* hold, and have alone ever held, and preserved the doctrine of

---

9. Adams, "Fighting Fire with Fire," 53–104.

10. Runciman, *The Great Church in Captivity*, 257.

11. For an introduction to the experience of Baptists in Eastern Europe, see Prokhorov, *Russian Baptists and Orthodoxy*; Corrado and Pilli, eds., *Eastern European Baptist History*; Jones and Randall, eds., *Counter-Cultural Communities*; Randall, ed., *Baptists and the Orthodox Church*; Bourdeaux, *Religious Ferment in Russia*.

12. Chute, et al., *The Baptist Story*, 33.

the gospel in all ages."[13] In Canada, Ontario-Baptist divisions in the 1920s led to some pretty harsh in-house rhetoric: "Nothing more venomous ever opposed the Gospel of Christ in the days of the Spanish Inquisition of the Bloody Queen Mary, than the venom which McMaster breathes forth."[14] And throughout the 1960s Canadian Baptists struggled with what made Baptists unique in the Protestant landscape.[15] Of course, not all shared such vitriolic rhetoric at all times, but it was common enough to create and exacerbate tensions.[16]

The above is a sweeping summary of 400 years, one which could be much more nuanced with a higher word count. But the simple point is that Baptists have a history of looking askance at other Christian groups, with the underlying assumption often being that only they are the New Testament church. The problem with such a reading is that one could be left with the impression that Baptists have a unique view of Christianity that shares little with other Christian communions. But that is not the case. In fact, as noted above, Baptists have a great deal in common with other communions.

IN THE COMPANY OF OTHERS

Baptists belong to a number of traditions and trajectories that place them in the company of other denominations. Such similarities cluster Baptists into various communities that transcend their own distinct denominational identity and provide an opportunity for a grander vision for the work of Christ's kingdom in the world. The following are examples of how Baptists share allegiances and ideals with the wider church universal.

Baptists are Protestant, and have much in common with other Protestants, such as the rejection of papal primacy, invoking the intercession of the saints, and purgatory. Like other Protestants, they also argue for the supreme authority of scripture, justification by faith, two ordinances, and the priesthood of all believers. These convictions put them into the

---

13. Kidd and Hankins, *Baptist in America*, 116. Emphasis in original.

14. Taken from the *Gospel Witness*, as quoted by Renfree, *Heritage and Horizon*, 222.

15. Rudy, "'The Ecumenical Movement, is it of God?'"

16. To be fair, Baptist were not alone in that regard. Harsh rhetoric often marked the discourse of other denominations as well.

Baptists and Others

same family of churches as Lutherans, Anglicans, Calvinists (Reformed churches such as Presbyterians), and Anabaptists.[17]

While technically not Anabaptists, Baptists are sometimes considered to be a part of the Anabaptist family (i.e., Mennonites).[18] They are similar to Anabaptists in that they both hold to a general Protestant position (e.g., authority of the Bible, two ordinances), observe a form of congregational government, believe in no state involvement in church life, and practice believer's baptism; however, as noted in a previous chapter, Baptists differ from Anabaptists in significant ways.

Baptists are dissenters, and belong to a number of denominations in that camp.[19] In principle, as dissenters they are opposed to a state church, and "dissent" from its strictures. Dissenters like Baptists want to preserve their religious freedom and the right to worship according to their conscience without state—or state church—coercion. As Michael Watts notes, what united dissenters from the sixteenth century through to the twentieth century was their refusal to submit their conscience to the whims of the state.[20] This conviction means that Baptists share much in common with churches outside of formal church establishment, such as Quakers, Methodists, Pentecostals, Presbyterians,[21] and Congregationalists.[22]

Baptists belong to the believers' church tradition.[23] They reject the notion of a territorial church comprised of those baptized into membership as infants by virtue of their living in a particular parish/territory, and espouse a believers' church comprised solely of those who profess faith

---

17. Some Anglicans and Anabaptists do not consider themselves to be Protestant, but that subject is for another book.

18. A number of research centres focus on both movements. For instance, see Acadia Centre for Baptist and Anabaptist Studies (Wolfville, Nova Scotia, Canada) and International Baptist Theological Study Centre (Amsterdam, Netherlands). In terms of history, the close relations (personal, structural, and theological) between Anabaptists and Baptist in eastern Europe has led to conflating the two movements.

19. The terms dissenter, free church, and nonconformist are usually used interchangeably, and primarily used in Britain. For further reading on dissenters, see Pope, ed., *T & T Clark Companion to Nonconformity*; Watts, *The Dissenters*; and Bebbington, *The Nonconformist Conscience*.

20. Watts, *The Dissenters*, 3.

21. Although the Church of Scotland—the official state church—is Presbyterian.

22. Although in the early decades of the New England colonies in America the Congregational Church was the established religion.

23. Durnbaugh, *The Believers' Church*.

and are baptized as an adult. It is a rejection of the notion of a Christian culture, or Christendom, where everyone is automatically a member of the church by virtue of infant baptism. This places Baptists in the same communities such as Pentecostals, Brethren, and Christian Missionary Alliance.

Most Baptists are evangelical. The English word "evangelical" is a transliteration of the Greek *euangelion* (the "good news" or the "gospel"). In the sixteenth century, the term became closely associated with the Protestant Reformation (a movement that stressed the "gospel"). On the continent to be "evangelical" meant that you were a Protestant (Lutheran or Reformed). In the eighteenth century in Britain and America the term was used differently—it was used to describe a movement that arose out of the Methodist Revivals and Great Awakening. David Bebbington defines the movement by a "consistent pattern of convictions and attitudes": biblicism (a reliance on the Bible as ultimate religious authority), conversionism (a stress on the New Birth), activism (an energetic, individualistic approach to religious duties and social involvement), and crucicentrism (a focus on Christ's redeeming work as the heart of essential Christianity).[24] While initially comprised of Church of England members, evangelicalism quickly became a movement led by Methodists and joined by Presbyterians and others over time, including Baptists. It is an ecumenical movement in that denominational distinctives are downplayed to highlight evangelical priorities such as missions, a hallmark of the movement.

Some Baptists are fundamentalists. Fundamentalism is a movement born in the late-nineteenth century in response to such issues as the advent of modern higher-critical approaches to the biblical text, the rise of Darwinism, the growth of liberal theology (or "modernism"), and other trends that were considered to be undermining the "fundamentals" of the faith.[25] This aspect of Baptist life links Baptists together with other fundamentalist churches in a network of like-minded churches, but it also separates them from the larger Christian community, including other Baptists, if there are any doctrinal disagreements.

Baptists are related to the ideal of Christian Restorationism. They are Restorationists at heart, but some press the principle more than others. The goal of Restorationism is to restore the New Testament church

---

24. Bebbington, *Evangelicalism in Modern Britain*. See also Noll, *The Rise of Evangelicalism*; Weber, "Premillenialism and the Branches of Evangelicalism," 5–21.

25. Marsden, *Understanding Fundamentalism and Evangelicalism*.

by doing only what the New Testament prescribes (that is why some Baptist churches called themselves "New Testament Baptist Church" or Primitive Baptists[26]), thus being the first-century New Testament church in the twenty-first century. This impulse places Baptists in a similar type of church as the Christian Churches (Disciples of Christ), and even Pentecostals, those who desire to emulate the church described in the book of Acts.

Baptists also share a great deal with other Christians such as Roman Catholics and Eastern Orthodox. For instance, like Catholics and Orthodox they share a common belief in the Trinity, the humanity and deity of Christ, the Lordship of Christ, the virgin birth, the need for the power of the Holy Spirit in a Christian's life, God's creation of the universe, and the reality of heaven and hell.[27] And while not always referring to the ancient creeds of the church, the contents of the Apostle's Creed, Nicene Creed, and Chalcedonian Creed are widely shared by Baptists.[28] This is made clear in article 38 of *An Orthodox Creed* (1678): "The three creeds, viz, Nicene Creed, Athanasius' Creed, and the Apostles' Creed, as they are commonly called, ought thoroughly to be received, and believed."

---

26. "Primitive Baptist" means something different in the Maritime Provinces. In the nineteenth century up to the late twentieth century, to be a Primitive Baptist meant you emphasized and reflected the simplicity of Henry Alline's ministry (they split from the Free Christian Baptist Conference of New Brunswick in the 1870s).

27. While most Baptists have been theologically orthodox, there have been heterodox movements, such as eighteenth-century Unitarianism among British Baptists.

28. "As to the theology of the confessions of orthodox Protestantism, we may distinguish in them three elements, the oecumenical, the Augustinian, and the evangelical proper. 1. The oecumenical element. In theology and Christology the Protestant symbols agree with the Greek and Roman Churches, and also in other articles of the Apostle's and Nicene Creeds from the creation of the world to the resurrection of the body. 2. The Augustinian element is found in anthropology, or the doctrines of sin and grace, predestination, and perseverance. Here the Protestant confessions agree with the system of Augustine, who had more influence upon the reformers than any uninspired teacher . . . 3. The Evangelical Protestant and strictly original element is found in soteriology, and in all that pertains to subjective Christianity, of the personal appropriation of salvation. Here belong the doctrines of the rule of faith, of justification by faith, of the nature and office of faith and good works, of the assurance of salvation." See Schaff, ed. *The Creeds of Christendom*, 1:210–11.

ECUMENICAL VISION AND DENOMINATIONAL IDENTITY

In the Western world, much of the animosity that marked Baptist engagement with other Christian groups is waning.[29] There are a number of inter-related reasons for this. First, denominational borders are becoming increasingly irrelevant, leading to fluid boundaries and migrating members. Simply stated, for a variety of reasons denominational distinctives do not matter like they used to.[30] Second, increasingly the secularizing of the West and the marginalization of Christianity is leading to an "ecumenism of the trenches."[31] Things are getting so bad that Christian divisions are no longer a "luxury" but a mortal threat; Christians simply must work together and share in the increasingly difficult task of Christian witness.[32] Third, rapid social changes are leading to ethical positions taking priority over denominational markers. For instance, Gerald Bray argues that "Today homosexuality is far more likely to divide Protestants from one another than episcopacy or infant baptism."[33] Fourth, dramatic changes within Catholicism since the Second Vatican Council (1962–65) have led to increasingly productive ecumenical dialogue between Catholics and Protestants.[34] Ancient hostilities and attitudes still exist, but the vitriol and violence has waned.[35]

This book is written in an ecumenical spirit that looks upon decreasing tensions between Christian communions as a positive development. While historical realities such as hostile secularization that led to the rapprochement among Christian groups do not have to be celebrated, the posture and telos of conciliation certainly should be. This book seeks to be ecumenical, in the best senses of the word. But, since certain streams of Baptists are suspicious of the ecumenical enterprise, perhaps it is best

---

29. In other parts of the world it is a different story. In some regions of the world Christians face horrible persecution and even genocide, whereas in other regions there is explosive growth of churches.

30. For instance, a number of denominations arose due to social conditions that no longer exist, and as a result the boundaries between some are increasingly irrelevant. See Niebuhr, *The Social Sources of Denominationalism* as to the social sources of many denominations.

31. This phrase is attributed to Timothy George.

32. *Havana Declaration* (2016); *Evangelicals and Catholics Together* (1994).

33. Bray, "English Protestantism to the Present Day," 106.

34. Noll and Nystrom, *Is the Reformation Over?*

35. Animosity is still high in South America, for the rapid growth of evangelicalism has led to some harsh responses from the Catholic majority.

to use the word "charitable." This project seeks to be charitable, building rather than burning bridges between Christian communions, seeking understanding, uniting when possible and differing if necessary, but being kind always. It is trying to model a synthesis of truth and love (Eph 4:15). Stated bluntly, the authors are not urging a return to old-school denominational flag waving, seeing all others as an inferior or corrupt version of the faith, and this work is not written as a condemnation of other Christian communities. It is, however, an attempt to educate Baptists as to their own tradition, and an effort to explain the Baptist position in a winsome, thoughtful, and compelling way.

SOURCES FOR BAPTIST CONVICTIONS

Baptists are convinced that the supreme authority for Christians is the Bible: "the Bible contained the charter, constitution, and by-laws of the true Church."[36] As stated in the *Second London Confession* (1689): "The Holy Scripture is the only sufficient, certain, and infallible rule of all saving Knowledge, Faith, and Obedience . . . the authority for which it ought to be believed, depends wholly upon God . . . because it is the Word of God." That said, Baptists have developed an abundance of confessions of faith and even catechisms that express the beliefs of a local church or associations. They have even adapted the statements of other denominations to fit a Baptist context; such as *An Orthodox Catechism* (1680) which was an adapted version of the *Heidelberg Catechism* (1563). With that in mind, then, we must be wary of identifying all Baptists as "people of the Book (Bible)" or being "non-creedal" as if Baptists have no use for formal theological statements. Baptists are a diverse group, and while some emphasize the "Bible only" for faith and practice, others include additional statements for guidance.

Baptist confessions, covenants, and ecclesiastical records are all helpful in providing sources for determining Baptist identity.[37] Confessions (sometimes referred to as Statements of Faith) can be written by individuals, congregations, associations, denominations, or institutions. Covenants (statements of how one should live in community) are most often produced by local churches. Ecclesiastical records are the multifarious sources produced by local churches, associations, denominations,

---

36. Brackney, *The Baptists*, 24.
37. These three categories are taken from Chute, et al., *The Baptist Story*, 327–30.

and so on. Adding to the more official confessions, covenants, and ecclesiastical records are hymnals, sermons, liturgies, periodicals, personal diaries, books, and oral histories of church members. A clue to the broad array of such published works can be seen in the reaction of Baptist opponents in the early-seventeenth century: it seemed that every day in England "the presses sweat and groan[ed]" with new Baptist books and pamphlets, and that they continually "vomit[ed] forth new streams of filth."[38] During the 1640s the government attempted to control those expressions of religious dissent, but was unsuccessful. For example, in 1643 one churchman chided Parliament for allowing heretical tracts: "I am not ignorant, what a numerous and almost infinite issue of bastard Books come daily to light: Even the very streets of the most populous Metropolis or Mother-City, being spread with petty Pamphlets. . . . We are overcloyed with bookes, our eyes are pain'd with reading, and our hands with turning over leaves."[39] All such material is fair game for those interested in gaining access to Baptist theological convictions.[40] Of course, the question of what determines "official" Baptist views is another question.

A FEW TERMS

Baptist theologians are another source for determining Baptist views, and there are an abundance of voices to consider in this regard.[41] But at this juncture we need to make a distinction between theology and polity. For our purposes, *theology* is a statement of what Baptists believe on a particular point of biblical teaching. For instance, believer's baptism is a central and unequivocal theological conviction of Baptists: baptism is only be administered to those who profess faith in Christ. *Polity* is how that theological conviction is applied or lived out in the life of churches. For example, some Baptist churches baptize anyone who profess faith in Jesus, regardless of age. Other Baptist churches recommend that a young child that professes faith in Christ be baptized once the child has matured (perhaps age 12 or 13). In this example, Baptists could agree on *theology*

---

38. McBeth, *The Baptist Heritage*, 66.

39. McBeth, *The Baptist Heritage*, 66.

40. Another factor to keep in mind is what Baptists officially hold as doctrine, and what Baptists in the pulpit or pew actually believe. The two are not always synonymous.

41. A good place to start researching the contributions of Baptist theologians is George and Dockery, eds., *Baptist Theologians*.

(believer's baptism) but disagree on *polity* (the age when one administers baptism). The distinction is an important one, for many disagreements among Baptists are often related to an issue of polity—even though it may seem at first glance to be theology. Of course, polity should always be derived from theology, for polity is a contextual manifestation and application of theological belief. Wise leaders always develop polity in light of theology, but also are keen enough to know when the issue is polity rather than theology.

A word on theology is in order. It is unwise to believe that dogma is passé or dangerous, for theology matters and should play an instrumental role in Christian discipleship.[42] In the realm of theology, of course, there are legitimate areas of disagreement that require vigorous and thoughtful debate. Denominational differences are important, and warrant theological distinctions being made. Yet, in writing about such important matters the authors seek to navigate between the proverbial dangers of Scylla and Charybdis. On the one hand, we abjure the error of thinking that dogma is merely a matter of perspective. While there is an element of truth to such a claim, we wish to avoid pushing postmodern perspectivalism to such an extreme that all truth claims are equally valid (or even that truth cannot be known). In other words, everything is not fair game. On the other hand, we wish to avoid such a rigid theological position that we cannot see the possible validity of other dogmatic positions. In other words, not every view that differs from Baptists is necessarily heretical. Consequently, we come wanting to avoid the radical extremes of empty-headed epistomological skepticism and hard-nosed epistomological certainty.

A word on the name "Baptists" is also in order. The title refers to their particular emphasis on believers' baptism by immersion. Baptists believe that the practice of the New Testament was just that, and any other view of baptism is a departure from New Testament teaching and practice. In that sense they make exclusive claims, just as other Christian communions do. The issues, as we see it, are not the claims *per se*, but the theological reasons for such claims and the spirit in which such claims are made: both are important. And it is our conviction that Baptists do have an important theological vision for the church. There are cultural reasons for being Baptist (e.g., Baptist parents), or pragmatic considerations for being Baptist (e.g., good music, like the pastor, get a job, only church in

---

42. Studebaker, "Theology: A Question of Discipleship"; Johnson, *Theology as Discipleship*.

town), but this book is written to provide readers with the theological justification for holding to the unique Baptist vision for the church. It is concerned with Baptist convictions and what they mean today.

Some have suggested making a distinction between (B)aptist and (b)aptist. The former refers to the movement itself, and those self-identified with a particular Baptist denomination. The small "b" baptist, on the other hand, refers to "all Christian movements which affirm believer's baptism, autonomy and freedom of conscience."[43] This distinction is important, for some are baptist in their beliefs, but are not Baptists in identity. For our purposes, we are detailing the distinctives of the Baptist movement.

BAPTIST DISTINCTIVES IN CANADA

One Baptist's reflections on Baptist identity strikes a negative chord: "What does it mean to be a Baptist? Some of us were raised in an environment where to be a Baptist meant to be in the 'No': no drinking, no smoking, no dancing, no rough language, no movies, no cards, no make-up, no parties, no loud music (unless it was hymns), in short, no fun."[44] Of course, there is more to Baptist identity than that—at least there had better be!

As one would expect, a global history of Baptist identifies commonalities among Baptists in different nations. For instance, H. Leon McBeth noted in his encyclopedic *The Baptist Heritage* that Baptists in different parts of the empire shared "common threads" that united their work.[45] What he had in mind was a mutual theology of Baptist distinctives (e.g., believer's baptism, congregational government, religious freedom) and common struggles (e.g., shortage of pastors and finances, minority status, theological battles). A number of recent global histories recognize that, in spite of the reality of common Baptist practices that most often mark Baptist life and thought, there are often important differences. As Bill Leonard argues, "amid certain distinctives, Baptist identity is configured

---

43. Wright, *Free Church, Free State*, xii. For a "baptist tradition" or "baptist vision" (all lower case), see also McClendon, Jr., *Doctrine: Systematic Theology, Volume II*.

44. Morrison, "What It Means to Be a Baptist in the 1990s," 29.

45. McBeth, *The Baptist Heritage*, 322.

in a variety of ways by groups, subgroups, and individuals who claim the Baptist name."[46]

So is there a "Baptist way," or "Baptist ways"?[47] There has been a remarkable diversity of people identifying as Baptist. Early Baptists may have been united by a common British heritage, but that did not necessarily lead to uniformity. In different times Baptists emphasized different priorities. For instance, as George Rawlyk notes, "Foot-washing was for some Canadian Baptists—a century or more ago—almost as important a sacrament as adult baptism and communion."[48] In his comments on Baptist diversity, Bill Leonard references eighteenth-century comments on the diversity of Baptists. The quote he provides paints a vivid picture of the variety of Baptists (or at least how Baptist unity was perceived by its critics):

> They don't all agree in one Tune. For one sings this Doctrine, and the next something different—So that people's brains are turn'd and bewildered. And then again to *see* them Divide and Sub-divide, split into parties—rail at and excommunicate one another—Turn (members) out of one meeting and receive (them back) into another. And a gang of them getting together and gabbling one after the other (and sometimes disputing against each other) on abstruse Theological Questions . . . such as the greatest Metaph[ys]icians and Learned Scholars never yet could define, or agree on.[49]

That observation from an American Anglican critic was close to the mark, for Baptists in the frontier were prone to splinter into factions. Regionalism, nationalism, ethnicity, to name a few non-theological factors, all played a part in shaping varying Baptist communities. As did attitudes to pressing social issues, such as slavery. Theological differences also played a critical role in creating a variety of Baptist trajectories. David Bebbington's identification of seven strands of Baptist theological traditions is helpful: within the world of Baptists one can find liberals, classic evangelicals, premillennials, a focus on charismatic renewal, Calvinists, those with an affinity with Anabaptists, and High Church

---

46. Leonard, *Baptist Ways*, xiii.

47. For different answers to this question, see Norman, *The Baptist Way* and Leonard, *Baptist Ways*.

48. Rawlyk, "Baptist Distinctives: Are There Any Left?" 9.

49. Leonard, *The Challenge of Being Baptist*, 1.

Baptists.⁵⁰ Barry Morrison's list detailing the diversity of Baptists is even longer: "There are General Baptists, Particular Baptists, Conservative Baptists, General Six-Principle Baptists, Seventh Day Baptists, Separate Baptists, Duck River Baptists, Free Will Baptists, Hard Shell Baptists, Independent Baptists, Regular Baptists, United America Free Will Baptists, Foot-Washing Baptists—not to mention the Two Seed in the Spirit Predestinarian Baptists and the National Baptist Everlasting Life and Soul Saving Assembly."⁵¹ But even with those distinctions and recognition of diversity, we are convinced that there are still common or core threads that make a Baptist a Baptist.

We could call these commonalities or common threads a Baptist tradition, or Baptist culture, or even a Baptist ethos. And in many ways these descriptors are helpful, for there is shared Baptist tradition, culture, and ethos. Yet we have chosen the term "distinctives" because we think that the term expresses the plurality of Baptist identity—there is more than one thing that makes Baptists Baptist—and connotes the idea that these are how Baptists set themselves apart from other Christian traditions. Stated simply, these are the things that Baptists believe are what make them distinct. That said, identifying Baptist distinctives is more than merely listing a bunch of autonomous theological ideas; it is also concerned with understanding how they are interwoven into a particular way of understanding the church. To use a baking metaphor, the recipe is more than the ingredients in their respective containers. Baptist distinctives need to be understood in relationship with one another, and how they mix and react together to form a particular vision for a certain kind of church.

There are two contexts for understanding Baptist identity, one old and one new. The first context is early seventeenth-century England. Where Baptists differ from other Christians is primarily related to issues of ecclesiology (theology of the church). Theirs was a radical and revolutionary vision for the church, one that was illegal in seventeenth-century England—a church comprised of believers only. While their opponents cast it in a negative light, Baptists were convinced that it was a positive vision for a church that, in some ways, had lost its way. As one author writes: "Baptists were not simply reacting negatively against forms of the church or of society which they found hard to accept as God's will; they

---

50. Bebbington, *Baptists Through the Centuries*, 265–73.
51. Morrison, "What It Means To Be a Baptist in the 1990s," 30.

were also discovering positive understandings of God's will for church and world which had been overlooked, neglected or suppressed in the church they inherited."⁵² They believed in baptizing adults who made a profession of faith, rather than baptizing infants who could not—and only such baptized believers were to be members of the church. They also rejected the Church of England episcopal hierarchy and ran their churches on a congregational model of church governance that left all decisions in the hands of each local church. Consequently, they were ground-breaking and outspoken advocates of religious freedom; the state was deemed to be a necessary God-ordained institution that needed to be supported, but it was to stay out of the affairs of the church. However one tries to understand Baptist convictions, one first needs to understand them in their original seventeenth century setting—a continuation of the English Reformation and a radical reaction to the apathy, abuses, and oppression of the Church of England.

The second context is twenty-first-century Canada. The seventeenth century is a long time ago, but the theological DNA of the movement continues in the life and practice of contemporary churches. However, that Baptist DNA has also been shaped by—and has adapted to—contextual factors. As David Bebbington notes, Baptist life is influenced by its environment, leading to local variations of Baptist identity: "The features of Baptist life in various lands were the fruit of their people's specific experiences, the interplay of a whole range of factors. Baptist identity was, in practice, multiform."⁵³ That reality applies to the Baptist context in Canada, with its regional, ethnic, theological, and linguistic variations. That being the case, a critical question to ask when thinking about identity is not just what Baptist beliefs meant in the seventeenth century, but also what they mean today for Baptists in the Canadian context. Yet even more specifically, we authors write from the world of the Canadian Baptists of Ontario and Quebec (CBOQ), a denomination within the larger umbrella of Canadian Baptist Ministries (CBM), a position that will nuance how we approach Baptist identity. Yet we recognize that there are regional variations among Baptists within Canada, and there are also Baptists outside the CBM family of churches, and those identities need to be understood according to their own contexts.

---

52. Wright, *Free Church, Free State*, xv–xvi.
53. Bebbington, *Baptists Through the Centuries*, 252.

Once again, we believe that there is a common core of Baptist convictions related to the Baptist vision of the church. What follows are four chapters related to the Baptist concept of the church. All four distinctives revolve around issues identified as central to Baptist identity, and all four are inter-related to the Baptist vision of a believer's church: (1) Church Membership; (2) Church Ordinances; (3) Church Governance and Issues of Authority; and (4) Church Coercion. Each one of these distinctives has a positive and negative aspect, for each distinctive was a reaction to what was seen to be a widespread corruption of the church, and a positive affirmation of what they considered the New Testament teaches.

- Church Membership (*stated negatively: no cultural Christians*) was a reaction to an established church and a parish system of being born and baptized into a church. The early church was comprised of those who were followers of Christ, and Baptists believed that the church today must be comprised of the same. It is significant that "every major Baptist confession of faith up to the present day affirms regenerate church membership." Put another way, one must *believe* before *belonging*.[54]

- Church Ordinances (*stated negatively: no babies and no sprinkling*[55]) were rooted in a belief that the church was comprised of believers, and its ordinances were for believers. Although sometimes what Baptists practice has been coined "adult baptism," the proper expression is believer's baptism. The key is chronology: *belief then baptism*, not *baptism then belief*.[56] Baptists are convinced that all descriptions of baptism in the New Testament are of those who had already become followers of Jesus.[57] Baptists understand immersion to be the best (and biblical) visual expression of a believers dying to sin and rising again in new life in Christ. For most of Baptist history, baptism (administered properly) was a prerequisite to membership.

---

54. Chute, et al., *The Baptist Story*, 331.

55. The technical term is "affusion."

56. The sociological aspects of belonging are important—people "belong" often before they get all their theological ducks in a row. However, the only theological point being made here is that baptism requires a confession of faith first, rather than a confession of faith from an earlier baptism.

57. Sometimes those who baptize infants are called "pedobaptists" and those who baptize believers only are called "credobaptists." However, some consider the use of "pedobaptist" to be pejorative.

Baptists have always agreed on the fact that only believers were to participate in communion.[58]

- Church Governance and Issues of Authority (*stated negatively: no prince, no pope, and no presbytery or synod*). There are a number of issues related to church governance and authority. Central to this concern is the nature of Christ's Lordship over the church. All Christian traditions believe that the church is Christ's bride, and that he is the Lord of the church (as well as the cosmos). How that Lordship is exercised, however, is the key for Baptists. In response to people who say that a bishop or pope is the head of the church, or that a temporal ruler is the head of the church (e.g., monarchy of England), Baptists say that Christ is the head. In response to those who say authority over the church is outside of the local church in a body such as a synod or presbytery, Baptists say the locus of authority is in a congregation. In response to those who say that tradition, councils, and/or creeds are authoritative, Baptists say that the ultimate authority for Christians is the Bible (where Christ gave his law): "the Bible contained the charter, constitution, and by-laws of the true Church."[59] As stated in the *Second London Confession* (1689): "The Holy Scripture is the only sufficient, certain, and infallible rule of all saving Knowledge, Faith, and Obedience . . . the authority for which it ought to be believed, dependeth wholly upon God . . . because it is the Word of God." That said, Baptists did develop confessions of faith and even catechisms that expressed the beliefs of a local church or associations.

- Church Coercion (*stated negatively: no violence for the faith*). Baptists were persecuted for their beliefs, and advocated for religious freedom. Baptists are very leery of coercion in matters of religion, and they have been advocates for religious freedom since their very beginning. It has sometimes been called a *voluntary* religion, for a person *voluntarily* seeks membership in a local church, a local church *voluntarily* associates with other Baptist churches, and members and churches *voluntarily* work together on various mission projects. Like Anabaptists, they said to the state and religious leaders "stop the coercion and leave us alone to handle our affairs."

---

58. Where they have not always agreed is on the relationship between membership, baptism, and communion.

59. Brackney, *The Baptists*, 24.

Unlike Anabaptists, they believed Christians had a role to play in government. Separation of church and state meant that the state was to stay out of the affairs of the church, but the church could still have a role to play in shaping the nation.

Each chapter will explore these views as they were developed in the seventeenth century, but also as they are practiced today in the world and by Baptists in Canada.

What is not included in the above distinctives are things such as Baptist spirituality,[60] and ways in which Baptists actually go about the "nuts-and-bolts" of church life in regard to the Lord's Supper, baptisms, weddings, funerals, worship, and ordination. There are a wide range of practices that vary from region to region, and local church to local church. What can be said is that the local traditions practiced by Baptists in such matters are derived from the above distinctives, and can only really be understood with them in mind.[61]

A few final comments on what some may see as glaring omissions. Some summaries of distinctives have the authority of the Bible and the Lordship of Jesus as two Baptist distinctives. Thus, a brief word of explanation is in order as to why we have not included them as "distinctives" in this list. Most certainly the authority of the Bible and the Lordship of Jesus have been and remain central to Baptist life and practice, as can be seen in Baptist confessions such as in the *Second London Confession* (1689) and the *Philadelphia Confession* (1742). In brief, Baptists believe that neither tradition or creeds or personal opinion trumps the scriptures: Christians must submit to its teaching. They also confess that Jesus is Lord of the church (as well as the cosmos) and that Christians have no higher authority—no other human and no organization (including the state)—trumps the Christian's loyalty and obedience to Jesus. Jesus is Lord, and to deny that is to reject one's Christian identity. However, the reason these convictions are not in the above list of distinctives is that they are not really distinctly Baptist. Christians of all stripes affirm

---

60. For further reading on Baptist spirituality, see Allen, "Mining Baptist History and Traditions for Spirituality"; Weber, "A Catholic Looks at Baptist Spirituality"; Grenz, "Maintaining the Balanced Life"; Hinson, "Baptist Approaches to Spirituality"; and Fiddes, ed., *Under the Rule of Christ*.

61. For a helpful summary of Baptist practices, see *Common Expression: A Canadian Baptist Manual for Worship and Service*.

the Lordship of Jesus, and the Baptist view of the scriptures is basically Protestant.[62]

What is unique about Baptist views of the Bible and the Lordship of Jesus is how such convictions manifest themselves in the life of local churches and the believer's life. Baptist distinctives revolve primarily around issues related to ecclesiology, and what is unique in the Baptist world is how that authority of the Bible and the Lordship of Jesus is lived out in Baptist life. For instance, what is unique is how Baptists think the Lordship of Jesus is exercised through congregational government (whereas other Christians see it being worked out through bishops or synods). Another example is how the Baptist emphasis on the Bible often manifests itself in an aversion to any structures or statements being authoritative in the local church or over a Christian's life. The tensions between personal convictions, congregational confessions, and denominational statements have never been resolved in Baptist life, but at the heart of the Baptist movement is a passionate desire to keep the locus of authority for the Christian rooted in the scriptures. Baptists have also developed leadership structures, however, none of those supplants the authority of scripture. These points will be made clearer as the following chapters explore four key distinctives of Baptist life and thought.

Another possible concern may be the omission of the priesthood of all believers as a distinctive. To be clear, this is not to negate or downplay the doctrine, rather, it is rooted in the recognition that virtually every Protestant denomination holds to some form or other of the doctrine. It is a distinctive of Protestantism more than of Baptists. That said, the doctrine manifests itself a certain way in Baptist life, and is key to understanding how Baptists live out their beliefs related to congregational policy, lay leadership, the role of clergy, the authority of church bodies, and so on. That will be made clear in the chapters below.

One last issue may be the omission of missions or evangelism as a distinctive. Brian Stanley summarizes well the importance of missions and evangelism when he writes: "If you wish to mobilize Baptists (and evangelicals as a whole) on an issue that divides the nation down the middle politically, the way to do it is to persuade them that liberty to preach the gospel is at stake."[63] Baptists are passionate about spreading the faith, and it that mandate has been a rallying cry and organizing

---

62. For a more detailed examination of Baptists and the Bible, see Bush and Nettles, *Baptists and the Bible*.

63. Stanley, "Baptists, Antislavery and the Legacy of Imperialism," 289.

principle for centuries. They have also been innovative pioneers in mission work, demonstrated by the work of people like William Carey in India. However, that passion for missions and evangelism is not unique to Baptists, for virtually every Christian tradition carries it out in some form or another. What should be noted, however, is how that passion is shaped and lived by Baptist ecclesiology.

CONCLUSION

This chapter has placed Baptists in the larger Christian world: what they share with other Christian groups, how and why they have often clashed with other denominations, and with what larger trajectories they resonate and often identify. It also cast a charitable vision for Baptist relationships with other Christian communions, all the while identifying Baptist distinctives. The chapters that now follow will detail a number of central Baptists distinctives and show how they are related to a unified vison for a believers' church.

4

Church Membership

A Believer's Church

BAPTISTS HAD A RADICAL vision for the seventeenth-century church: they called for a church comprised of believers only. The phrase commonly heard in Baptist circles is "a regenerate church" or "a believers' church." The concept was not unique to Baptists—as they shared it with the Anabaptists—but it was uncommon and controversial for the time. In the years since, it has come to occupy a central part of Baptist ecclesiology. Baptists reject the idea that one can be born into a church; instead, they defend the idea that people may only join the church if they have made a conscious decision to follow Christ and have displayed evidence of that transformation.

EARLY BAPTISTS AND REGENERATE CHURCH MEMBERSHIP

Among the earliest Baptist principles was the idea that a church should be comprised solely of believers. While this idea may not seem too controversial today, it was a provocative proposal in the early-seventeenth century. It stemmed from an objection to a parochial church and the parish system, wherein one's place of birth determined to which church he or she belonged: each newborn was baptised into the church with the expectation that as children grew they would also grow in faith. One's religious practice was less a matter of choice or conviction and more a way of life. Prior to the Reformation, this meant that virtually everyone in the West was part of the Roman Catholic Church; and, even in the wake of the Reformation, reformers such as Martin Luther, John Calvin, and Ulrich Zwingli retained this practice.

Objection to these religious structures and adherence to the concept of a "believer's church" was not unique to the Baptists. In the 1520s, a divergent stream of the Reformation rejected the parish system and instead vied for a church comprised strictly of those who had made public declarations of faith through "believer's baptism." Contemporary opponents later labelled them pejoratively as the "Anabaptists" (the "rebaptizers").[1] The Swiss Anabaptists' *Schleitheim Confession* (1527) clearly captures their distinctive ecclesiology, which prioritized baptism as being for those who have "learned repentance and amendment of life, and who believe truly that their sins are taken away by Christ."[2] Today theologians consider both Baptists and Anabaptists to be a part of "the believer's church movement."

While the degree to which one can (or should) identify the Baptists as a relative of the Anabaptists is subject to considerable debate,[3] it is clear that each group emphasized that the "true" church was to be limited only to sincere believers. They found support for their position throughout the Bible, which showed that "no one can see the kingdom of God without being born from above" (John 3:3). In John Smyth's *Short Confession of Faith* (1609), he notes simply that the church was to be "a company of the faithful; baptised after confession of sin and of faith, endowed with the power of Christ."[4] Practically identical to this view, in Thomas Helwys' *A Declaration of Faith of English People Remaining at Amsterdam in Holland* (1611), he notes that the church is "a company of faithful people separated from the world by the word and Spirit of God, being knit unto the Lord and one unto another, by baptism."[5] As one Baptist historian sums: "Baptists reversed the traditional sequence in the relationship of baptism and faith. They did not see baptism as a

---

1. For a good overview, see Estep, *The Anabaptist Story*.

2. *The Schleitheim Confession of Faith* (1527), 248.

3. See Bebbington, *Baptists Through the Centuries*, 37–38. See the discussion on this in chapter one.

4. Smyth, *A Short Confession of Faith* (1609), article 12.

5. Helwys, *A Declaration of Faith of English People Remaining at Amsterdam in Holland* (1611), article 10.

foundation of faith at birth, but rather as a practice adopted as a consequence of faith."[6]

As these examples show, the early Baptists highlighted two requirements for admittance into the church as members: first, evidence of their faith; and second, believer's baptism.[7] In his *Certain Queries or Points now in Controversy Examined* (1645), Thomas Collier wrote simply: "none are to be baptized, but those that are able to manifest faith and turning to God" and "none are to be admitted [to the church] before Baptisme."[8] Indeed, from the first, like the Anabaptists, these early Baptists argued that believer's baptism was the means by which they could display the evidence of their faith. What constituted the "proper" Baptist view of baptism is the subject of the following chapter.

While the majority of Baptists did limit membership to those who had received believer's baptism, there were some who opted instead to form "open" or "mixed" congregations, which admitted even those who had received only infant baptism into the membership roll. The most visible advocate of this practice during this era was John Bunyan, the author of the religious literary classic *Pilgrim's Progress*. While pastoring at a nonconformist church in Bedford, England, he published a book entitled *Differences about Water Baptism, No Bar to Communion* (1673), in which he responded to many of his Baptist contemporaries. In it, he plainly stated that "Baptism makes thee no Member of the Church, neither doth it make thee a visible Saint; It giveth thee, therefore, neither right to, nor being of Membership at all."[9] Drawing on the scriptures (e.g., 1 Cor 12:13), he claimed that there was only one necessary baptism, and that it was by the Holy Spirit. "Water-Baptism hath nothing to do in a Church, as a Church," he wrote, "it neither bringeth us into the Church, nor is any part of our Worship when we come there; how then can the Peace and Unity of the Church depend upon Water-Baptism?" Instead, he maintained, the church gathers through the "Unity of the Spirit."[10]

Bunyan's perspective was not particularly well received by the majority of his Baptist contemporaries. Perhaps his most famous antagonist was William Kiffin, a Particular Baptist preacher, who wrote *A Sober*

---

6. Pitts, "Arguing Regenerate Church Membership," 35.

7. Birch, *To Follow the Lambe*, 38.

8. As quoted in Birch, *To Follow the Lambe*, 38. We have reversed the order in which they appear in the original source.

9. Bunyan, *Differences of Judgment*, 14.

10. Bunyan, *Differences of Judgment*, 28.

Discourse of Right to Church-Communion (1681) as a direct response to him. In it, he maintained that the open view was "dangerous, as [it would bring] many unregenerate Members into the Church."[11] Earlier, on another occasion, Kiffin, along with two fellow Particular Baptist preachers—Benjamin Coxe and Hanserd Knollys—published a tract entitled *A Declaration Concerning the Public Dispute* (c. 1646), wherein the Baptist authors firmly set forth their arguments against infant baptism.[12] Among other things, they observed that "it was impossible for Baptists to accommodate infant baptism since they [infants] were incapable of displaying observable signs of faith in Christ."[13]

Another important aspect of early Baptist ecclesiology was the use of covenants. A year or two before the Gainsborough Separatists under Smyth were exiled to Amsterdam, they formed a covenant with one another. They pledged to come together "into a Church estate, in the fellowship of the gospel, to walke in all his [Christ's] wayes . . . according to their best efforts, whatsoever it should cost them."[14] As discussed elsewhere in this book, it often cost them quite a bit, including imprisonment and death for some. This event predated their acceptance of believer's baptism by two years, but Paul Fiddes has identified it as "a defining moment" in the Baptist story. He notes that it shows the Baptists' continuity with their Separatist heritage, as it borrows from covenants of earlier Separatists, such as Robert Browne, who articulated a covenant on two different dimensions: one horizontal and one vertical—meaning, one with other believers and one with God.[15] This same practice filtered into various Particular and General Baptist covenants moving forward.

Unlike confessions, which dealt primarily with theology, covenants tended to focus on practical or relational elements of church life. There was some confusion as to the role that confessions and covenants should play in the life of the church, as it became common for seventeenth-century Baptist churches to print a confession and their covenant on

---

11. Kiffin, *A Sober Discourse of Right to Church-Communion*, 7.

12. In 1645, the Baptist authors were supposed to publically debate Edmund Calamy, a Presbyterian elder, over the issue of infant Baptism. Fearing a violent response from the public, the London authorities opted to cancel the debate. Kiffin, Coxe, and Knollys published this work as a summary of what they had hoped to talk about at the debate. On this debate, see Birch, *To Follow the Lambe*, 25.

13. Birch, *To Follow the Lambe*, 44–45.

14. As quoted in Fiddes, *Tracks and Traces*, 21.

15. Fiddes, *Tracks and Traces*, 22.

succeeding pages, which even led some congregations to require their members and pastors to assent to both.[16] In spite of this confusion, covenants were to play an important and unique role in the life of the church: they outlined both the members' commitment to God and to one another. This ideal reflected Helwys' above-cited statement that the church would be a community "knit unto the Lord and one unto another." As such, they provided many of these early Baptists with "a strong sense of identity and community."[17]

These early Baptists believed that if believers came together in community under a shared set of principles they might also mature in Christ. As the first Baptists in Massachusetts wrote in 1663: "We also know that it is our most bounden duty to walk in visible communion with Christ and each other."[18] By virtue of its role in the life of the church, the covenant also provided the rule against which believers were sometimes disciplined. For Baptists, the church covenant was the mode by which a church maintained its regenerate church membership and encouraged participation within the church.[19]

REGENERATE CHURCH MEMBERSHIP AND BAPTISTS IN CANADA

Many of the considerations related to church membership have been relevant for Baptists in Canada. For much of their history, each of the largest Baptist bodies across the country have agreed that baptism is the best way for believers to provide evidence for one's faith. In 1799, for example, the statement of faith for the Baptist church in Hatley, Quebec read: "We believe we have no right to a visible standing in the Church . . . till we have been baptized upon a profession of faith in the name of the Father, the Son and Holy Ghost."[20] In the same way, in 1917, one western Baptist

---

16. Fiddes, *Tracks and Traces*, 45–46. For modern application, Fiddes has helpfully clarified that a confession should provide the *context* for believers to covenant with one another, but it should never be a *requirement* to live in community. See Fiddes, *Tracks and Traces*, 47.

17. Leonard, *Baptist Ways*, 45.

18. "Organizing Covenant of the Founders of the First Baptist Church in Swansea, Massachusetts" (1663).

19. Deweese, "Church Covenants," 44–45.

20. As cited in Renfree, *Heritage and Horizon*, 102.

wrote, among other things, that there is "No membership in the church without baptism."[21]

Since around the mid-twentieth century, some Baptists in Canada have been much more open to other approaches to membership—including, significantly, ones that do not involve baptism. Various pressures and circumstances have led Baptists to consider new ways of linking baptism with membership. These considerations became prominent in the mid-twentieth century, when a number of Christians from the United Church of Canada sought to transfer their membership into Baptist churches. On the east coast, Baptists confronted this change when a large conservative cohort succeeded in passing a motion on the floor of convention that all future voting delegates at convention needed to be baptized by immersion.[22] Debate over this motion has occurred at various points in the years since, including as recently as 2003, when a study group with interested persons on either end of the issue came together and issued "the Amherst Statement," which read in part:

> All churches in our Convention practice regenerate church membership. These churches hold to the believer's church principle that only those who have been born anew by the Holy Spirit through faith in Jesus Christ are eligible for membership.
> All churches in our Convention practice believers' baptism. Except for exceptional circumstance, such as the physical inability of the candidate, baptism is by immersion.
> Baptist unity in Christ does not require uniformity in everything. One example is how our churches accept regenerate people into membership who come from other Christian traditions.[23]

This statement exhibited the significant diversity that exists in Baptist life in Canada in the twenty-first century.[24] While the majority of Baptist churches still require baptism for membership, the fluidity of people

---

21. D. G. Macdonald, "What is Close Communion?" *Western Baptist*, September 1917, 7.

22. Hobson, ed., *Year Book of the United Baptist Convention of the Atlantic Provinces, 1971*, 21a–22a.

23. "The Amherst Statement" (2003), in Gardner, ed., *2004 Year Book of the Convention of Atlantic Baptist Churches*, B-29.

24. Perhaps it is worth noting that denominational distinctions are less of a factor for many churchgoers, as people tend to move freely between churches with wildly different theological views on things such as baptism.

Church Membership

moving from church to church from non-Baptist traditions means that this question will remain a pressing one into the forseeable future.

Today Baptist churches in Canada—like Baptists elsewhere in the world[25]—typically extend membership in one of several different ways. First is believer's baptism upon confession of faith. As already mentioned, this position has characterized much of the conversation on membership throughout Baptist history. Second is by a letter of transfer or dismissal. In this case, the person seeking membership would ask their former church to write a letter attesting to the fact that he or she is a "member of good standing" in their faith community. Third is by Christian experience. This option is available to believers who (for one reason or another) cannot supply a letter from a previous church. This may be because they were not already a member of a different church, or perhaps because their old church has since closed down. Fourth is membership by exception. This option is typically reserved for those who are unable to receive believer's baptism by immersion. Perhaps that person has a fear of water or, as noted above, perhaps he or she is paralyzed and is therefore unable. In such rare cases, typically each church has a process by which they determine how to extend membership to that person, but usually the decision falls to the leadership team, the board and deaconate, or the members themselves. Of course, each way requires that the potential member is indeed a believer.

In the same way that Baptists in Canada reflected the early Baptist views on the necessity of a believing church, so too have they reflected a "covenant community." The earliest Baptist churches in Canada rallied around a shared declaration of the gospel. Denominational records from the early twentieth century show that the Baptists in central Canada encouraged new churches to use John Newton Brown's *Covenant* (1853) in their churches. After affirming the importance of baptism in forming the community, it reads:

> We engage, therefore, by the aid of the Holy Spirit to walk together in Christian love; to strive for the advancement of this church, in knowledge, holiness and comfort; to promote its prosperity and spirituality; to sustain its worship, ordinances, discipline, and doctrines; to contribute cheerfully and regularly to the support of the ministry, to expenses of the church, the relief of the poor, and the spread of the Gospel through all nations.

---

25. E.g., Maring and Hudson, *A Baptist Manual*, 72.

> We also engage to maintain family and secret devotions to religiously educate our children; to seek the salvation of our kindred acquaintances; to walk circumspectly in the world; to be just in our dealings, faithful in our engagements, and exemplary in our deportment; to practice temperance in all things and to be zealous in our efforts to advance the Kingdom of our Saviour
>
> We further engage to watch over one another in brotherly love; to remember each other in prayer; to aid each other in sickness and distress; to cultivate Christian sympathy in feeling and courtesy in speech; to be slow to take offense, but always ready for reconciliation and, mindful of the rules of our Saviour, to secure it without delay.

It closes with the pledge that if one is to leave that community, he or she will join another church "where we can carry out the spirit of this covenant and the principles of God's Word."[26]

Whereas covenants were meant to draw Baptists together in community, occasionally in the life of the Baptists in Canada they also caused difficulty within the church. Because covenants set a standard for membership, they also inherently emphasized discipline, which unfortunately, eventually led many churches to downplay the importance of the church covenant. From 1850 to 1870, for example, Baptists in the Maritime Provinces developed negative feelings toward church covenants. From their perspective, the use of covenants had taken a decidedly legalistic hue. Rather than draw believers together, they believed that a covenant's primary purpose was to discipline those within the congregation.[27] Unfortunately, increasingly Baptists used the covenant as "a document of correction rather than prevention."[28]

CONSIDERATIONS FOR THE FUTURE

Baptism and Varieties of Membership

There is no unified understanding on which approach to membership is best and, because each church has a wide range of freedom, Baptists

---

26. Brown's *Covenant* is published in full in Hammett, *Biblical Foundations for Baptist Churches*, 137.

27. Deweese, "Church Covenants," 44–45.

28. Moriah, "Christian Discipline," 174. See also, Moriah, *The Thirteenth Discipline*.

in Canada across the theological spectrum usually demonstrate one of three types of membership. First is *closed membership*, which are those churches that emphasize the necessity of believer's baptism as a requisite for membership. Typically churches that operate under this model also prioritize baptism by immersion. Second is *open membership*, which are those churches that dictate that believers of every kind are able to receive full membership to a church. It does not, as some have supposed, mean that membership is "open" to unbelievers. One must provide evidence of regeneration in order to enter into this membership. This approach might be broken down further, as there are some churches that will accept any form of baptism and there are those that do not require baptism at all. Third is *associate membership*, which are those churches that seek a middle-ground to the previous options. If one is a Christian but has not received believer's baptism, they are given an "associate" membership; whereas those who have received believer's baptism are eligible for "full" membership. Those who receive associate status are limited in what their membership provides, including in things like voting at business meetings.

Baptist churches across Canada have reflected each of these views at various points, and there is considerable diversity between the conventions, fellowships, and unions. In 1978, for example, as many as 73 percent of eastern Baptist pastors and 92 percent of Fellowship Baptist pastors were in favour of closed membership; whereas only 40 percent of central Baptist pastors and 33 percent of western Baptist pastors believed the same.[29] Recent debates among Fellowship Baptists over accepting other forms of baptism besides immersion indicate that shifts are taking place even among an historically conservative denomination.[30] Each of these approaches has pros and cons. For example, although closed membership upholds the Baptist's emphasis on believer's baptism, it may also give the church the appearance that it is exclusive and unwelcoming to other Christians. Conversely, while open membership retains the idea that all are "equal at the foot of the cross," it might be argued that it downplays the role of believer's baptism. Finally, although the associate membership approach might appear like a good balance of the two, it could create a kind of "caste" system. How a church operates, or whether it uses one of these models, ultimately comes down to the church in question:

29. Beverley, "Survey of Baptist Ministers," 273.

30. For one side of the debate, see Belyea, Carter, and Frey, eds., *Baptism Is . . . The Immersionist Perspective.*

each congregation needs to approach these issues in a biblically and theologically responsible way, ensuring that their view is firmly rooted in scripture. Differences among Baptists may occur, but at least let them be based on different interpretations of scripture, not mere pragmatics or careless reasoning.

The Role of the Covenant in the Church

If the conversation around baptism and church membership has amplified in recent years, the discussion on church covenants among Baptists in Canada has practically been on mute. Because of the negative connotations, generally Baptists are less likely to emphasize their role as a covenant community. With the comparative decline in Canadian church membership since the mid-twentieth century, churches may have downplayed the role of the covenant because they do not wish to expedite the process by which people are leaving the church and not returning. Of course, this does not negate the fact that churches that do not have (or display) an official covenant may in fact have an unofficial one. What kind of culture has this church cultivated? Does it have a certain way it expects its members to act or believe?

The negative views of covenants neglect its role: it is all about community. When a Baptist congregation comes together, believers grow personally, they grow with one another, and they grow closer to God. They become a united front in the mission to serve God and spread the good news. At the same time, in the context of a covenant community, where the believer invites others on their spiritual journey, the idea of "discipline" is more in line with the idea of instruction, and comes from a deeply personal place of investment in the person's life.

Considerations Moving Forward

The decline in church membership in Canada since the mid-twentieth century is well documented;[31] however, it is also worth noting that many

---

31. Several interesting studies on Canada's changing religious demographics have been written in recent years, including Clarke and Macdonald, *Leaving Christianity*; and Thiessen, *The Meaning of Sunday*. Sociologists Sam Reimer and Michael Wilkinson suggest that while evangelicals have faired "comparatively well" in the general downward trend in church adherence, they appear to have "plateaued." See Reimer and Wilkinson, *A Culture of Faith*.

thriving congregations have a growing number of people that participate in the life of the church but for one reason or another have decided not to become members. In these cases, while the total number of congregants may have increased, the number of members has plateaued or declined. There are multiple possible influencing factors for this trend. A church might not have clear processes for inviting people to become members of the congregation; or perhaps potential members are skeptical about the role of membership in any religious organization and "just want to follow Jesus." Whatever the cause of the decline in membership, these situations provide evidence for the fact that statistics may not be the greatest gauge of a congregation's health.

One question with which congregations are wrestling is the precise nature of church membership. Some churches require high levels of commitment, responsibility, and accountability as entry points to congregational membership. They emphasize the challenge and responsibility of discipleship and the cost of following Christ. Those churches underscore that their members have to give their finances and their time to the church, and they will hold members accountable if they do not follow through on these obligations. The rationale is that people are drawn to exclusivity—that high standards and values can be aspirational and inspiring. By contrast, other churches see membership as more of an entry into church life and that discipleship is for believers regardless of their spiritual maturity. They emphasize that Christ's invitation to new life extends widely and they do not want to create unnecessary barriers or expectations that might keep people from experiencing new life in Christ. They do not want to set up unnecessary boundaries that might keep people from fully participating in the life of the congregation.

Some Baptist churches have responded to the challenge of getting new members by assessing the language they use. Certainly "member" remains quite standard, but for some it sounds antiquated and smacks of other relatively unimportant commitments, such as having an "Amazon" account or gym membership. A variety of alternatives have cropped up in recent years in an effort to more precisely address what the church expects of its congregants. Some churches use the language of "partnership" or more covenantal language to indicate that their members are to *partner* with them and with one another in the work of the gospel. Of course, many Baptists have opted to retain the term "membership" because they see it as more biblical: "Now you are the body of Christ, and individual members of it" (1 Cor 12:27).

CONCLUSION

Baptists in Canada have always maintained that the church should be a community of believers only. For much of their history, many have also recognized the important role that the covenant plays in that community. As one Canadian Baptist theologian summed in the mid-twentieth century: "God intends a community in covenant relationship with Himself, composed of individuals in responsive and responsible obedience to Him and therefore knit to each other in the closest kind of fellowship."[32] In spite of this shared belief, Baptists in Canada have disagreed on the best way to approach the question of membership—closed, open, or associate? The following chapter explores another topic that is deeply related to this question: the ordinances. As Baptists parsed the meaning of "baptism" and "communion" in their communities, it raised other significant questions with regard to membership and the nature of the church.

---

32. Aldwinckle, *Of Water and the Spirit*, 11.

5

Church Ordinances

Baptism and Communion

LIKE MANY OTHER CHRISTIANS, Baptists in Canada practice two ordinances: baptism and communion (the latter known alternatively as "the Lord's Supper"). Some churches exercise other spiritual habits that they consider ordinances, such as washing feet and laying on of hands; however, these are not universally practiced.[1] As Benjamin Keach, a Baptist preacher, explained in 1677 in one of the earliest Baptist catechisms: "Baptism and the Lord's Supper differ from the other ordinances of God in that they were specially instituted by Christ to represent and apply to believers the benefits of the new covenant by visible and outward signs."[2]

In a number of other church traditions, believers identify these practices as sacraments. Historically speaking, this is one area in which the majority of Baptists have differed from many of their Christian brothers and sisters, as they have preferred the term ordinance to sacrament. For most Baptists, the term ordinance refers to those practices established by Christ that believers are to exercise as a sign of their faithfulness, whereas a sacrament is a rite through which grace is imparted to the participant. The two terms are not necessarily mutually exclusive (as the practices themselves could be both an act of obedience *and* an occasion to receive grace),[3] but most Baptists remain uncomfortable with the idea of grace

---

1. Brackney, *A Capsule History*, 51.

2. Keach, *The Baptist Catechism* (1677), question 99.

3. See Cross, "Baptism Among Baptists," 147–48. Even some Baptists in Canada have submitted to this perspective, as one statement of faith from the Baptist Union of

being mediated through the events themselves and therefore do not use the "sacrament" designation.[4] As various scholars have shown in recent years, there is historical precedent in the Baptist community for identifying baptism and communion as sacraments; however, for the purposes of this study, this chapter uses the term "ordinance" throughout for consistency.[5] This chapter assesses baptism and communion individually, showing how they are interrelated, and explores why Baptists still practice them today.

BAPTISM

As might be expected for a group called "Baptists," the act of baptism is central to the denomination's identity. In fact, it led one prominent Canadian Baptist leader to conclude: "Any discussion of Canadian Baptists has to begin with a discussion of baptism."[6] Like many topics explored in this book, baptism is not unique to Baptists and indeed virtually all Christians employ some form of baptism, but there is significant diversity in how believers understand and practice it. At the same time, not all Baptists agree on baptism, as Anthony R. Cross has written:

Western Canada said in the early-1970s: "The Lord's Supper has been described as a 'memorial feast.' It is that, but it may and should be more; to the honest seeker it may well be a means of grace, a time when his Master draws very near." As republished in "What Baptists Believe," *Atlantic Baptist*, 15 September 1974, 1.

4. There is some debate over the use or rejection of the term "sacrament" among Baptists in Canada. Those who are more ecumenically minded find it too isolating, as it creates yet another point of contention to overcome when dialoguing with other believers, which serves further to distance Baptists from the larger body of Christ. For an example, see Morrison, "Tradition and Traditionalism in Baptist life and Thought," 39–51. For a discussion on this matter within the larger Baptist community, see Harmon, *Baptist Identity*, 42–44. From a surface level, the use of ordinance over sacrament moves Baptists away from even having a shared vocabulary with other Christians, which also frustrates ecumenical conversations. Allison Trites, the longtime Professor of New Testament at Acadia Divinity College, once described the development and use of "ordinance" in the Baptist tradition by writing: "Understandably the word *ordinance* was born of reaction to superstition, but it is hardly a suitable word to articulate the mysteries of the faith. In the fear of saying too much, it has said too little, for it tends to become a barren euphemism that conveys little more than the simple dimensions of sentimental memory." See Trites, "An Assessment."

5. On the historical precedent, see Fowler, *More than a Symbol*; Cross, *Baptism and the Baptists*; and Cross, "The Myth of English Baptist Anti-Sacramentalism," 128–62.

6. Jones, *What Canadian Baptists Believe*, 17.

Church Ordinances

there is no single Baptist theology and practice of baptism, only theologies and practices, and this diversity accords with Baptist ecclesiology which continues to tend toward independency, each local church and individual minister exercising their liberty in the administration and interpretation of Christ's laws.[7]

What is important about the Baptist view is the approach to baptism, which may be summed by answering two basic questions: *who* should be baptized, and *how* should a person be baptized?

Early Baptists and Baptism

Central to the Baptist understanding of who should be baptized is a rejection of "infant baptism" (sometimes identified pejoratively as "pedobaptism") in favour of "believer's baptism" ("credobaptism"). The key is chronology: *belief then baptism*, not *baptism then belief*. For much of Baptist history, Baptists have viewed baptism as a public declaration of an inward change. In 1611, Thomas Helwys described it as "the outward manifestation of dying unto sin and walking in newness of life."[8] A person should receive baptism only after making a personal decision to become a Christian. This particular interpretation places Baptists into a camp known as the "believers' church."

The rejection of infant baptism was one of the earliest defining Baptist traits. As explored in an earlier chapter, the Gainsborough Separatists, under the leadership of John Smyth, fled from England in the early-seventeenth century and settled in Amsterdam. Here, Smyth rejected infant baptism. In a controversial move, he baptized himself ("se-baptism") and then baptized each member of his congregation. This practice was an active protest against the established Church of England. Although Smyth would later depart from this community in an effort to join the Mennonites, his followers retained their new religious identity, even when they returned to England the following decade.

To reinforce their position, Baptists pointed toward the fact that there is no New Testament teaching that supports the baptism of infants, and that all descriptions of baptism in the New Testament are of those who consciously made the decision to become followers of Jesus. In Matt

---

7. Cross, *Baptism and the Baptists*, 455.
8. Helwys, *A Declaration of Faith of English People Remaining at Amsterdam in Holland* (1611), article 14.

28, commonly identified as "the Great Commission," Jesus instituted the basic framework that Baptists have followed in their understanding of baptism. He said: "Go therefore and make disciples of all nations, *baptizing* them in the name of the Father and of the Son and of the Holy Spirit, and teaching them to obey everything that I have commanded you (Matt 28:19–20, emphasis added)." Significantly, in this important passage, belief precedes baptism—meaning one must become a disciple before being baptized. Likewise, Baptists have pointed to a number of other instances in the New Testament, such as those demonstrated in the early church:

> "So those who welcomed his message were baptized." (Acts 2:41)
>
> "And immediately something like scales fell from his eyes, and his sight was restored. Then he got up and was baptized." (Acts 9:18)
>
> "Paul said, 'John baptized with the baptism of repentance, telling the people to believe in the one who was to come after him, that is, in Jesus.' On hearing this, they were baptized in the name of the Lord Jesus." (Acts 19:4–5)
>
> "And now why do you delay? Get up, be baptized, and have your sins washed away, calling on his name." (Acts 22:16)

Baptists have always maintained that the New Testament clearly shows a pattern wherein baptism is predicated on belief.[9]

For those early Baptists, therefore, baptism became a sign of the true church. As Helwys described, "the church of Christ is a company of faithful people separated from the world by the word and Spirit of God, being knit unto the Lord and one unto another, by baptism."[10] This

---

9. Some Baptist theologians have taken this a step further and pointed out that each of these examples from the New Testament (and many others) seem to indicate that conversion and baptism are sequential, yet *connected* events. This reflects a more sacramental view that envisions baptism as a "meeting place" of faith and grace (e.g., Fowler, *Rethinking Baptism*, 29; and Beasley-Murray, *Baptism in the New Testament*, 263–66). Among the most significant modern interpreters on this point is the Fellowship Baptist theologian Stanley K. Fowler. (See Fowler, *More than a Symbol*.) If Fowler and others are correct on this point, it opens a number of new ideas for Baptists to debate and, in the very least, raises a topic with which Baptists may need to engage. In any case, it is as Cross has noted: "In both interpretations of baptism, non-sacramental and sacramental, faith is key, and Baptists of both schools of thought oppose the view that baptism's efficacy operates *ex opere operato*, that is, in mechanical isolation from the faith of the believer." See Cross, "Baptism Among Baptists," 147.

10. Helwys, *A Declaration of Faith of English People Remaining at Amsterdam in*

stood in contrast to the dominant view of Christendom,[11] in which one's baptism as an infant meant that membership was practically automatic and universal, and based largely on his or her proximity to the established church. The emphasis on the necessity of one's baptism as a believer, later identified as "closed" membership, was the most pronounced one among early Baptists; but it was not the only one, as some "open" or "mixed" congregations in the seventeenth century made a point to include those who practiced infant baptism.

As early Baptists established the importance of a believing church, it was necessary for them to determine *how* they should baptize. Throughout history, Christians have employed several different forms of baptism, which typically fit into three categories: (1) pouring, or "affusion"; (2) sprinkling, or "aspersion"; and (3) immersion. For Baptists today, immersion has become the standard mode of baptism, but that was not always the case. When Smyth baptized himself and his congregation, he did so by pouring. This mode remained an accepted Baptist practice until the mid-seventeenth century.

It was not until the early 1640s that Baptists adopted immersion. A Particular Baptist named Richard Blunt was among the first to raise the question of baptizing by plunging the believer under the water. He pointed specifically to two passages, Col 2:12 and Rom 6:4, each of which highlighted being "buried" with Christ in baptism. Convicted by his new perspective, he, along with around fifty others, withdrew from the "JLJ" church in Southwark, London in 1640, although they did not immediately join a new church. Blunt travelled to the Netherlands to fellowship with a group of Mennonites who practiced immersion, presumably to learn from them.[12] When he returned, he baptized Samuel Blacklocke, a teacher and fellow layperson, and together they baptized an entire congregation of upwards of forty people.

The Blunt-Blacklocke baptisms were the first recorded occasions of believer's baptism by immersion in England, but the practice soon spread like wildfire. Shortly thereafter, employing the same logic as Blunt, William Kiffin, an early-Particular Baptist preacher, contended that baptism was done through "dipping [the] Body into [the] Water, resembling Burial

---

Holland (1611), article 10.

11. See Cross, "Baptism Among Baptists," 139–40.

12. Chute, et al., *The Baptist Story*, 22–23.

and rising again."[13] Similarly, in the *Somerset Confession* (1656), the Particular Baptist authors dictated that a believer needed to be "buried under the water."[14] Following this stipulation, the *Second London Confession of Faith* (1677/1689) wrote simply that "Immersion . . . is *necessary* to the due administration of this ordinance."[15] From their perspective, there was no ambiguity in the text—immersion was non-negotiable. As Baptists began to grow in numbers, increasingly they practiced immersion as the standard mode of baptism. Baptists have variously pointed to the fact that the word used in the New Testament, *baptizo*, when rendered literally means "dip" or "immerse." Moreover, they have pointed toward Jesus' own baptism for further evidence: when John the Baptizer baptized Jesus in the Jordan River, the text notes that he came "up out of the water" (Mark 1:10).

In England, where the established church baptized infants, the dissenting opinion on baptism was not well received. In fact, by moving to a system that rejected infant baptism, it raised a host of theological and pastoral issues. One of the reasons infant baptism had entered the church was in an attempt to find reassurance amid the high infant-mortality rates. Christians had come to believe that if a priest could baptize an ill newborn before the infant died, God would extend his grace and the infant would be saved from perdition. This created an issue for the Baptists: what would happen if a baby, born in a credobaptist home, died prematurely? Smyth went as far as to respond: "infants are without sin."[16] Likewise, other Baptists in the seventeenth century wrote that children that died in infancy had "not actually transgressed," and that they would be subjected only to "the first death, which comes upon them by the sin of the first Adam, from whence they shall be all raised by the second Adam."[17] Later Baptists disagreed that infants were sinless, but did maintain that they were innocent. The Particular (Calvinist) Baptists' *Second London Confession of Faith* (1677/1689) maintained: "Elect Infants dying in infancy, are regenerated and saved by Christ through the Spirit."[18] By being able to circumvent this significant theological conundrum, they

13. Kiffin, "Kiffin Manuscript," (n.d.).
14. *Somerset Confession* (1656), article 24.
15. *The Second London Confession of Faith* (1677, published 1689), article 29.4.
16. Smyth, *A Short Confession of Faith* (1609), article 5.
17. *A Brief Confession of Declaration of Faith* (1660), article 10.
18. *The Second London Confession of Faith* (1677, published 1689), article 10.3.

were able to focus on what they considered the real problem: they believed that one needed to make the conscious decision to be baptized—a position that earned them the moniker "Baptists."[19]

Baptism in a Canadian Context

Baptists in Canada reflected this emphasis on believer's baptism by immersion from their earliest days. In 1800, it was this view that led Anglican Bishop Charles Inglis to criticize the New Lights-turned-Baptists in Nova Scotia by writing about their "rage for dipping."[20] In that region, as with elsewhere, the Baptist position sparked an intense public debate over baptism.[21] The emphasis on "dipping" was similarly important to Baptists across modern-day Canada. In 1838, one central Baptist explained:

> A word may be applied to a number of things and actions that bear some affinity or resemblance to each other, but never does *light* mean darkness, or *darkness* light—cold heat, heat cold—immersion sprinkling, or sprinkling immersion. No more can *baptizo* mean *rantizo* [sprinkle]; or else the language can no more be a sure and certain vehicle for the conveyance of human thoughts, far less for the general publication of a revelation from heaven, intended to make men wise to salvation, through the faith that is in Christ Jesus.[22]

Even in the early-twentieth century, while various Christians across the country discussed the merits of ecumenical cooperation and organic union, non-Baptist denominations recognized that "believer's baptism by full immersion [was the] Baptists' foremost distinctive and the primary obstacle to union with them," with one Methodist perceptively

---

19. On the development of the term, "Baptist" and how it came into common usage, see Brackney, *Historical Dictionary*, 41–43.

20. As quoted in Saunders, *History of the Baptists*, 115. It is likely that this "rage" effectively solidified the Baptist place of prominence in the Maritime Provinces, as many during this period saw immersion as an opportunity for a post-conversion religious experience on par with (or at least similar to) the intense passion they had experienced during the new birth. It became the most effective form of "the visible gospel" and allowed Baptists to become "the religious tradition most solidly rooted in the emerging colonial religious culture." See Goodwin, "Footprints," 193–94.

21. See Goodwin, "The Baptismal Controversy," 3–20.

22. W. Fraser, "Baptism," *The Canadian Baptist Magazine and Missionary Register*, April 1838, 250.

describing it as a Canadian Baptist "shibboleth."²³ This same emphasis led the Fellowship of Evangelical Baptist Churches in Canada to identify as "a company of immersed believers" in their founding affirmation of faith in 1953.²⁴

As this reference to the Fellowship suggests, the connection between baptism and church membership has been prominent in Baptist thought in Canada for many years. Initially, most churches limited membership to those who had received believer's baptism by immersion. As explored in the previous chapter, since around the mid-twentieth century, in general, Baptists in Canada have been much more open to other approaches to membership—including, significantly, ones that do not involve baptism, let alone immersion. Among these external considerations, Baptists in Canada have raised several pertinent questions: should Baptists exclude Christians who have received believer's baptism by a mode other than immersion?²⁵ Should Baptists exclude Christians who seek to transfer their membership from other, non-credobaptist traditions?²⁶ The responses to these questions have varied considerably, as some opted for open membership (all believers) or associate membership (mixed tier system of baptized and non-baptized), while others retained closed membership (baptized believers only). This decision ultimately comes down to each individual church, although, as noted above, sometimes the larger denominational body places restrictions for fellowship.

COMMUNION

The second ordinance that Baptists in Canada observe regularly is communion.²⁷ Like baptism, communion is not unique to Baptists and, again

---

23. Jones, "The Canadian Baptists of Western Canada," 61. The "shibboleth" quote is cited from the same source.

24. Fellowship of Evangelical Baptist Churches, *Affirmation of Faith* (1953), available online: www.fellowship.ca/WhatWeBelieve. For a study on this topic from a Fellowship perspective, see Belyea, Carter, and Frey, eds. *Baptism Is*.

25. This consideration was the primary one that drove the recent discussion on baptism among the Fellowship of Evangelical Baptist Churches.

26. This consideration became prominent among the Canadian Baptists in the mid-twentieth century, when a number of Christians from the United Church of Canada sought to transfer their membership into Baptist churches.

27. Other church traditions use the term "Eucharist" to describe this practice; however, it is not very common in Baptist circles. Those Baptists that do use it might prefer it because they have roots in another tradition, or perhaps they are making a

Church Ordinances

like baptism, Baptists have held a variety of opinions on how to properly practice it.[28] Most Baptists have viewed communion as a memorial event, wherein believers gather in "community" (communion) to remember and declare Christ's sacrifice by eating bread and drinking wine—commonly called the "elements"—which represent Christ's body and blood respectively. (Today, Baptists tend to use grape juice instead of wine, which is a decision that is largely a relic of the temperance movement.) While the earliest Baptists were much more concerned with defending their position on baptism,[29] the topic of *who* should be admitted to the communion table became a matter of central importance for them.

Early Baptists and Communion

Communion has been a part of Baptist life since the beginning of the Baptist story. Echoing his description of baptism, Helwys called communion "the outward manifestation of the Spiritual communion between Christ and the faithful."[30] It was an occasion for believers to gather together with one another and in Christ. Baptists drew their basic framework from the descriptions of the Last Supper in the Gospels (Matt 26:26–28; Luke 22:14–20; and Mark 14:22–25) and from Paul's first epistle to the Corinthians (1 Cor 11:23–29). Central to the latter passage was the command to "examine yourselves, and only then eat of the bread and drink of the cup" (1 Cor 11:28). Much like baptism, Baptists maintained that one's participation in communion should be contingent upon his or her profession of faith. This lined up with Paul's entreaty to "examine yourself" and "discern the body" before taking part in communion. The emphasis on "the spiritual preparation of the believers" led many Baptists to prefer Paul's description of communion to those found in the Gospels.[31]

---

conscious effort to be more ecumenical.

28. For example, some churches pass a tray with the elements, while others ask the congregants to move to the front of the sanctuary or meeting place to collect the elements. Some dip the bread in the wine or juice, while others take them separately. By 1880, fearful of spreading diseases, many Baptist churches moved to using small, individualized glasses. See Brackney, *Historical Dictionary*, 262.

29. Grace, "Early English Baptists' View of the Lord's Supper," 179

30. Helwys, *A Declaration of Faith of English People Remaining at Amsterdam in Holland* (1611), article 15. We have modernized the English.

31. Brackney, *Historical Dictionary*, 262. This is visible in the supporting passages for *The Faith and Practice of Thirty Congregations, Gathered According to the Primitive*

Given their historical context, it is helpful to view much of the early Baptist discussion of communion against a backdrop of the Reformation-era debates on the topic. One of the major points of departure from Roman Catholicism during the Protestant Reformation was on the doctrine of transubstantiation, which was the view that the bread and wine literally become the flesh and blood of Christ when consecrated during mass (though they keep the physical appearance of bread and wine). Among the earliest Baptist confessions and statements of faith, they articulated a clear distaste for this interpretation. In the *Second London Confession* (1677/1689), the Particular Baptists stated their position rather bluntly:

> That doctrine which maintains a change of the substance of Bread and Wine, into the substance of Christ's body and blood (commonly called Transubstantiation) by consecration of a Priest, or by any other way, is repugnant not to Scripture alone, but even to common sense and reason; overthrows the nature of the ordinance, and has been and is the cause of manifold superstitions, yes, of gross Idolatries.[32]

Contemporary General Baptists likewise decried the idea of transubstantiation, and also added an admonition against consubstantiation, which held that Jesus was in, around, and among the bread and wine, writing in *The Orthodox Creed* (1679) that this view was "not consonant to God's Word."[33]

These early Baptists instead preferred a much more symbolic view of communion. The Particular Baptists wrote that it was not for the "remission of sin," but rather "only a memorial" of Christ's sacrifice, and that the bread and wine "still remain truly and only Bread and Wine, as they were before."[34] They saw Christ as host of communion, but that his presence was not in the elements themselves.[35]

Pattern (General Baptist Confession) (1651), article 52.

32. *The Second London Confession of Faith* (1677, published 1689), article 30.6. We have modernized the English.

33. *The Orthodox Creed* (1679), article 33.

34. *The Second London Confession of Faith* (1677, published 1689), articles 30.2 and 30.5.

35. Ulrich Zwingli emphasized the spiritual elements of the Lord's Supper over the material ones, which has led some to suggest that Baptists simply inherited a Zwinglian tradition. Yet, it would be more accurate to say that the Baptist view is a "reductionist version of Zwinglian symbolic memorialism." Harmon, *Baptist Identity*, 42. As Brackney explains: "His position meant that in the re-enactment of the Lord's Supper believers felt the powerful presence of Christ in their midst. The more that

Church Ordinances

For many early Baptists, the primary question concerning communion revolved around who showed evidence of the necessary "spiritual preparation," and therefore whom they should invite to the table. One of the most popular early opinions among seventeenth-century Baptists was that communion was only for those who had received believer's baptism by immersion and thereby had been accepted as a member to the church. This view was known as strict or closed communion, and appeared in both General and Particular Baptist circles. For example, the Particular Baptists added to a revised version of the *First London Confession* (1646) that only after one had received believer's baptism could he or she "partake of the Lord's Supper."[36] Likewise, in 1679, the General Baptists wrote that "*no unbaptized*, unbelieving, or open profane, or wicked heretical persons, ought to be admitted to this ordinance to profane it."[37]

The closed perspective was not the only view, as other early Baptists advocated for a non-restrictive table and maintained that believers of all stripes could receive communion, regardless of baptism or membership. This view was known as open communion. As discussed in the previous chapter, one of the best-known early advocates for this position was John Bunyan, author of *The Pilgrim's Progress*, who wrote several manuscripts against the closed position. In 1673, he noted succinctly, "the Church of Christ hath not Warrant to keep out of their Communion the Christian that is discovered to be a visible Saint by the Word, the Christian that walketh according to his Light with God."[38]

In spite of Bunyan's impassioned plea, the majority of early-English Baptists remained closed communionists. In direct response to Bunyan, in 1681, Kiffin questioned: "if Unbaptized Persons may be admitted to all Church Priviledges [sic], does not such a practice plainly suppose that it is unnecessary? For to what purpose is it to be Baptized . . . if he may enjoy all Church Priviledges [sic] without it?"[39] This remained a controversial topic in Baptist circles for generations; however, the hard stance that Kiffin took slowly lessened over time, to the degree that perhaps one of the

---

the congregation celebrated the Supper the more of the special presence of the Lord Jesus they enjoyed. Obedience, then, became a secondary issue for those in the true Zwinglian tradition." Brackney, *A Capsule History*, 50.

36. *The First London Baptist Confession of Faith* (1644, updated 1646), article 39. See footnote b in Lumpkin, ed. *Baptist Confessions of Faith*, 167

37. *The Orthodox Creed* (1679), article 33. Emphasis added.

38. Bunyan, *Differences of Judgment*, A2.

39. Kiffin, *A Sober Discourse of Right to Church-Communion*, 13.

primary contributions English Baptists made to the nineteenth-century Baptist community in Canada was their stance on open communion.

Communion in a Canadian Context

The open-closed question was so central for Baptists in Canada that it led William H. Brackney to identify communion as "One of the defining issues in early Canadian Baptist identity."[40] From the late-eighteenth century into the nineteenth, the majority of Baptist churches in Canada followed the closed tradition. In 1809, for example, the Regular Baptists in the Maritimes withdrew fellowship from any churches unwilling to accept closed communion.[41] They stipulated that "altho [sic] many unbelievers may creep into the Visible church, . . . we believe that none but true Believers have a Right to the Sacraments," adding, "the Lord's Supper was Instituted by Jesus Christ only for his children," which they believed could be demonstrated only by receiving believer's baptism.[42] In central Canada, beginning as early as 1837, talks of uniting Baptist associations were stifled over "the communion question," which took over fifty years to resolve.[43] This reflected the tension between their American roots, which were committed to a closed communion, and their English influences, which were largely oriented toward an open communion. The debate was clearly visible in the eventual fate of the Canadian Baptist College in Montreal, which closed in 1849 largely over its position on open communion.[44]

From the early-twentieth century up to the modern day, increasingly Baptist churches across Canada have reevaluated their position and many have opened the table to believers of all convictions. Some conservatives have retained their preference for closed communion, but this position is not as ubiquitous as it once was. Harry Renfree has suggested that while Baptists today may view the early Canadian Baptists' prohibitive table as "shortsighted" because of how many churches practice open

---

40. Brackney, ed., *Baptist Life and Thought*, 489.

41. Goodwin, *Into Deep Waters*, 53.

42. "The Church Articles," Minutes of the Nova Scotia and New Brunswick Baptist Association, 27–29 June 1808, printed in Brackney, ed., *Baptist Life and Thought Source Book*, 489–91.

43. Renfree, *Heritage and Horizon*, 102–3.

44. Wilson, "British Influence," 26. For a brief discussion of this point, see chapter 2—on the history of Baptists in Canada—in this volume.

communion now, it was perhaps "vital to saving the infant Baptist body from the gradual dilution and decline that would have resulted from persisting 'mixed' membership and lack of common purpose."[45]

ORDINANCES TODAY

While it is clear that these ordinances played an important role in the history of the denomination, some may question why they remain central today. This chapter briefly considers their contemporary relevance and concludes with some possible considerations for how Baptists in Canada may need to engage these concepts in the future.

Even though some churches are moving away from baptism as a requirement for membership, usually they retain a strong emphasis on the significant place that it plays in Baptist life. Indeed, it was this emphasis that led George Rawlyk to remark that baptism is "one important, formative distinctive from the past that is still profoundly important" for Baptists today.[46] There are several reasons for its continued place of prominence. When one receives baptism they are joining in the death and resurrection of Jesus. In the words of a nineteenth-century Canadian Baptist, it is "a solemn profession of the believer's faith in Christ, as delivered for our offences, and raised again for our justification . . . we are therein said to be risen with Christ, that we should walk in the newness of life."[47] Moreover, baptism highlights one's place in the church. When one receives baptism he or she is committing to serving Christ in community. These two features are what George Beasley-Murray called the "indivisibility of the two aspects of baptism: it is baptism to Christ and into the Body." He continued:

> It is at once intensely personal and completely corporate, involving the believer in relationship simultaneously with the Head and with the members of the Body. . . . We are called to recognize therefore that a purely private relationship to Christ cannot exist, nor a bestowal of the Spirit given to be enjoyed on our own, as it were, in isolation from the Christian fellowship.[48]

45. Renfree, *Heritage and Horizon*, 60–61.
46. Rawlyk, "Baptist Distinctives," 2.
47. "The Baptists," *The Canadian Baptist Magazine and Missionary Register*, July 1839, 3.
48. Beasley-Murray, *Baptism in the New Testament*, 282. See Cross, "Baptism Among Baptists," 150–51.

In the same way that baptism has remained a staple to Baptist practices in the twenty-first century, so too does communion remain an important part of Baptist life. By participating in communion, believers are once again announcing that they belong both to Christ and to his body. God did not intend for the believer to travel the Christian journey discretely or alone; it was intended it to be a communal activity. By gathering together at communion (in "community"), believers celebrate with like-minded people and experience fellowship in the larger church body in a tangible way. Christ's death and resurrection is the rallying point of the Christian faith, so by coming together as one to remember and reflect on that sacrifice, Baptists remain fixated on the love of their saviour and declare it "until he comes."

Considerations for the Future

There are several questions that Baptists in Canada need to confront as they move forward. For baptism, several of these issues have already appeared in this chapter, such as whether or not churches should accept non-credobaptist baptisms or non-immersion baptisms. Another question that Baptist churches may be required to face is that of re-baptism—should Baptists ever re-baptize someone? What if it was a choice a person made as a child and did not fully comprehend the decision he or she was making? This question may lead to a related discussion on age restrictions. On this topic, one prominent Canadian Baptist observed, some churches baptize "at age five or six or seven, which as far as I am concerned means infant baptism."[49] While the implementation of an age restriction is to ensure that the individual receiving baptism is fully cognizant of the decision he or she is making, it can be problematic, because if one sets too restrictive of an age limit the practice becomes "adult baptism" rather than "believer's baptism."[50] How should Baptists approach this tension?

Baptists across Canada have answered these questions and others with significant diversity. A number of Baptists in Canada maintain that if you have received believer's baptism in another church, you do not need to be baptized again; however, if you were baptized as an infant, those same churches may encourage you to receive baptism as an adult. Other churches will not allow you to become a member unless you have

49. Perkin, "The Baptists," 32.
50. Cross, "Baptism Among Baptists," 149.

been baptized within *their* church, as they identify external baptisms as "alien baptisms."[51] These churches are not as common in Canada, but they do exist.

Likewise, as Baptists move forward, there are several considerations they must address with regard to communion. While the question of open and closed communion seems settled for many Baptist communities, it will remain necessary for churches to articulate their position (and to make it known each time they set the table) as they move into a context that may become increasingly hostile to a Christianity deemed exclusive. Another area perhaps worth addressing is that of spiritual preparation—what does it mean to "examine yourself" and "discern the body"?

Different churches have different ways of conducting communion. Some churches pass a tray (or multiple trays) that contains the elements and those who participate remain seated, while others have the elements at the front of the sanctuary and call believers forward to take them. Another related question revolves around frequency: how often should a church set the table? Some churches observe communion once a month, while others prefer each week. Each has its benefits and drawbacks. For example, increased regularity offers believers the opportunity to reaffirm their commitment to Christ and to each other more often, but at the same time it may be cautioned that, "something repeated too often may lose its power to speak to us." These are questions that each church must address individually. In any event, it is clear that "The important thing is that it should be held regularly and that careful attention be given to interpret its meaning to a congregation."[52]

Another question worth reflecting upon is the matter of who is responsible for officiating or administering the ordinances. Traditionally, it is an ordained pastor who administers them; however, there are some notable exceptions to this common practice. Some churches do not have an ordained pastor—or a pastor at all—and therefore must find an alternative approach. Those churches might rely on their deacons or elders to administer the ordinances. Other churches discard this practice knowingly, adding that on the basis of the priesthood of all believers *any* Christian can administer them. Generally speaking, Baptists are more flexible on this question than some other Christian traditions that stipulate that only ordained clergy are to preside over the ordinances.

51. Jones, *What Canadian Baptists Believe*, 28–29.
52. Maring and Hudson, *A Baptist Manual*, 167.

A related discussion might surround whether the ordinances should be limited to the local church worship service, or whether it is correct to practice them wherever a body of believers is gathered. Should Baptists take communion at convention gatherings or at association meetings? Some Baptist convention bodies in Canada hold a communion service at their annual gathering, but they are quite intentional about how they do it. Atlantic Baptists, for example, usually have a closing communion service *hosted* by one of the local churches, which they simply invite others to lead. This approach offers a kind of communal experience while also naming that the practice belongs to the local church. This is a good, balanced perspective, but there are some other nuances with which Baptists must grapple on this question. Outside of the question of a convention gathering, could a group of friends from different churches perceivably take communion together? What about at a youth group or a summer camp? How about a Bible study group? These questions approach the concept on a much more pedestrian level, but they provide insight into how this question might be directly relevant to those in the pew.

Because Baptists in Canada (or anywhere) are not monochromatic, it is impossible to provide a single, sweeping response to these questions—except to say that each Baptist needs to weigh the matter against his or her conscience. Further, these matters should be discussed in consultation with a larger community, which will include the church body, and may even extend to the wider denomination itself.

CONCLUSION

These ordinances are significant because Jesus Christ instituted them and they remain relevant in the life of the church. A 1798 catechism for children noted succinctly that Christ gave these ordinances "To show that his disciples belong to him, and to remind them of what he has done for them."[53] While Baptists in Canada have debated these practices—and have even divided over them—they have always been central to their identity. As Baptists navigate the new religious climate in Canada, they will need to engage the matters discussed in this chapter, especially as they relate to baptism, and weigh them against their consciences and received Baptist practice. Moving forward, they will need to thoughtfully

---

53. *A Catechism for Girls and Boys* (1798), question 128.

consider how to balance showing grace to newcomers while retaining Baptist convictions and practices.

6

Church Governance and Issues of Authority

THE BAPTIST VISION OF church governance today is not unlike many other modern denominations and Christian groups; however, their original emphasis on congregations operating as localized and independent bodies was a radical vision in the seventeenth century. This chapter looks first at how early Baptist churches were governed and how they approached issues of authority. Next it approaches how some Baptists in Canada organized themselves as local congregations that associated with other like-minded congregations. Finally, it explores some of the challenges and opportunities for Baptist congregations and associations navigating ministry in the twenty-first century.

EARLY BAPTISTS AND CHURCH GOVERNANCE

When Baptists began gathering in the seventeenth century, their vision of church was radically different from that of other contemporary Christians. The Roman Catholic Church exercised an episcopal model of governance that placed authority with its centralized leader, the Pope (bishop of Rome), who provided leadership through a structure of cardinals, bishops, and priests. Meaning, only those in authority made the decisions on issues of doctrine or practice. The Church of England (which had separated from the Roman Catholic Church in 1534) likewise had an episcopal model of governance, with authority under the English monarch instead of the Pope, and was governed by archbishops, with bishops presiding over local dioceses. Throughout Europe there were other Protestant state churches with different approaches to church governance, but, significantly, all of them placed the locus of authority outside of the local church. For example, the Church of Scotland, like other churches in the Reformed tradition, followed a presbyterian model, which involved a group of regional representatives—both clergy and lay people—who would gather to make decisions for the larger body as well as local churches. In this model of governance, significant decisions made by the local church needed to have approval from the presbytery.

It was against this historical backdrop that the Baptist tradition emerged. They disagreed on several key points; in response to those who said that a pope, bishop, or temporal ruler was the head of the church, Baptists argued that Christ alone is the head; and in response to those who said authority over the church was outside of the local church in a body such as a synod or presbytery, Baptists argued that the locus of authority is in each congregation. Additionally, Baptists differed from other churches by their reticence in ascribing tradition (including creeds and councils) any significant authority. Instead, Baptists said that the ultimate authority for Christians is the Bible, where Christ gave his law. Put another way: "the Bible contained the charter, constitution, and by-laws of the true Church."[1] As Baptists stated in the late-seventeenth century: "The Holy Scripture is the only sufficient, certain, and infallible rule of all saving Knowledge, Faith, and Obedience . . . the authority for which it ought to be believed, depends wholly upon God . . . because it is the Word of God."[2] In other words, Baptists believed that Christ had established a congregational model of governance for his church and that each local church should be capable—through the power of the Spirit and the instruction of the Bible—to make its own decisions without outside interference.

Localized congregations could make their own decisions, they could respond to the needs of the community, and they did not have to wait for permission from bishops or synods. Today, Baptists often call this idea the "autonomy" of the local church; however, this term was not used by early Baptists and emerged later.[3] Baptists have more consistently

1. Brackney, *The Baptists*, 24.

2. *Second London Confession of Faith* (1677, published 1689), article 1.1. Of course, as this reference makes evident, Baptists did develop confessions of faith and even catechisms that expressed the beliefs of a local church or associations, but they were always intended as *descriptive* documents (what does the church or body believe at this particular time) not necessarily *prescriptive* ones. We have modernized the English.

3. The term "autonomy" is not indigenous to the Baptists and was originally a term

referred to this principle as the "independence" of the local congregation. This allowed early Baptist churches to be nimble and adaptive (not to mention free from oppressive and coercive states and church bodies), but it also required great energy to keep these independent congregations operating.

For most Baptists, the claim to independence came with a caveat, as they routinely sought to associate with other Baptist churches for fellowship and support, which resulted in a lingering, unresolved tension with regard to the relationship of the local congregation with the larger Baptist community.[4] One of the first statements to summarize Baptist thought on the issue was *The First London Confession of Faith* (1644/1646). In it, the Particular Baptist authors affirmed that Christ had empowered each local church to choose those who should be acknowledged as qualified for building up his church:

> That being thus joined, every Church has power given them from Christ for their better well-being, to choose to themselves meet persons into the office of Pastors, Teachers, Elders, Deacons, being qualified according to the Word, as those which Christ has appointed in his Testament, for the feeding, governing, serving, and building up of his Church, and that none other have power to impose them, either these or any other.[5]

The authors of this confession appealed to the early church in the book of Acts, among other New Testament passages, as the example of how the early church received instruction through the Holy Spirit for discerning who should provide leadership for the church (e.g., Acts 1:2; 6:3; 15:22, 25). Yet, it is significant that alongside their statement on the prerogatives

---

from the field of social psychology used to describe, simply, one's self-governance. It did not appear in Baptist circles until the influential Southern Baptist scholar Edgar Y. Mullins employed it to describe the independence of the local church around the turn of the twentieth century. See Brackney, *A Capsule History of Baptist Principles*, 57.

4. Nigel Wright has identified the issue thus: "It is an enduring and continually repeated flaw in this way of being church that autonomy becomes independency. Each church does what is right in its own eyes. This is sometimes flaunted as the 'Baptist way' and defended against those who want to 'meddle and interfere' in the life of the local church. If there is any point at which the Baptist/baptist tradition needs to learn from the wider church it is in the recognition that we are part of a movement sweeping forward through time from Christ and his apostles in the power of the Spirit and that we are eccentric and potentially heretic in so far as we neglect the Body of Christ in all its dimensions." See Wright, *New Baptists*, 54.

5. *London Confession of Faith* (1644), article 36.

of the local church they added that while each congregation is responsible for seeking the Lord independently, they are to associate with other congregations as members of one body under the Lordship of Christ:

> And although the particular Congregations be distinct and several Bodies, every one a compact and knit City in itself; *yet are they all to walk by one and the same Rule, and by all means convenient to have the counsel and help one of another in all needful affairs of the Church, as members of one body in the common faith under Christ their only head.*[6]

Recognizing the temptation for believers to divide into fractions over different teachings, the authors drew from a few passages from 1 Corinthians to call the churches to seek counsel from others for their common faith (e.g., 1 Cor. 4:17; 14:33, 36; 16:1). They recognized that they were not only independent, but they were also to be *inter*dependent.

This form of extra-congregational reliance in Baptist circles is sometimes called "the associational principle."[7] The earliest Baptists recognized the important practical benefits of voluntarily coming together into a larger body. Associational meetings

> became forums for discussing theological and disciplinary queries, and so for establishing a "Baptist viewpoint." . . . meetings discussed such issues as the gathering of churches, believer's baptism, communion with the unbaptized, the ordination of ministers, the maintenance of the ministry, the place of the magistrate, missionary activity, liturgical usages—such as vocal ministry, breaking bread, psalm-singing, foot-washing, anointing the sick, ecclesiastical discipline, the grounds and manner of exclusion, domestic duties and relationships.[8]

In England, pastors and congregants would often gather each year for fellowship, preaching, and discussion. It was their practice to read letters that contained updates from each church, and after the gathering they would draft a letter that summarized the responses to any of the significant controversies they discussed—which they grounded in scripture—and then circulate it among each of the churches. As William H. Brackney has observed, after the Act of Toleration received royal assent

---

6. *London Confession of Faith* (1644), article 47. We have modernized the English.

7. E.g., Brackney, *A Capsule History of Baptist Principles*, 59–68; and Brackney, *Voluntarism*, 38–41.

8. Briggs, "The English Baptists," 395.

in 1689, "a second layering" developed to the English Baptist practice of associationalism. He notes that they began by attempting "to form funds for ministerial training" and soon thereafter identified "the need to care for clergy widows and support for weaker congregations." These kinds of "[m]inisterial associations . . . gave structural integrity to the Baptist movement by the mid-eighteenth century."[9]

INDEPENDENCE AND ASSOCIATION AMONG BAPTISTS IN CANADA

From their beginnings in the eighteenth century, Baptists in Canada have generally strived toward a balance between independence and interdependence. The earliest Baptist churches in the Maritimes "recognized each other as sister churches, maintained autonomy, [and] exchanged ministers."[10] They formalized this practice in July 1797 when a number of Baptist and New Light Congregationalists in Nova Scotia issued the following statement: "being agreed together in our minds to walk together in fellowship as ministers of Jesus Christ, have agreed to hold a yearly conference to know our minds and the state of the different Churches standing in connexion, by their delegates being sent by them."[11] As explored in an earlier chapter, it was during this time that the antinomian debacle swept through the region. The churches that made up the proposed association were those that had grown out of the revivals of the previous decades and its members were therefore perhaps most predisposed to antinomianism. The new association effectively safeguarded those churches from such a damaging heresy, as they kept one another in check by godly fellowship, and, if necessary, corrective discipline through exhortation (or—in a worst case scenario—even dismissal from the association).

By 1800, the Baptists in the east set out on their own and formed the Nova Scotia Baptist Association. They wrote:

> That such a combination of Churches is not only prudent but useful, as has been proved by the experience of many years in England and America. Some of its most obvious benefits are—union and communion among the several Churches,— maintaining more effectually the faith once delivered to the

---

9. Brackney, *Voluntarism*, 38–39.
10. Thompson, "The Status," 95.
11. As quoted in Levy, *The Baptists*, 70.

saints,—obtaining advice and counsel in cases of doubt and difficulty, and assistance in distress,—and in general being better able to promote the cause of God.

That such Association is entirely consistent with the independence and power of particular Churches, because it pretends to no other powers than those of an advisory council, utterly disclaiming all superiority, jurisdiction, coercive right or infallibility.[12]

The formation of these associations came not long after the formation of the churches themselves, which highlights the important status that they ascribed to the associational principle.

Baptists in the central region were not far behind their Maritime counterparts. The first Baptist association in the area was the Thurlow Association, which was comprised of three Baptist churches located near the Bay of Quinte in modern-day Ontario: the churches at Thurlow, Hallowell, and Cramahe-Haldimand. That association met for a number of years, but after the War of 1812 prevented regular meetings, they reorganized in 1819 as the Haldimand Association. Baptists in the central region were not necessarily threatened by the same doctrinal issues as the Baptists in the Maritimes, but rather their implementation of the associational principle was a happy inheritance from their American Baptist forebears. Unsurprisingly, they adopted their threefold form of organization: First was the local congregation, led by the minister and deacons; second were the associations, regional bodies comprised of churches; and third were the mission societies, which were generally supported by the associations. Yet, while affirming the importance of these forms of organization, they never deviated from their emphasis on the self-governance of the local congregation: "anything resembling a chain of authority from smaller units of organization to larger, or from larger to smaller, was instinctively avoided."[13]

While American Baptists influenced their structural organizations, English Baptist practices were also very pronounced. Similar to the early English Baptist associations that usually met each year, Baptists in modern-day Canada routinely selected a time for an annual meeting. For many, the best choice was to meet in late spring, after the farmers had planted their crops and during the warmer weather, which made travel

---

12. "Association of Baptist Churches of Nova Scotia" (1800), Article 1 and 2, as republished in Bill, *Fifty Years*, 36–37.

13. Ivison and Rosser, *The Baptists*, 164.

easier. The associational body usually designated a pastor to "preach the introductory sermon," and, for safe measure, they would also select a "back-up" person assigned to preach if the first person was suddenly unable. In 1870, for example, at the Huron Association meeting in Ontario, the sermon title was "The duty of Canadian Baptists to send the gospel to the heathen," which reflected their emphasis on mission work.[14]

Likewise, following the early English Baptist association model, it was common for Baptists in Canada to compile a circular letter from reports from each congregation. One person (and a designated back-up person) would be assigned to write the circular letter. In 1876, there is a listing of the twelve different association gatherings that occurred in the central region that year, each with the subject of the circular letters. Some examples of the topics from each of the associations include: (1) Working for Jesus; (2) Hold fast and strengthen; (3) Church Discipline; (4) Training of Young Converts; (5) Christian Devotion; (6) Consecration; (7) Systematic Beneficence; (8) Toronto Association as a Mission Field; (9) Church Finances; (10) Christian Work; (11) Weekly Communion; (12) Divine Assurance.[15] Perhaps worth noting, of course, is that of the topics listed in these circular letters, many are topics that Baptists continue to discuss today.

The fact that the early Baptists in Canada prioritized associations while also protecting the authority of their localized independent expressions shows that they believed there was something important in gathering together with other Baptists for fellowship, support, and mission. What was it? In the nineteenth century, when compared to the number of Roman Catholics, Anglicans, Presbyterians, or Methodists in Canada, Baptists (aside from those in New Brunswick and Nova Scotia) were relatively small in number. Therefore, fellowship with likeminded believers was particularly important in the early days. Early Baptist churches in Canada found conditions primitive and challenging and they needed support from each other. Many of the pastors worked what is commonly called "bi-vocationally," and many provided oversight for multiple congregations. Gathering with other churches reminded them that they were a part of something bigger than their own challenges. Moreover, they organized around mission as sending bodies and found that conversation helped them recognize that they were part of something bigger. It is clear

14. *Baptist Register*, 1870, 96.
15. *Baptist Register*, 1876, 94.

Church Governance and Issues of Authority

that these Baptist congregations—each independent—associated with other Baptists for both theological and practical reasons.

For Baptists in Canada, the topics of independence and associationalism have often become major talking points during times of change or reorganization. In the Maritimes, leading up to the union of the Regular Baptists and the Free Baptists in 1905–1906, a proper balance between the two principles became a significant concern because Free Baptists were known to exercise stronger denominational control than the Regular Baptists. For example, while each Regular Baptist church selected their own pastor and ordained him as they saw fit, the Free Baptist District Meetings had the right to relocate a pastor and they had control over the ordination process. As a result, when the groups came together, they enshrined what they believed was a good compromise into the first article of their *Basis of Union*: "Each church is independent, but the churches are interdependent. All the power the more general bodies have over the less general and the individual churches is to advise and to enforce advice with the strongest moral motives."[16]

In the west, the Baptist Union also addressed this tension when they considered reorganizing in the 1950s in 1960s. In the planning stages, they commissioned a report that outlined six Baptist "Basic Imperatives," among which they wrote:

> It is imperative that we recognize our responsibility to each other. While we glory in the independent local church, we gladly discipline our liberties that Christ might be glorified. Therefore in carrying on our enterprises we accept the democratic judgment of Convention decisions; thus we recognize the Holy Spirit in our midst, and become conscious of the Church as a single body.[17]

---

16. "United Baptist Convention of the Maritime Provinces Basis of Union (Doctrinal Statement and Church Polity)" (1906), Article 1. As the convention matured, by 1922, they were willing to give the larger body more authority in the ordination process, and formed a standing, centralized examining council to test potential ordinands (who would then be ordained by the local congregation). See Beals, ed., *The United Baptist Year Book of the Maritime Provinces of Canada, 1922*, 125. Admittedly, this became a sore-spot for some in the convention, and led an emerging fundamentalist cohort (which was, as noted in an earlier chapter, very much a minority) to criticize the convention for removing authority from the local church. See Murray, "Exodus to Exile," 282–303.

17. "Basic Imperatives" (1959), as cited in Thompson, *The Baptist Story in Western Canada*, 237.

Further, they wrote that "the churches in the New Testament era are in a formative period so far as organization is concerned; they are seeking for a balance between local independence . . . and centralized control," which the Baptists believed was an equally important balance in the contemporary world because it "would keep the organization adaptable enough to meet the needs of an imperfect world, yet completely faithful to the conviction that Christ is the Head of His Body, the Church."[18] By the mid-1960s, some in the Union were even ready to identify the term "Autonomy" as a "bogey-man word" that was unhelpful and tended to keep Baptists apart, rather than draw them together.[19]

Even those Baptists that separated from the convention Baptists in the early twentieth century formed unions and associations of their own. Following the schism of 1927, which birthed the Union of Regular Baptist Churches of Ontario and Quebec, the fundamentalists formed a number of shared initiatives, such as the Women's Missionary Society and the Fundamentalist Baptist Young People's Association. In spite of several internal schisms between 1931 and 1949 (discussed in an earlier chapter), in general they remained oriented toward working together in the faith. Since coming together with the Fellowship of Independent Baptist Churches of Canada (from whom they had earlier divided) to form the Fellowship of Evangelical Baptist Churches in Canada in 1953, they have emphasized that each local church is "a sovereign, independent body,"[20] while also coming together on an annual basis to fellowship with one another (as their name suggests) and collectively discern faithful practices moving forward.[21]

Of course, there are those Baptist churches in Canada (typically those that are more fundamentalist in nature) that have elected not to work within bodies larger than the local congregation. Even the majority

18. Gregory, ed., *Year Book 1960–1961 of the Baptist Convention of Ontario and Quebec. 1961*, E-8.

19. Thompson, *The Baptist Story in Western Canada*, 264–65.

20. Fellowship of Evangelical Baptist Churches, "Affirmation of Faith" (1953), available online: www.fellowship.ca/WhatWeBelieve.

21. For example, when the formerly-independent Fellowship Baptist Church in Melvern Square, Nova Scotia joined the Fellowship in 1969, they did so with the knowledge that they would receive "help through materials and encouragement while being able to have input in the greater work in Canada, all the while maintaining their independence." Simply, as the pastor stated at the time, "we were tired of being alone." Put another way: "The church realized the need for interdependence in the body of Christ." Lockey, "Fishing for Men," 49.

of these churches, however, tend to practice what Brackney calls "selective associationalism,"[22] which means they still solicit support from their likeminded counterparts in the region and even occasionally work alongside them for various ministries.

Regardless of what type of Baptist, there were some core essentials to Baptist views of independence and association. It was certainly a system of governance that provided freedom, but it was freedom for both local churches and associations to act in ways that both deemed to be correct. Local churches were free to run their own affairs without an outside body telling them what to do. Local churches were free to join an association on the basis of agreement with the association's statement of faith (and maybe a covenant if it had one). Local churches were free to leave an association without penalty or coercion. However, associations (or denominations) were also free to expect local churches within its membership to hold to the agreed upon statement of faith, and also free to dismiss local churches that did not. There are ample examples of all these "freedoms" being acted upon in Baptist life in Canada.

ORGANIZATIONAL CONTRASTS

In some ways, congregations have changed a great deal over the last four centuries and in other ways they are very similar. A congregation is a community of believers trying to faithfully live out the "good news" of the gospel. That community is comprised of unique gifts and talents, ideas and expressions of faithfulness to God and scripture. Jesus said, "for where two or three gather in my name, there I am with them" (Matt 18:20). Following this principle, Baptists believe that Jesus is present when believers gather, but that there will also be a need for some kind of organization, regardless of how organic that might be. What is astonishing for Baptist churches today is the difference between life in the seventeenth century versus life in the twenty-first century.

Organizational Structures

One significant difference between seventeenth-century Baptist life and today is the organizational structures, such as those involved in stewarding finances. In the seventeenth century, congregations functioned by

22. Brackney, *Historical Dictionary of the Baptists*, 222.

receiving tithes and offerings through cash money or some kind of gift (i.e., food or service). By contrast, Baptist churches in the twenty-first century are navigating how to receive charitable donations in multiple formats: cash, cheques, electronic funds transfers, online giving, bequests, gifts in kind, stock or securities transfers. All of these are made under increasingly specified regulations by governing bodies. As independent, not-for-profit organizations, Baptist congregations are required to meet demanding organizational fiduciary responsibilities around duty of care, fiscal stewardship, and risk management. Leaders within congregations have often looked to business models and the not-for-profit sector to find guidance in running their independent organization.

While all congregational models of governance keep discernment and decision making within the local congregation, few Baptist congregations have the exact same structure. Over the last fifty years, there have been a number of different approaches to the congregational model. This is not only due to local traditions, but also to the size of the congregation. Some congregations are board-driven, meaning the congregation elects leadership teams that seek the Lord's leading in decision making, primarily as it relates to the direction of the congregation's mission and to providing protection in the areas of policy and operations. Each church identifies these teams by a different name, including Elders' Board, Deacons' Board, Board of Management, Board of Directors, Vision Team, Leadership Team or Council, and many others. Perhaps the key point in the diversity of names is that even while Baptists hold to a model of congregational governance there are a variety of ways of doing that. There is no one congregational model of governance. The key theological consideration is that, while the church has pastors, elders, and/or deacons who have responsibilities to lead, the congregation must also be brought into the decision making of the church.

Another area in which there is some debate revolves around *who* should be permitted to serve on the leadership team. Many of the more conservative churches, for example, do not allow women to serve in these positions, whereas many others do. There are differences between the various conventions, unions, and fellowships, but there are plenty of disagreements within these bodies as well.[23] Some churches partially cir-

---

23. This is well illustrated in a recent study of "first" Baptist churches in the Maritimes, in which the respective authors observe that First Cornwallis (in Upper Canard, Nova Scotia) admitted women to the deaconate as early as 1919, and Brunswick Street (in Fredericton, New Brunswick) did not accept female deacons until 2010.

cumvent the issue by having both a deacons' board and an elders' board, where women are permitted to serve on one, but not the other. This may work for some, but for others it inadequately addresses a contentious topic. This is an important issue with which churches need to grapple, but as of yet there is no consensus on the issue.

Ordination

Like virtually all Christian denominations, Baptists ordain their clergy and other leaders such as missionaries. For Baptists, the process revolves around the notion of publicly recognizing those called by God to be set apart as leaders. It does not grant "special" powers to the minister, nor does it make clergy more "special" in God's eyes. It is also not a statement that the call of God on clergy is "superior" to the work that everyone else does in life. It is, however, a recognition that God gifts and calls certain people to carry out leadership roles in the church (with all the weight of responsibility that comes from such service). The biblical support for such an act can be seen in Old Testament examples of leaders being ordained, such as the laying on of hands on Joshua (Num 27), or the New Testament examples of Paul (Acts 13:1–3) and Timothy (1 Tim 4:14). The key, Stanley Grenz notes, is "a divine call and the confirmation of the local body."[24] Baptists require both in the process of ordination, and that process is usually marked by years of prayer, interviews, training, and discernment. That process does not guarantee the success or orthodoxy of all leaders, but it is a way of trying to ensure that the church is led by people who fulfil the biblical qualifications for leadership (1 Tim 3:1–3; 4:7–16; Titus 1:5–9). The actual body that ordains is the local church, although it is usually carried out in conjunction with some type of associational and/or denominational ordination council. Some Baptists only ordain pastors, and perhaps missionaries. Others even ordain elders and/or deacons, and, in some cases, that ordination is for life (even though their term in office may be limited).

But what about the priesthood of all believers? Ordaining pastors in no way is supposed to supplant the work of all Christians to act as priests to one another (e.g., praying, interceding, discipling, etc.), nor does it

---

See Lohens, "First Cornwallis Baptist Church," 152; and Atkinson, "Brunswick Street Baptist Church," 134.

24. Grenz, *The Baptist Congregation*, 67.

intend to undermine the conviction that each Christian can directly approach God through Christ without a human intermediary. What is does mean is that the pastor has been recognized by the congregation to be gifted, empowered, and called to lead in the church, so that the body of Christ is built up and equipped (Eph 4:11–13). Ultimately, it is a recognition of one called to service.

Professionalization of Clergy

The role and function of clergy has also changed significantly over the years. Early Baptist ministers often had a basic theological education at most (in some frontier conditions, perhaps none). It was not uncommon for members of a church to identify an individual whom they believed was a promising congregant with natural gifts, and thereby grant that person a license to preach. "Proof of a man's fitness for ordination lay not in his formal training or educational qualifications," writes one study on Baptists in Canada, "but in whether he possessed sufficient natural gifts to justify the church in setting him apart."[25] Many of these leaders received little or no pay from the congregation and had to earn an income elsewhere. Those who were fortunate were given living quarters.

By contrast, clergy today are often required to have a relatively robust theological education (although a trend in the last decade is to move away from the three-year MDiv as a requirement for ordination to an acceptance of the two-year MTS—a marked decrease in theological training). There has been an increasing desire for the professionalization of clergy that includes raising the quality of renumeration for clergy. While clergy have benefited from receiving pay that is more comparable to other professions, there have also been challenges for smaller congregations to fulfill this requirement. There are employment standards required by governments, insurance regulations, pensions, and benefits. While these standards and requirements help raise levels of support for clergy, they also can become significant challenges for small churches that have not really seen their mandate as being employers.

While congregational independence is still the norm for Baptists, there is an increasing need for congregations to work together to provide support for what they are unable to do on their own. One example is in the area of clergy pension and benefits. An independent Baptist church

---

25. Ivison and Rosser, *The Baptists*, 121.

may not have the infrastructure to be able to secure and deliver a pension and benefit package to its employees. Conversely, beginning in 1956, Baptists belonging to the Federation (and then Canadian Baptist Ministries) have offered a Canada-wide pension plan for pastors and missionaries in order to provide more protection for widows and children.[26] There are a host of other issues related to clergy on which Baptists have chosen to work together with larger association bodies, such as working with government agencies to provide clergy with licenses to perform legal marriages, gathering clergy together for training opportunities, and accreditation and discipline.

Buildings

Throughout much of Christian history, congregations have sought to worship in spaces dedicated for that purpose. While many congregations have decided to forego the stained-glass, gothic cathedrals of yesterday in favour of homes or other locations, many churches throughout the years have chosen to build worship spaces and spaces for Christian education. Baptists followed the examples of other denominations in constructing buildings, although often the buildings were far more modest due to limited financial resources.

In the nineteenth century, as Canada was becoming a nation, many congregations built in or near the centre of the city or town. Such a visible presence was important and reflected the church's role in society, but it also provided the congregation itself with a sense of stability—its central location was a rallying point for many. There was a second church building construction boom in the 1950s and 1960s throughout suburban neighbourhoods in Canada as urbanization patterns changed. Today some Baptist congregations are rethinking their approach to building ownership. Many see the cost of construction, renovations, and maintenance as too prohibitive. With many churches experiencing a decline in financial offerings, and with many churches reporting occupancy-usage rates of the sanctuary between only 5 percent to 7 percent of the time, churches are discerning if they could or should use their buildings for such things as community hubs.

---

26. Bentall, *From Sea to Sea*, 46.

Discernment Practices

Baptists say that Christ is the head of the church and that the locus of authority is the local congregation; however, that does not mean that a local congregation is the complete picture of the body of Christ. No congregation has all the necessary spiritual gifts, wisdom, or perspective to be a complete picture of the bride of Christ. They need to seek wisdom and insight from associations, regional, and national bodies. At a local level there is a tremendous need for the congregation to develop healthy discernment practices.

Since local congregations are required to follow the leading of Christ through scripture and the guidance of the Holy Spirit they take the call to developing healthy discernment practices very seriously. Reading scripture and appropriately responding as a leadership team and a congregation are important in seeking how to move forward through tough situations. Discerning what God is saying in scripture becomes a key gathering principle. The congregations that are able to deal with the internal and external challenges of ministry are the congregations that are able to keep the vision of Christ as articulated in scripture as their focal point. Congregations that are not able to keep focused on a clear vision or mission often become unhealthy or divided.

Of course, relying on scripture for authority in the local congregation is not always so clear-cut. Many contemporary issues are subject to interpretations because the scriptures do not address every question that gets raised in congregational life. Baptists have kept central theological tenets; however, they have often differed on how best to live these in practice. For instance, believer's baptism is a central component of congregational life, but, as mentioned in a previous chapter, there is no standardized age for when children or young people can or should be baptized. That is up to a local congregation to discern an appropriate age. Another example might be the call to develop disciples of Jesus. This is an important part of spiritual formation, but there is no single approach on how this is best accomplished. Some churches have highly-developed training programs that include Bible study and service, whereas other congregations simply rely on Sunday worship gatherings as their primary discipleship strategy.

THE SHIFTING ROLE OF ASSOCIATIONS

In addition to the theological vision that the local congregation needs to be in relationship with other congregations to be a fuller picture of the Body of Christ, Baptists also gathered for four very practical reasons: Christian fellowship, ministry support, shared mission, and accountability. As more and more Baptist churches emerged in Canada in the early-nineteenth century, the need to be in relationship with other Baptist churches was vital for their growth and survival. However, some of the needs of local churches have changed throughout the last two centuries as the Canadian Christian community and Canadian society has shifted.

Early on in their history, Baptist churches in Canada realized they needed to work together with other churches that were relatively close geographically. Communication and travel were often unreliable and limited because of the costs, distances, and weather. For churches to associate together they needed to do so deliberately. The boundaries for early associations in Upper Canada developed along railroad routes. By contrast, today, with cheaper travel costs and methods of communication, churches are no longer threatened by the same kinds of isolation. Baptist churches are navigating new realities when it comes to the role of the church and fellowship among churches and with other churches in the association. There is no longer the same need for fellowship that churches can get from other Baptists as there once was. Since Jesus prayed for unity of the believers in John 17 there has always been a call for Christians to be one. Baptist congregations and associations are going to have to navigate their historic origins and identity while exploring the call to be more kingdom-focused rather than church-centric.

Another factor is the increase of resources that are available from businesses, ministries, educational institutions, mission agencies, parachurch ministries, and interdenominational church networks to support the work of local congregations. Today, churches have a plethora of support options and mission opportunities that can be tailored to the gifts, needs and desires of local churches. This increase of ministry resources means that the need for support to the ministry or organizational life of Baptist congregations now often extends beyond Baptist associations.

The denominational dividing lines were more pronounced throughout the religious landscape of Canada in the 1800s. Today, due to decades of ecumenical conversations among denominations and the rise of national transdenominational groups (e.g., The Evangelical Fellowship of Canada, The Canadian Council of Churches), there appears to be increased willingness for denominations to work together. Likewise, on the local level, pastors now often gather with ecumenical pastoral groups or as part of citywide gospel movements (e.g., TrueCity Hamilton, Love Ottawa). Churches have often elected to work with other local congregations across denominational boundaries to work on mission or social projects. Consequently, the amount of time and energy Baptist churches have to participate in the life of their Baptist association is dwindling.

Baptist associations continue to gather around common areas of mission with other Baptist churches. Many gather to support camp ministries, recognizing that, while a local congregation may not be able to run summer camps, together with other churches they can. Many associations continue to work together on church-planting initiatives—again, while one congregation might not be able to support a church-plant alone, there are associations of Baptist churches working together to resource church plants.

In addition to fellowship, support, and mission, Baptist churches continue to gather for mutual accountability. Baptist churches that associate with others voluntarily grant their association the opportunity to provide accountability and they will submit, to varying degree, to the authority of their association. At times, when pressing social issues arise, leaders will gather together to study and define how their churches can respond to the identified issue. As a result, the association can provide theological oversight and even offer the role of discipline to a pastor or church that has stepped outside their identified statement of faith or theological boundaries. As independent churches, there can be various levels of commitment and willingness to submit to the authority of an association, even within an association. Each Baptist denomination has a different practice with regard to the level of authority of its associations, and tensions can exist between those who want an association to have more authority "to solve" a problem and those who want the local church "to be free" to deal with its own affairs without the interposition of an authoritative association. That said, associations aim to work with dissenting churches in a pastoral and redemptive manner, reserving the right and freedom to dismiss churches (or pastors) that do not agree upon a mutually shared theological statement.

CONCLUSION

Since Baptist roots began as "Separatists" that found their distinctiveness by modifying other church traditions and expressions of faith, there has always been an impulse towards independence. The independence of each congregation to seek the Lord and to govern itself according to the teaching of the scriptures through the power of the Holy Spirit has always been vital; however, with that independence is also the impulse to associate with other churches for increased effectiveness and co-operation. A concern for churches relinquishing responsibility or support to associational bodies is that,

> efficiency may become more important to us than people. Baptists have consistently emphasized the equality of all church members and involvement of members in decision making whether it be in the local church or in transcongregational organizations. Streamlining our organizations for the sake of efficiency may reap benefits in the short term, but in the long term may mean the spiritual dwarfing of our people through lack of involvement and responsibility.[27]

The dance between independence and association has led to a great deal of diversity and at times fractured community; however, the call to live under the Lordship of Christ, through covenant living is a compelling vision for the twenty-first century. As independent localized mission posts, Baptist churches can be adaptable to respond to the needs of communities with the hope of Christ. The Baptist associations that are able to navigate the complexities of divergent views, with a faithfulness to and unity in Christ, will have the opportunity to live with a renewed radical vision.

---

27. Thompson, "The Status," 106.

7

Religious Liberty

BAPTISTS WERE BORN IN a world where coercion was the order of the day. From the late-fourth century on, Christians in the West had become accustomed to a partnership between church and state that enforced religious conformity. As the centuries progressed, heresy trials, witch hunts, and inquisitions were instigated to weed out those considered suspect, and even crusades were launched against Christian movements deemed heretical. "One king, one law, and one faith" was reckoned essential, and divergent Christian movements were considered to be a threat to the political, social, and religious order, and any such unrest would lead to civil unrest. As a result, religious uniformity was considered indispensable for a peaceful social order. As Edwin S. Gaustad writes, "Indeed, at that time hardly anyone believed in religious liberty. And not only did they not believe in it, they were horrified by the prospect of it. The common assumption was that if religious liberty prevailed, churches would close, governments would fall and all moral standards collapse."[1] It was into this world that the Baptists put forth their provocative proposal of religious liberty.

HISTORICAL CONTEXT

Many of the prevailing assumptions of church-state relations were embodied in the sixteenth-century Reformation. Catholics used state power to suppress the spread of Protestantism, and many Protestants did the

---

1. Gaustad, *Roger Williams*, 83–84.

Religious Liberty

same to their competitors.[2] John Calvin's support for the burning of Michael Servetus was a clear statement that coercion would continue to be a part of how the Reformed churches dealt with dissent. Martin Luther's conception of the "Two Kingdoms" initially led to him being opposed to state coercion of religious dissent, but, by the end of his life, he contradicted his own position by advocating harsh penalties on Jews. Anabaptists were a glaring exception to the rule, for they decried any such coercion.

In Reformation-era England, Anglicans and Puritans considered the welfare of the church to be one of the responsibilities of the state. Thomas Cartwright wrote in *The Holy Exercise of a True Fast, Described Out of God's Word* (1610) that magistrates were "Fathers and Nurses to maintain and cherish the church."[3] That general sentiment was widely shared, and many were convinced that "the magistrate was a tool in the hands of God both to establish true religion and to punish false religion"[4] (although there was no consensus as to just how that church-state partnership was to actually work). The church and the state were deemed to be divinely ordained separate spheres, with priests and magistrates to deal with issues pertaining to their respective spheres.[5] In an age that looked to magistrates to protect and even advance the Reformation, a pressing question was "should the church look to the state to advance reform, or should the church act without the state's support or approval?"[6] One consequence of the notion that a state needed to ensure the practice of right religion was the implementation of various laws. For example, religious conformity to the Church of England was expected in the realm, and individuals could not worship as they saw fit. Catholic worship was

---

2. For a helpful book on views of persecution and toleration in the sixteenth century, see Bainton, *The Travail of Religious Liberty*.

3. We have modernized the English.

4. Lee, *The Theology of John Smyth*, 246. For extensive background on the development of religious liberty in England, see the four volumes of Jordan, *The Development of Religious Toleration in England*.

5. For instance, magistrates were not to preside over the sacraments of the church, and priests were not to attempt to act as magistrates by bearing the sword. Each were to operate in their own spheres, but cooperation was the ideal relationship between the two.

6. For instance, Robert Browne, a separatist calling for reform, argued that the church should advance its own reform without the state's support, even if it meant separating from the Church of England. See Browne, *A Treatise of Reformation without Tarying for Anie*. Browne's views would influence Baptists' views a few decades later.

banned, as were any separatist church meetings: the Church of England was the established church and they tolerated no dissent.[7] In that context, Baptists were born, and quickly persecuted. And it was in that trajectory of a 1,200-year tradition of church-state coercion of religious dissent that the Baptists forged their vision for religious liberty.[8]

EARLY BAPTISTS AND RELIGIOUS LIBERTY

Key Figures and Confessions

In 1611, Thomas Helwys led his small band of followers back from Holland to England. Soon thereafter he published his famous work *A Short Declaration of the Mystery of Iniquity* (1612), perhaps the first work in English advocating for full religious liberty.[9] Helwys affirmed the classic distinction between the two spheres, that of the state and that of the church. But he then went on to call for the state to stay out of matters related to the human conscience:

> [O]ur Lord the king has no more power over their [Roman Catholic] consciences than over ours, and that is none at all: for our lord the king is but an earthly king, and he has no authority as a king but in earthly causes, and if the king's people be obedient & true subjects, obeying all human laws made by the king, our lord the king can require no more: for men's religion to God, is between God and themselves; the king shall not answer for it, neither may the king be judge between God and man. Let them be heretics, Turks, Jews, or whatsoever it appertains not to the earthly power to punish them in the least measure. This is made evident to our lord the king by the scriptures.[10]

---

7. The established church in Scotland was Presbyterian. For a detailed analysis of seventeenth-century English thought related to liberty, see Cragg, *Freedom and Authority*.

8. Baptists were not the first to advocate for religious toleration, for they inherited much from the Anabaptists in this regard. Their calls for religious freedom would also share much with the Enlightenment's aversion to compulsion.

9. For a helpful and detailed summary of the early development of Baptist positions on religious liberty, see Cross, "'Christ Jesus . . . exalted . . . farre aboue all principalities and powers,'" 3–22.

10. Helwys, *A Short Declaration of the Mystery of Iniquity* (1611/1612), 69. We have modernized the English.

Religious Liberty

While John Smyth remained in Holland and sought membership with the Mennonites, he echoed the same sentiment in regard to the state staying out of matters of conscience:

> That the magistrate is not by virtue of his office to meddle with religion, or matters of conscience, to force and compel men to this or that form of religion, or doctrine, but to leave Christian religion free, to every man's conscience, and to handle only civil transgressions (Rom. 13). Injuries and wrongs of men against men, in murder, adultery, theft, etc. for Christ only is the king, and lawgiver of the church and conscience (Jas 4:12).[11]

Not surprisingly, Helwys' attack on the Church of England's establishment being bolstered by the state's sword, and the concomitant call for religious liberty, got him into trouble with the authorities. He was arrested and died in Newgate Prison in London in 1616. Upon Helwys' imprisonment, leadership of the church passed into the hands of John Murton (or Morton). A decade later, in 1626, he, too, died in prison. Obviously advancing the notion of religious freedom was not going to be easy.[12]

Another important figure in the development of early Baptist views of religious conscience was Leonard Busher, the "premier political theologian of the early Baptists."[13] In fact, it has been argued that his work is the "first clear enunciation of unqualified liberty of conscience" in the English language.[14] His *Religious Peace; or, a Plea for Liberty of Conscience* (1614) detailed a notion of religious liberty predicated on the priority of respecting human conscience.[15] In the sphere of civil activities, the state had the authority to make laws and enforce compliance. As for spiritual convictions and matters of conscience, the state (and established church)

---

11. Smyth, *Propositions and Conclusions* (1612), article 84. John Smyth's views on church-state relations mirrored Helwys in a number of ways, although Smyth's embracing of the Anabaptist position on pacifism and refusal to serve as magistrates was a critical distinction between Helwys and the Baptist position(s). See Lee, *The Theology of John Smyth*, ch. 7.

12. For some easily accessible source readings on early persecution of Baptists, see Brackney, ed., *Baptist Life and Thought*, 71–80.

13. Yarnell, "Political Theology among the Earliest Baptists," 23.

14. Whitley, "Leonard Busher, Dutchman," 112, as quoted in Yarnell, "Political Theology among the Earliest Baptists," 24.

15. There is no extant version, but it was republished in 1646 and that later edition is extant.

had no right to coerce. Any attempt to enforce religious orthodoxy by the sword was a sinful and destructive overreach by the authorities:

> persecution for difference in religion is a monstrous and cruel beast, that destroys both prince and people, hinders the gospel of Christ, and scatters his disciples that witness and profess his name. But permission of conscience in difference of religion, saves both prince and people; for it is a meek and gentle lamb, which not only furthers and advances the gospel, but also fosters and cherishes those that profess it.[16]

Decades later, during the tumultuous years of civil war, Busher once again entered the fray and wrote church leaders at Westminster Assembly. In his *An Exhortation unto the Learned Divines Assembled at Westminster* (1643), he reiterated his call for liberty of conscience and cast a vision for "both liberty of preaching (i.e. the freedom of speech) and liberty for printing (i.e. the freedom of the press)."[17] Others also called for liberty of conscience.[18]

Advancing the notion of religious freedom was also not easy in the New World, as Roger Williams—the "prophet, pioneer, and apostle" of liberty[19]—discovered.[20] In March 1636, Williams and a few friends from Salem planted a church just outside the Massachusetts Bay colony jurisdiction, which is the church some consider to be the first Baptist church in America. Over the next few years he worked towards developing a colony that practiced religious freedom. In 1643, he travelled to England to formalize Rhode Island's legal status. While in England he published his famous *Bloudy Tenent of Persecution for cause of conscience discussed* (1644). John Cotton sought to refute his arguments in his *Bloudy Tenent washed and made white in the Bloud of the Lamb* (1647), to which Williams responded with *Bloudy Tenent yet more Bloudy* (1652).[21] Much was

---

16. As quoted in Brackney, ed., *Baptist Life and Thought*, 78. We have modernized the English.

17. Yarnell, "Political Theology among the Earliest Baptists," 32.

18. For a collection of such petitions and exhortations, see Underhill, ed., *Tracts on Liberty of Conscience and Persecution, 1614–1661*.

19. Strickland, *Roger Williams*.

20. Baptists claim Williams as one of their own, but Williams was a seeker and remained a Baptist for only a time. For biographies of Williams, see Barry, *Roger Williams and the Creation of the American Soul*; and Gaustad, *Liberty of Conscience*.

21. For further background and sources, see Greene, ed., *Roger Williams and the Massachusetts Magistrates*.

at stake in those exchanges, but at the heart of the debate was the right of the state to use coercion to enforce religious conformity. Williams' argument was that the state had a God-given responsibility to legislate and use the sword in regard to civil affairs, but, when it came to matters of conscience, the state (and any state church) had absolutely no jurisdiction. The conscience was free from the sword of the state, and could only be changed through the Word of God and the Holy Spirit. William's view was not widely accepted at the time, and he continued to face restrictions and hardships due to his dissenting religious views.

Not surprisingly, convictions on religious liberty made their way into Baptist confessions. The *London Confession* (1644/1646) affirmed Baptist recognition of the civil magistrate's legitimate authority to use the sword for the "punishment of evil doers."[22] And in most matters, Christians were obliged to obey the state, for it was deemed to be God's servant to ensure and advance civil justice. However, if the state overreached and demanded something against God's law, then obedience to the state was simply not an option; arrest or even martyrdom were considered to be better than going against conscience and the Word of God. In regard to the protection of conscience, magistrates had a "duty to tender the liberty of mens' consciences. Eccles.8:8 (which is the tenderest thing unto all conscientious men, and most dear unto them, and without which all other liberties will not be worth the naming, much less enjoying) and to protect all under them from wrong, injury, oppression and molestation."[23] The forty-sixth article of *An Orthodox Creed* (1678) made an unambiguous statement on the importance of liberty of conscience:

> The Lord Jesus Christ, who is King of Kings, and Lord of All . . . is only Lord of Conscience, having a peculiar right so to be: He having died for that very end, to take away the Guilt, and to destroy the filth of Sin; that keeps the Consciences of all Men in Thraldom, and Bondage, till they are set free by his special Grace. And there he would not have the Consciences of Men in Bondage to, or imposed upon, by any Usurpation, Tyranny, or command whatsoever, contrary to his revealed Will in his Word, which is the only Rule he hath left, for the Consciences of

---

22. *London Confession of Faith* (1644/1646), articles 48 and 49.

23. The *Second London Confession* also affirmed that God was the sole Lord of the conscience. See *Second London Confession* (1677/1689), article 21.2.

all Men to be ruled, and regulated, and guided by, through the assistance of his Spirit.[24]

The *Philadelphia Confession* (1742) echoed and elaborated on those earlier sentiments. God had established the civil authorities, and Christians were enjoined to obey them. However, the power of the state had limits, as did Christian obedience to the state. No Christian needed to heed a state that required going against the Word of God, and no state had jurisdiction over a person's conscience:

> God alone is Lord of the conscience, and hath left it free from the doctrines and commandments of men which are in any thing contrary to his word, or not contained in it. So that to believe such doctrines, or obey such commands out of conscience, is to betray true liberty of conscience; and the requiring of an implicit faith, an absolute and blind obedience, is to destroy liberty of conscience and reason also (James 4:12; Rom. 14:4; Acts 4:19, 29; 1 Cor. 7:23; Matt. 15:9; Col. 2:20, 22, 23; 1 Cor. 3:5; 2 Cor. 1:24).[25]

Baptist ministers such as American pastor John Leland embraced such ideals and passionately advocated for religious freedom in the colonies (and then in the nascent American nation). Baptist statements since those early years have echoed the same refrain. For example, the Baptist World Alliance's yearly statements on religious liberty and justice mirror those earlier calls for freedom.[26]

Convictions

Baptist convictions on liberty were a combination of both pragmatic and theological concerns, primarily motivated by a passionate desire to follow the New Testament's teaching. That said, Baptist views resonated with—and were reinforced by—the Enlightenment's concern for religious liberty.[27] For instance, Baptists would have agreed with philosopher Denis Diderot who said, "The mind can only acquiesce in what it accepts as

---

24. *An Orthodox Creed* (1678), article 46.
25. *Philadelphia Confession* (1742), 21.2.
26. www.bwanet.org.
27. Eventually, Baptists would sometimes find themselves allied with ardent Enlightenment figures on that very issue. For example, see Kidd and Hankins, *Baptists in America*, chapter 4.

true. The heart can only love what seems good to it. Violence will turn a man into a hypocrite if he is weak and into a martyr if he is strong . . . Teaching, persuasion and prayer, these are the only legitimate means of spreading the faith."[28]

The pragmatic aspect of Baptist convictions revolved around the belief that coercion simply did not work, and would, in fact, make matters worse for the faithful by tarnishing Christian witness and emboldening opponents of the church. It would also have the deleterious effect of driving good citizens into exile (something deemed to be morally repugnant, as well as harmful to a nation). To persecute for matters of conscience was also to act like "Turks" and Catholics, behaviour considered unbecoming for *true* Christians.[29] In sum, the gains from persecution for conscience were superficial or fleeting, and, at the end of the day, it was a net loss.

As important as such pragmatic concerns were in the formation of Baptist beliefs, the Baptist vision for religious liberty is rooted in particular theological convictions, without which the Baptist position would be unrecognizable. More specifically, beyond pragmatics the Baptist view on religious liberty is an amalgam of ideas regarding a proper view of the state's role, New Testament gospel ministry, natural law, God's care for the oppressed, and soul competency.

First, the state's role needed to be understood properly to ensure religious liberty. In spite of how it may have appeared to critics, Baptists were not fifth columnists seeking to undermine the civil authority of the magistrates at the behest of a malevolent foreign power, nor were they end-times fanatics abandoning all civil responsibilities as they looked forward to an apocalyptic showdown when Christ returned. Rather, like centuries of Christians before them, like other magisterial reformers during the Reformation, and even like the Church of England from which they were separating, they believed that God had established the state to restrain evil and to promote human flourishing. A part of that divinely ordained mandate was to enact laws for the good of citizenry, and even to use the sword for the defence or promotion of justice. Baptists also envisioned politics as a legitimate sphere for Christians to serve in as magistrates and soldiers, and they deemed the notion of a just war to be a legitimate Christian position.

---

28. As quoted in Bokenkotter, *A Concise History of the Catholic Church*, 234.

29. For a helpful summary of pragmatic concerns, see White, "Early Baptist Arguments for Religious Freedom," 3–10.

At the heart of the theological matter was who was responsible for what. Baptists wanted a recalibration of the church's view of church-state relations, and their concomitant means and ends, in order to recover a more biblical understanding of the church's role in enforcing its own affairs under the authority of Jesus—the Lord of the conscience.

A significant Baptist departure from the orthodoxy of the day was their claim that the state's authority—and right to coerce—did not extend into the realm of the conscience. Christians were enjoined to obey the state in all matters, except when the state passed unjust laws or sought to operate outside its legitimate sphere such as in the realm of the conscience. For instance, Williams divided the Ten Commandments into two sections: the first table was to God, the second table to others. The civil authorities could punish in regard to the second, but in no way were the civil authorities to coerce in regards to the first. Any attempt to promote, or defend, the faith by force was a confusion of responsibilities and an inappropriate use of the sword. It was also ultimately destructive of faith and witness.

It is here that state coercion intersects with the Baptist view of church governance and the nature of church life: only the church was to oversee the affairs of the church. The state was to provide protection for all citizens, but it was to keep its hands off the church when it came to matters of conscience. Jesus was Lord of the conscience, and he exercised that Lordship through the Word and Spirit, in the context of a church of believers. No state, no magistrate, and no bishop (hand-appointed by the state) had any power over doctrinal matters. Nigel Wright's summary of this position is exactly right, and worth quoting in full:

> For Baptists, freedom has been paramount, freedom in the first instance from "sacred power," simply to be the church under the Lordship of Jesus Christ and to do those things its Lord asks of it as they are interpreted by a properly informed conscience. The corollary of this is a political one: it is wrong for princes and rulers to play God, and to seek to determine what people believe and how they think, to enforce religion or ideology. So the notion of the free church requires a kind of counterpart in a free state. This is the insight the first Baptists stumbled across, however imperfectly they grasped it. It is truly revolutionary and has shaped political discourse ever since.[30]

---

30. Wright, *Free Church, Free State*, xxi.

Religious Liberty

Second, the New Testament, it was argued, demonstrated that Jesus himself did not coerce, nor did the early church expect or teach that the state had any role to play in the internal functions, convictions, or discipline of the church. Religious liberty, it was argued, was simply an assumption of the earliest Christians. It also seemed to be an assumption of early Christian missionaries in the book of Acts, for the faith was spread (and defended) by active efforts of men and women who preached, taught, organized, and argued in the power of the Spirit—not the power of state—for the veracity of their apostolic message. That model of ministry was a hallmark of early Baptist ministry, as exemplified by Williams' conflict with the Quakers. Consider Gaustad's account:

> In his old age, Williams rowed some 30 miles from Providence to Newport to engage the Quakers in vigorous debate, attempting to show them the error of their ways. See, some commentators say, he did not really believe in religious liberty, because he told the Quakers they were wrong! What a dreadful misunderstanding this is. Yes, Williams told the Quakers they were wrong and for several days debated their religious principles with them. But no, he did not prevent their moving to and thriving in Rhode Island. And he did not allow the hand of the state ever to be raised against them. Nor did he fine, jail, whip, or hang any Quakers, or permit others to do so. Williams, who cared deeply about his own faith and his own conscience, would, with equal passion and devotion, ever care about and protect the consciences of others.[31]

That concern for the protection of liberty of conscience in the spread of the gospel has been a part of Baptist DNA since the movement's inception.

Third, much of Baptist commentary on religious liberty in the contemporary world references human rights. For instance, the Baptist World Alliance encourages Baptist congregations to observe Human Rights Day (December 10), the anniversary of the formation of the Universal Declaration of Human Rights (10 December 1948). This language reflects the rise of human rights in Western discourse and international law in the modern age, but is also rooted in an ancient notion of natural law. Natural law, as understood by theologians such as Augustine and Aquinas, is the belief that God has endowed the natural world with laws that can be known by human reason.[32] Human value, dignity, and free-

---

31. Gaustad, *Roger Williams*, 106–7.
32. Some would argue that this is what Paul was talking about in Rom 1:20.

dom are part of that world created by God and the "rights" of humans are something that must be respected. Not all Baptists are supportive or in agreement with notions of natural law, and the Baptist view does not rise or fall solely on such arguments.[33] However, the Baptist position is bolstered by contemporary notions of natural law and human rights, and Baptist discourse certainly draws upon it.

Fourth, Baptists believe that God is concerned for the marginalized and oppressed, and that passion is at the heart of contemporary concern for religious liberty and human rights. Athol Gill argues that this is matter of reflecting the "heart of God":

> For many of us, Christian concern for human rights has been awakened by the frightening injustice and sometimes overwhelming oppression of the world in which we live, but it is important for us to realize that this concern for human rights is ultimately grounded in the nature of God the creator and redeemer. As a result it can never be reduced to the level of an optional extra or even be considered simply as a necessary implication of the gospel. Social justice and the quest for human rights are at the heart of the gospel; they reflect the heart of God.[34]

The argument is simply that the Old Testament prophets made it clear that God was concerned for the oppressed, and that rulers had better take care of those under their watch—especially the most vulnerable. Oppression, injustice, cruelty, and the like, were simply anathema, and God's heart was for liberation and liberty. The message and ministry of Jesus was in the same vein, for the coming of the kingdom associated with justice.

Fifth, Baptist assumptions on religious liberty are based on the notion that each and every soul is responsible before God for how one lives one's life, and for what one believes. Not only that, but each and every person has the right and ability to relate directly to God without human intermediaries. The following statement from the Southern Baptist Convention expresses well this notion of human accountability directly to God and the need for religious liberty:

> God alone is Lord of the conscience, and He has left it free from the doctrines and commandments of men which are contrary

---

33. Mitchell, "National Law and Religious Liberty," 111–24.
34. Gill, "Human Rights," 244.

> to His Word or not contained in it. Church and state should be separate. The state owes to every church protection and full freedom in the pursuit of its spiritual ends. . . . The gospel of Christ contemplates spiritual means alone for the pursuit of its ends. The state has no right to impose penalties for religious opinions of any kind. The state has no right to impose taxes for the support of any form of religion. A free church in a free state is the Christian ideal, and this implies the right of free and unhindered access to God on the part of all men, and the right to form and propagate opinions in the sphere of religion without interference by the civil power.[35]

Of course, the implication is that the state should stay out of matters related to theological convictions, whether heretical or orthodox. And most certainly churches should not urge the state to get involved in such matters.

It should be noted that Baptists did not think that their views on religious liberty were a novelty. Rather, they could be seen to be supported by not only by the Old and New Testaments but also the church fathers such as Tertullian and Lactantius.[36] For instance, consider Tertullian's exhortation for religious freedom in the second century:

> However, it is a fundamental human right, a privilege of nature that every person should worship according to their own convictions; one person's religion neither harms nor helps another person. It is assuredly no part of religion to compel religion—to which freewill and not force should lead us—the sacrificial victims even being required of a willing mind. You will render no real service to your gods by compelling us to sacrifice. For they can have no desire of offerings from the unwilling, unless they are animated by a spirit of contention, which is a thing altogether undivine.[37]

With that type of commentary it is clear that calls for religious liberty had a long pedigree, and Baptists saw themselves as simply calling the church back to its roots.

---

35. *The Baptist Faith and Message* (2000), article 17.
36. Lactantius, *Divine Institutes* 54.
37. Tertullian, *To Scapula*. See also Tertullian, *Apology* 24.

BAPTISTS AND RELIGIOUS LIBERTY TODAY

Not Easy to See Clearly

Baptists today continue to be shaped by that theological DNA, and those familiar with the tradition are well aware that Baptists are sensitive to matters of religious liberty. Over the centuries, expressions have developed around the issue, some of the more well-known being "soul liberty," "soul competency,"[38] and the "separation of church and state." At the heart of such expressions is the conviction that no person should be coerced in matters of conscience. Jesus is the Lord of the conscience, and no other could make such a claim. The state, and/or established churches, were in no way to meddle in the internal matters of the church, but especially in regard to matters of conscience. Any such attempts were an over-reach of the state's divinely ordained responsibilities.

The problem, of course, is the difficulty of seeing clearly in the midst of powerful, and corrupting, cultural norms, and, like every other religious group on the planet, Baptists are not immune to the consequences of living in a fallen world. Incongruities and tensions abound: they opposed many core Enlightenment assumptions, but supported Thomas Jefferson for religious freedom; they argued for religious liberty, but many supported slavery; and they provided safety for indigenous Americans, but supported their relocation to make room for European colonists.[39] Even Williams disenfranchised African Americans and Catholics in his nascent colony.[40] Sadly, there are other such examples.

A further demonstration of how difficult it is to see clearly sometimes is when coercion seemed necessary for liberty. Religious liberty has been central to Baptist convictions on war and peace, and that concern was central to shaping attitudes toward conflicts.[41] If the British Empire furthered the cause of liberty, was support for the advance of empire a necessity? If godless communism was a great evil, then was support for Hitler the best option? If the war for liberty against Germany needed conscription, was the suppression of conscientious objectors acceptable?

---

38. A major proponent of the notion of "soul competency" was Southern Baptist leader, E. Y. Mullins. See Mullins, *Axioms of Religion*.

39. Kidd and Hankins, *Baptists in America*.

40. Yarnell, "Political Theology among the Earliest Baptists," 33.

41. Heath, "Engaging War and Empire."

Religious Liberty

There are more such examples, but the point is clear. It is oftentimes quite difficult to know the right way forward to advance the cause of liberty, and, ironically, the very thing that you think is promoting liberty may, in fact, be taking it away from others.

Another area of possible gain is that of receiving funding from the government. For instance, many churches receive government grants for students involved in summer ministries. It is the state's God-given responsibility to protect its citizens—Baptists included. However, is it the role of the state to fund the ministries of the church? Baptists have disagreed on this point, and the issue is not going away any time soon. Those who argue against receiving funding do so out of a desire to keep the state out of the affairs of the church (i.e., not taking money gives the state less leverage over what goes on in the church), and out of a conviction that the ministry of the church is the church's responsibility. Those who argue for it do so from pragmatic considerations (i.e., funding is needed, and it is for a good cause), and from the belief that tax money should be available to all tax-paying citizens—religious people included. Whatever side one comes down on, it should be noted that the historic concerns over government coercion of churches are somewhat mitigated if churches remain free from the government holding the purse strings.[42]

One last area of possible gain is in partnership with the state to create a "Christian nation." Baptists in Canada at the end of the nineteenth century entered into an informal establishment with other major Protestant denominations (Methodist, Presbyterian, and Anglican) to do just that. The dream was a Christian nation, but the cost was a partnership with the state that led to compromises on Baptist views on church-state relations and the implicit coercion that came with such a partnership. In fact, many dissenting bodies in the Anglophone world did likewise.[43]

There are a number of popular myths and misunderstandings when it comes to Baptist views on the state. For instance:

---

42. One recent discussion is if churches accept property tax exemption, clergy residence exemption, or even be offering charitable tax receipts. Some Baptists argue that such tax exemptions are really government sponsorships. Some Anabaptists have gone so far as to not claim their clergy residence deductions on their personal taxes.

43. Heath, "Dissenting Traditions and Politics in the Anglophone World," 61–90. The rise of the religious right in the United States, headed by prominent Baptists such as Jerry Falwell, is an American example of this tendency. See Sutton, *Jerry Falwell and the Rise of the Religious Right*. For the larger context, see Marsden, *Religion and American Culture*.

- Baptist have a low view of the state
- Baptists should not be involved in politics or enter the public square
- Baptists are inherently pacifists
- Religious liberty means no church discipline
- A commitment to religious liberty means no evangelism

As noted above, Baptists have a high view of the state, one that recognizes its God-given role in promoting justice and human flourishing.[44] The state is a valuable, essential, and legitimate authority, and Christians must obey laws that do not transgress God's laws. They believe that the state has a God-given role to use the sword for the cause of justice. They also believe that Christians can be magistrates and even soldiers in the cause of justice; however, Baptists also argue that the state needs to stay out the affairs of the church, and let the church (or whatever religion) believe what it must without state coercion. The state's sword is to protect all citizens, including Christians, but that same sword is not to be used to enforce religious orthodoxy. Stated differently, church discipline is an internal matter. Yet, keeping the state out of the affairs of the church does not mean that Baptists are to withdraw from the public square. "Separation of church and state" (to use an American expression)[45] means that the state is to stay out of the affairs of the church, but Christians as citizens could still have a role to play in shaping the nation. Christians are free to serve at all levels of government, not in order to create a theocracy but simply to promote justice for all. Finally, religious liberty does not preclude church discipline for sin or heresy, although the state has no mandate or role to play in such matters. Nor does it preclude evangelism—it merely means that the gospel must be shared with kindness, not coercion. As one Baptist pastor stated (with a tone of superiority): "Other churches may employ carnal weapons, and inflict pains and penalties, to promote their prosperity; but Baptist churches, if they flourish, must succeed by moral suasion and the grace of God."[46]

---

44. For instance, see *Philadelphia Confession of Faith* (1742), chapter 25.

45. There are various western models of church-state relations besides the American model. See Soper, et al., *The Challenge of Pluralism*.

46. Jeter, *Baptist Principles Reset*, 129. (His point about Baptist methods is valid, his criticism of other denominations reflects the nineteenth century Baptist hostile posture towards other denominations.)

Religious Liberty

Global Context and Organizations

In spite of their failure to always live up to their ideals, Baptists continue to identify religious liberty as one of their defining characteristics. The importance of religious liberty is rooted in the ideal that no one's conscience—Christian or otherwise—should be compelled by the threat of violence, but it is also a pressing pragmatic necessity since Baptists face uncertainty and persecution in various places around the globe. Tensions with the Orthodox Church in Eastern Europe have a long history, and Baptists have sought, and sometimes gained, relief from restrictions. However, present tensions and suffering continue. For instance, as a small minority, Baptists often face legal restrictions and persecution in the Ukraine and Russia. Elsewhere, Baptists in India face the burning of churches and threats of physical violence. Myanmar is not a safe place for Baptists, and being a small minority makes them vulnerable. Baptists in Nigeria are a large community, yet their size does not protect them from vicious attacks from Islamic militants. In these places, and elsewhere, Baptists make appeals to government to lift restrictions and grant religious liberty to themselves and to any other disenfranchised groups. Helping small and marginalized groups of Baptists in such calls for religious liberty are large organizations like the Baptist World Alliance. Many denominations have committees or organizations appointed to lead the charge on such matters, such as the Southern Baptist Ethics & Religious Liberty Commission. Local churches can partner together in the cause of liberty and justice with collective organizations such as Canadian Baptist Ministries.

CONCLUSION: BAPTISTS IN CANADA AND RELIGIOUS LIBERTY

From the question of church establishment in the nineteenth century to the persecution of Baptists in Quebec in the early-twentieth century, Baptists in Canada have had to deal with a variety of issues related to religious liberty. Fortunately, Baptists have had a number of prominent leaders who made their mark advocating for liberty. Watson Kirkconnell, university president and professor, spent decades advocating for those on margins of Canadian life, and fighting for democracy against communist tyranny during the Cold War.[47] Prime Minister John Diefenbaker spearheaded the development of Canada's first Bill of Rights, passed by Parliament in 1960. It was a ground-breaking effort to protect the rights of minorities and human rights in general. Both of these examples are public demonstrations of historic Baptist convictions in regard to the importance of liberty.

In the twenty-first century, domestic tensions and uncertainty remain in areas such as education, hiring, access to government services/funding, church discipline, and social mores. The jury is still out on the impact of church incorporation on the church-state relationship, but that could also exacerbate problems of state involvement in church affairs in the future. The post-Christendom trajectory of Canada may also lead to situations whereby Baptists feel their once-held freedoms are being challenged by a state not so amenable to conservative religious sensibilities. As for the international scene, Baptists in Canada will continue to read of restrictions and even repression of Christians in general, and Baptists in particular, in some parts of the world. Those reports of the suffering of Baptists (and any people—Christian or not) are cause for Baptist advocacy and offers of support.

There is no easy solution to issues related to religious liberty, and not all Baptists will agree on proposed solutions. But what is certain is that Baptists should work with their local church and denominational organizations (and other organizations as well) to create conditions that promote a healthy and vibrant society where people can thrive without state coercion on matters of conscience. The mandate for Baptists is clearly stated in the *London Confession* (1644/1646): "so it is our duty not to be wanting in nothing which is for their honour and comfort, and whatsoever is for the wellbeing of the commonwealth wherein we live."[48] They must also avoid the temptation to expect or even enlist the state to aid in the promotion of Baptist mission: expecting government to protect the freedom to worship according to conscience is a legitimate expectation, but expecting that same state to coerce in matters of conscience is unconscionable.

---

47. Heath, "Watson Kirkconnell's Covert War against Communism," 64–79.
48. *London Confession of Faith* (1644/1646), article 48.

8

Baptists and the Future

BAPTISTS FACE UNIQUE CHALLENGES and opportunities around the globe. In some parts of the world, the church (including Baptists) is under pressure, and persecution is a clear and present danger. Yet, in other regions, the church is surging in numbers and Baptists are riding the wave along with other Christian denominations. The future for Baptists in those diverse communities will be shaped by countless factors, and time will tell what the future holds.

Some of what Baptists face in Canada is what all churches face in the West. And, of course, other challenges are unique to Canada. Canada has changed and Canada is changing. Since the early days of Canadian Confederation through to today there have been significant shifts in urbanization patterns, ethnic diversity, economic trends, emergent technologies, among a myriad of other cultural changes. Religious affiliation patterns have changed, particularly with the rise of Canadians that do not identify with any religion (from 4 percent in 1971 to 24 percent in 2011).[1] Questions of power and authority, and the ways different cultural groups interact, have evolved since the mid-twentieth century. Gradually, all churches have found themselves on the margins, shifting from the gilded halls of power to the backwaters. They are no longer "nation builders" as formerly understood for much of Canadian history. In fact, increasingly it is argued that religion should have no voice at all in the public square. Some even vehemently argue that "religion poisons everything" and that religion is extremely dangerous and a form of child

---

1. Statistics Canada, 2011 National Household Survey and Statistics Canada, 2001 Census.

abuse.[2] These shifts have led to the descriptions of the cultural milieu of twenty-first century Canada as "Post-Christian," "Post-Christendom," "Post-Denominationalism," and/or "Post-Colonial." While identifying the full array of shifts in the Canadian landscape and accompanying terminology is beyond the scope of this chapter, Canada is changing and those changes affect Baptist congregations.[3]

TAKING THE PULSE

At the end of the second decade of the twenty-first century, it is worthwhile to "take the pulse" of Baptists. There is good and bad to report. The percentage of Baptists in Canada has fallen from 5 percent of the total population in 1921 to less than 2 percent in 2011 (635,840).[4] However, the precipitous post-1960s drop off in numbers—experienced by virtually every Protestant denomination—seems to have leveled off. Baptist churches continue to close, in both rural and urban centres, with even iconic churches closing down and selling the property. The decline of numbers and churches has led to agonizing denominational soul searching over how to adjust its ministries to reflect decreased financial giving. That said, there are positive signs of growth among the various Baptist communities. Church plants proceed apace, with denominations committing significant resources and attention to such promising endeavours, and some older churches are experiencing renewal and stabilizing growth. Reginald Bibby demonstrates how religion for many remains a vibrant part of their lives, and how the arrival of Christian immigrants has bolstered the churches with new members and vitality.[5] For instance, much of the CBOQ's growth over the past few decades has been among the Chinese and other ethnic communities.[6] While the splintering propensity of Baptists remains a threat, enmity between Baptist groups seems to have waned over the decades, with promising signs of mutual respect and even partnership between once alienated people.

2. A common refrain of "New Atheists" such as Richard Dawkins and Christopher Hitchens. For instance, see Hitchens, *God Is Not Great*.

3. For a helpful examination of religious demographics in Canada, Clarke and Macdonald, *Leaving Christianity*.

4. Statistics Canada, 2011 National Household Survey.

5. Bibby, "Post-Christendom in Canada? Not So Fast," 125–41.

6. Conservative estimates have the number of congregants in Chinese churches at about 25 percent of the total number of congregants in CBOQ.

Baptists and the Future

CHALLENGES, OPPORTUNITIES, AND BAPTIST DNA

The future is filled with opportunity. But one must not be Pollyanna, for there are challenges ahead. What follows is a summary of what are some of the most significant challenges and opportunities. Many are what all Canadian denominations face; what we aim to do is identify how Baptist identity and distinctives inform a response and help chart a way forward in complex situations. There is no way these few pages can "solve" all the challenges, but an identification of what Baptist DNA can provide is a starting point for churches that are seeking to move forward to the future with courage, confidence, wisdom, and faith.[7]

New, No, or Loss of Religion

The religious mosaic of Canada is changing, and that brings opportunity and challenges. The arrival of significant numbers of new Canadians who belong to another world religion is readily apparent. The rise of those who identify with no religion (often referred to as the "Nones"[8]) has also risen significantly in the last few decades. The loss of faith of their youth has been especially troubling for churches that seek to "pass the baton" to the next generation.

Baptists have recently invested a great deal of thought and energy with regard to the last point. According to *Hemorrhaging Faith* research, one in ten Catholic and Mainline Protestant and four in ten Evangelical Canadian young adults raised in churches reported attending religious services at least weekly as they entered into adulthood.[9] Young people raised in the church simply are not staying in the church. In the follow-up study, *Renegotiating Faith*, attention is given to Emerging Adulthood, a life stage that delays by five to seven years a shift to traditional notions of adulthood.[10] This delay has impacted commitments to faith: "Emerging adulthood works against young adults' staying engaged in their faith and the life of the church because it disrupts their access to Christian communities and makes it difficult for them to negotiate meaningful roles

---

7. For helpful commentary on how Baptist distinctives may shape contemporary challenges and opportunities, see Blythe, "Eating Forbidden Fruit."
8. White, *The Rise of the Nones*.
9. Penner, *Hemorrhaging Faith*, 22
10. Hiemstra, *Renegotiating Faith*, 10.

in those communities."[11] These conclusions were alarming, and, in April 2016, the Canadian Baptist Youth & Family Team pulled together fifty influential CBM leaders from across the country to ask the question, "What must we do to reach and engage young people with the person and message of Jesus?"[12] They produced a report called *The Imaginative Hope Report: Revealing the Obstacles and Opportunities to Reaching and Engaging the Next Generation with the Gospel*. This report identifies seven obstacles "to reach the next generation with the gospel of Jesus," and Baptists were encouraged to begin the hard work of reaching this generation with the gospel.

Baptist life has a robust tradition of carrying out missionary work. Their first attempts at organization were motivated by it, immense personal and financial sacrifices were made for it, and innovative methods marked their efforts to do it. Rather than lament "the way it was" or "the way it should be," Baptists today can draw on their rich tradition of missions to forge new ways of connecting with others and discipling their own. It should also be noted that the congregational model makes for a fluid system of governance that should—in theory—allow for local churches to carry out rapid, innovative, and local context-specific outreach. There are approximately two thousand Baptist congregations in Canada. That means that there are two thousand local churches that are free to adapt to local contexts in order to carry out their mission and mandate—and of course, free as well to partner together on larger issues that require cooperation. There has never been a one-size-fits-all solution to mission and church planting. Baptists have sought to be faithful to their calling but also to recognize that there is an obligation to being responsive to the community's traditions, customs, and vernacular. That localized approach fits well with trends such as "buy local," "live local," and the "100-mile diet."

Reconciliation with Indigenous Peoples

As noted in a previous chapter, in response to the Truth and Reconciliation Commission of Canada's calls for action, Terry Smith, the Executive Director of CBM, issued an apology to Canada's indigenous population for past injustices inflicted by the church in general, and Baptists

---

11. Hiemstra, *Renegotiating Faith*, 161.
12. Canadian Baptist Youth & Family Forum, *Imaginative Hope*, 5.

in particular. That recognition and apology is an important marker highlighting how Baptists have come a long way since the days of a national vision marked by a distinctly Anglo-Saxon imperial identity. The challenge is to make good on the promise to do and be different. The difficulties facing indigenous communities are significant, and only the investment of significant resources and the growth of loving relationships will demonstrate the sincerity of such statements. One positive indicator is the focus on indigenous studies at various theological institutions, including Acadia Divinity College, which has partnered with the North American Institute for Indigenous Theological Studies (NAIITS) to offer graduate training in Indigenous Community Development.

Move to the Margins

Baptists in Canada belonged to an unofficial religious establishment for the nineteenth and much of the twentieth centuries, but those days of Christian prominence are gone. While Canada is still demographically Christian (69 percent on the last census), the churches' relationship with power has certainly shifted. No longer is the nation self-identified as "Christian," and no longer is Christianity the unofficial religion of the land. In that sense, Canada is in Post-Christendom, for the medieval synthesis of church and state has been jettisoned, and all religions are—or are supposed to be—on an equal standing. Some have called this a "move to the margins," a place where churches operate without power and privilege. Life on the margins is made even more difficult by the significant shifts in social mores, especially in areas of human dignity, sanctity of life, and sexuality. Conservative churches increasingly find their beliefs on such issues place them even more on the margins, with significant tensions swirling around a matter of faithfulness to scripture and yet grace towards those who differ.

Baptists should be well prepared for life on the margins, for they were an illegal movement born in adversity, had their martyrs, and were convinced that the true church does not need to be propped up by the state. More specifically, the Baptist model of church life and governance assumes a church of believers, led by believers, supported by believers, without any outside control of the state (and/or hostile religious body). They are often willing to receive state money (e.g., tax exemption, tax credits, summer student grants), but when "push comes to shove," they should be willing to accept the loss of such perks rather than risk state intrusion into church life. They are also ardent advocates for religious liberty, calling on government to not overstep its authority by seeking to coerce in matters of conscience. They also should be ardent defenders of *any* matter of conscience—be it Muslim, Hindu, Jewish or other—that is being coerced by the state. Baptists in the Middle East, Asia, or elsewhere know how their tradition can inform their response to pressures that come from living on the margins. However, Baptists in Canada have lived a privileged life for much of their experience, and a future on the margins is a rude awakening.

The challenge is to embrace the new status, and, as Jarold Zeman writes, the question is if Baptists in Canada "have the courage to be a minority."[13] In fact, the shift in status can open up new possibilities for a church no longer bound by a nation-building ethos that had lost some of its prophetic edge. What is helpful here is Hans Mol's paradigm of how religion can perform a "priestly (legitimating)" or "prophetic (critical)" role.[14] The shift from priest to prophet may be difficult, but it allows for a freedom to explore new avenues for engaging Canadian public life not from a position of an insider with power ("priest") but rather as an outsider from the margins ("prophet").

Post-Denominationalism

Denominational identity simply does not matter like it used to. Increasingly people migrate from denomination to denomination without a care for (or knowledge of) differences in denominational distinctives. On the one hand, such a telos towards Christian unity should be celebrated. As Nigel Wright notes, "In essence, the breaking down of denominational barriers must surely be welcomed as a good and enriching thing. There is one Lord, one faith and one baptism and so for any kind of barrier to be broken down in the church of Christ must be counted a good thing."[15] This phenomenon is more than just the movement of theologically unaware and/or spiritually shallow "church shoppers" (although, to be honest, that may be part of it), it is also born out of an important recognition that the kingdom of God is bigger than one denomination. On the other

---

13. Zeman, "The Courage to be a Minority," 105–11.
14. Mol, *Faith and Fragility: Religion and Identity in Canada*.
15. Wright, *New Baptists*, 47.

hand, this is troubling for Baptist identity and the preservation of distinctives that are considered to be foundational for living as the church was meant to live. The questions facing denominational-identity gatekeepers revolve around "How will you make people aware of Baptist history and polity in your local church?" "Why does it matter?" and "What role will denominational identity and affiliation take in your ministry?"

However, a few comments are in order with regard to the alleged immediate demise of denominations. Nigel Wright's summary is helpful:

> Firstly, although we may be in a postdenominational age, it should not be imagined that denominations are about to go out of existence.
>
> Secondly, the postdenominational claim must take into account the fact that denominational structures still function with a high degree of vitality in the contemporary world and are able to gather and mobilize large numbers of people for valuable and productive purposes.
>
> Thirdly, new movements that define themselves as post-denominational often come to display characteristics that can clearly be described as denominational.
>
> Fourthly, it needs to be affirmed that the issues and questions out of which denominations have emerged have not gone away.[16]

Denominations seem to be here to stay, for the time being anyway. But what is also here is a fluidity to membership that (1) raises questions about the relativizing of the value of "Baptist" identity, and (2) places pressure on expecting new members to hold to views that are—in some cases—matters seen to be convenience not conscience. That said, the fact that many non-Baptist churches practice Baptist distinctives such as believers' baptism and some form of congregational government makes migration less of an issue in some cases.

Women in Ministry

Another topic with which Baptists in Canada have always wrestled is that of women in ministry. Mark Noll has identified the issue of women in ministry as a decisive turning point in Christian history. He writes:

---

16. Wright, *New Baptists*, 49–52.

> A twentieth-century development that has been too diffuse to associate with a single, discrete moment may yet be of momentous significance for the Christian future. . . . Whether the commissioning of single women missionaries (which has been controversial in both Catholic and Protestant worlds), the ordination of women to pastoral office (which is till fiercely debated in the West at the end of the twentieth century), or the new social and economic roles opened to women in Western societies (which has engendered intense discussion over "family values"), attention to women's public Christian activities has been a source of friction and hope throughout the century.[17]

Like other denominations, Baptists in Canada have embraced—or resisted—evolving views of women in culture and the church.

The role of women in ministry continues to divide Baptists in Canada. Convention Baptists recognize the ordination of women, while other Baptist denominations such as the Fellowship Baptists do not. At the present time there is no hope for a consensus on this issue, for both sides consider it to be an issue of fidelity to the teaching of the Bible. And because Baptists on either side believe the fidelity of the Bible is at stake, passions can still lead to uncharitable assumptions and remarks toward one's opponents.

In spite of this difference of opinion, there is a way forward, or at least a way to find some common ground. Baptists of all stripes have a rich history of women serving in a wide variety of ministries and functions. For instance, the role of women in Baptist missionary work has been stellar and essential for its success. In Luke 21:2 is the story of a widow that gave her last "mite" to support the work of God. The first known Baptist "Female Mite Society" was in Saint John, New Brunswick in 1818.[18] From that point on, women were instrumental in helping raise funds to support missionary work throughout the world. The first Canadian Protestant single woman missionary was Minnie B. DeWolfe who was sent by the Atlantic Baptists to work with the Karen people in Burma under the American Baptist Missionary Union.[19] Many others followed in her wake. David Bebbington provides a helpful taxonomy of the roles of women in Baptist churches:

- Piety (devotional life, Bible study, prayer, discipleship)

17. Noll, *Turning Points*, 304.
18. Barnes, *Our Heritage Becomes Our Challenge*, 10.
19. Barnes, *Our Heritage Becomes Our Challenge*, 11.

- Print (significant writings by women—poetry, stories, hymns, biographies)
- Parent (this was deemed to be primarily the role of a mother)
- Philanthropy (a very prominent role in this area—especially in the nineteenth century)
- Missions (they were the "mainstay of home support" for missions, and played a significant role in the nineteenth century missions movement—support and actual mission work overseas)[20]

Baptists in Canada and elsewhere remain divided on the issue of women's ordination, and the issue will not be solved in these brief pages. But what all can recognize is that Baptist women have played a critical role in the past, and have one to play in the present and future as well. Reminding women of the varied and rich history of women's contributions to the church's mission can inspire women in new and fresh ways to find their calling in the kingdom regardless of whether or not they are ordained.

Technology

Technology is rapidly changing the way humans interact, organize, and learn. There is much to be gained by applications of new technology to church life, yet advances do lead to difficulties. For instance, in the past, Baptist associations and institutions served a vital purpose in regard to community and education. Today local churches "no longer need denominations as they once did."[21] Baptist pastors do not have the same need for meeting at associations for fellowship when they can go online and connect with anyone, anywhere, anytime, in any weather (a big deal in the Canadian winter!). Associations were already struggling to find a place in modern Baptist life, and recent technology has simply made it even more challenging for old structures to work in a digital age.

That said, the upside is that technology opens up new possibilities. Social media allows for communication across oceans and continents in ways that Baptists of previous generations could only dream of. For instance, in the nineteenth century, people deemed the speed by which information traveled by undersea cable to the distant colonies of the British Empire to be a marvel almost beyond imagination. In 1803, news

20. Bebbington, *Baptists Through the Centuries*, 164–71.
21. Leonard, *The Challenge of Being Baptist*, 111.

arrived to Australia from Britain ten months old. By 1850, it was four months old when it arrived in Australia. After the Suez Canal opened, the news would arrive in forty-four days. After the installation of cable in 1872, news could arrive within hours.[22] Today's face-to-face, real time communication is a boon for those seeking community and information. Theological education can be global, with a professor lecturing in Vancouver with virtual students engaging from Nigeria, China, Lebanon, Bolivia, and Russia. Leaders can provide leadership from a distant location. Pastors can connect with one another, congregations can connect directly with missionaries, ministers can see insights into their congregations through social media (which might be a shock in some cases!), and so on. Advances in technology also allow for the proliferation of mission trips. A recent example of the value and possibilities of technology are readily apparent in the global pandemic of 2020. With the social gathering restrictions that were brought on churches with COVID-19, churches were able to adapt to continue Sunday gatherings utilizing video technology and streaming. Baptists have a history of innovation, and that will help chart a way forward.

Divisions

Baptist history in Canada has been marked by encouraging unions, such as the one that occurred in the early-twentieth century in the Maritimes; however, for much of the twentieth century, Baptists have lived in the shadow of the theological battles and splintering that occurred in the 1920s (and carried over into subsequent decades). Although the vitriol has waned, and crosspollination of Baptists in local church life is now a common occurrence, the Baptist witness is still weakened by divisions, suspicions, and duplication of ministries.

On the one hand, at the heart of those theological battles was a passionate concern to defend the inspiration and authority of the Bible. The very first Baptist confessions made it clear that the Bible was the supreme authority for Christians, and those alarmed with theological innovations sought to defend a cardinal doctrine of the church. The importance of the Bible was a catalyst for the unease, and in that sense the Baptist DNA served them well. However, on the other hand, another catalyst for the divisions was a Baptist over-emphasis on the local church apart from any

22. Inglis, "The Imperial Connection," 21–38.

concern for the unity of the universal church. Stated differently, Baptists have invested a great deal of energy emphasizing the freedom of a local church, but very little attention is given to the universal church. And that "go it alone" mindset that is unconcerned about the universal church can contribute to divisions. The way forward in the midst of contemporary theological issues—of which there are some pressing—is not to abandon Baptist convictions regarding the authority of the Bible or the freedom of the local church. Rather, it is to add to such historic convictions a revitalized commitment to the unity of the universal church, and a pledge to do all that one can to promote and preserve it.

One good coming out of the churches' move to the margins in a post-Christendom West is what has been described as an "ecumenism of the trenches."[23] The basic idea being that, besides the move to the margins in regard to power, the dramatic demographic shifts in regard to the number of Christians in the nation has led to denominations recognizing that they no longer have the "luxury" of waging internecine warfare. There are much greater issues to be faced, and far better uses of resources, than waging war over what—in the big picture of the larger Christian tradition—often seem to be secondary issues.

CONCLUSION

This book began by talking about the revolutionary, radical, and illegal vision of the church displayed by the early Baptists. In closing, it is worth noting the words of wisdom of Albert Outler in reference to a different denomination, that of Methodism.

> Neither the Wesley theology, nor his methods are simple panaceas. They are not like the TV dinners that can be reheated and served up quickly for immediate use. They call for imaginative updating in the new world cultural contexts . . . Wesley's vision of Christian existence has to be reconceived and transvalued so that it can be as relevant in the experience of the late 20th century as it was to alienated English men and women in 1740![24]

The denomination may be different, but the principle is the same. The methods of Baptist forbearers are not "simple panaceas" and past actions cannot just be reheated like a TV dinner. The Baptist vision "has

---

23. Attributed to Timothy George.
24. Outler, "The Wesleyan Quadrilateral in Wesley," 17.

to be reconceived and transvalued" for the twenty-first century, that is the challenge. And if Baptists are to survive, and even thrive, they must regain their radical vision and spiritual zeal. While freedom of religion in Canada provides Baptists with opportunity to worship without fear of persecution, what is the Baptist revolutionary and radical vision for the church today? Some might answer that its radical vision should be preserving an understanding and commitment to the Word of God. Others might say its radical vision should be in fighting for the freedom and equality of every individual. Some see protecting congregational autonomy as vital. Others emphasize associating with likeminded believers and the call to unity in Christ. Others might claim the call to evangelize Canada for Jesus is the radical vision for the church today. For Baptists in Canada to continue to make an impact they will need to discover how their historical identity has prepared them for the future.

Appendix A

Baptist Landscape in Canada in 2020

- Canadian Baptist Ministries (*1000+ churches*)[1]

    a. Canadian Baptists of Atlantic Canada (*approx. 500 churches*)[2]

    b. Canadian Baptists of Ontario and Quebec (*approx. 340 churches*)[3]

    c. Canadian Baptists of Western Canada (*approx. 175 churches*)[4]

    d. Union of French Baptist Churches/l'Union d'Églises Baptistes Françaises au Canada (*approx. 30 churches*)

- Fellowship of Evangelical Baptist Churches (*over 500 churches*)
- Canadian National Baptist Convention (*over 400 churches*)[5]
- Baptist General Conference of Canada (Swedish origins) (*approx. 108 churches*)
- Seventh Day Baptists[6]

---

1. In 1995, the Canadian Baptist Federation joined the Canadian Baptist International Ministries to form the Canadian Baptist Ministries (CBM). The CBM is not a denomination in and of itself, but an umbrella organization that coordinates the home and foreign missions and relief work of the CBM denominations.

2. Formerly United Baptist Convention of the Maritime Provinces; United Baptist Convention of the Atlantic Provinces; and Convention of Atlantic Baptist Churches.

3. Formerly Baptist Convention of Ontario and Quebec (BCOQ).

4. Formerly Baptist Union of Western Canada (BUWC).

5. Formerly Canadian Convention of Southern Baptists.

6. Many seventh-day local Baptist churches belong to the Seventh Day Baptist General Conference of the United States and Canada.

Appendix A

- North American Baptist Conference (German origins) (*approx. 46 churches*)[7]
- Ukrainian Evangelical Baptist Convention of Canada (*approx. 10 churches*)
- Sovereign Grace Fellowship of Canada (*15 churches in Ontario and New Brunswick*)
- Union of Slavic Churches of Evangelical Christians and Slavic Baptists of Canada (*11 churches*)
- L'Association des Églises Missionnaire Baptiste Landmark du Québec or Landmark Missionary Baptist Association of Quebec (*10 churches*)[8]
- Atlantic Association of Free Will Baptists[9]
- Various Independents

---

7. These belong to the North American Baptist Conference, with over 400 churches in United States and Canada.

8. "Landmarkism" comes from Prov 22:28: "Remove not the ancient landmark, which thy fathers have set." (KJV)

9. These Baptists were part of the Primitive Baptist Conference of New Brunswick, Maine, and Nova Scotia until 1981, when they joined the National Association of Free Will Baptists and became the Atlantic Association of Free Will Baptists. Since then, the Free Will Baptists have planted a few churches in the Maritimes. Numbers uncertain.

Appendix B

Writing Your Local Church's History

The writing of a local church's history is a worthwhile experience for those involved in the research. Sifting through records and pieces of evidence is certainly a daunting task at times, but the end result is a deeper appreciation for the church's history and identity, and a sense of God's providential care for his church. Once finished, the history can serve the church in many ways. A local church's history can provide an orientation to the church's uniqueness and mission for newcomers, portray the record of faithful lives, describe the reasons for some of the problems that the church faces, list the pastors and leaders who have previously ministered, or remind the present-day church of its original vision and purpose.

While there is no one way that a history must be written, the following are some brief things to consider when going about compiling and writing such a history. If you are uncertain about doing historical research, take a look at Gordon L. Heath, *Doing Church History: A User-friendly Introduction to Researching the History of Christianity* (Toronto: Clements, 2008) for a brief and helpful primer.

STAGE ONE: PRELIMINARY WORK

- Ask why you are doing it. Do not use the book to make a point, condemn a person, or save your job.
- Will it be a chronicle or a history? Chronicles tend to be "just the facts," while a history will interpret. A chronicle tends to be "safer" and less controversial than a history.

- Don't recreate the wheel. See if you already have a written history. If you do, why not simply update the history (some are years old and could benefit from someone filling in the history up to the present day).
- Some churches are fortunate enough to have an unofficial historian already present. You would be wise to work with such a person.
- Is someone going to be paid to write it? If so, who has final editorial power? Related to this is the question of whether or not it will be an "official" history. If so, the church leaders usually will want a final say as to the content.
- Who will publish it? Who will pay for publishing? Will it be print-on-demand (a growing preference for small circulation books)?

STAGE TWO: GATHERING THE SOURCES

Whatever your grand intentions, your history will be limited by what sources you are able to get your hands on. One of the first things to do in this stage is to begin making a list of sources available, and their locations. There are a variety of sources that should be consulted, and the following is a brief list of the types of things that you need to track down. Remember that you must be diligent and try to get as much evidence as possible. Another thing to consider is that you should try to get a variety of perspectives on issues—especially controversial ones.

- Will you be relying on oral sources? If so, who should you interview? Try to make a recording of interviews (make sure you get permission to do this) for future reference. In fact, oral histories are an important type of historical storytelling in and of themselves.
- What is at the denominational archives? Contact the Baptist archives and visit to see what it holds. (Some Baptist churches also have material at local town or county archives—check there too.)
- What do the association minutes say about your church? The archives may have these records, or the association itself may have copies of past minutes.
- What founding and legal documents can you obtain? For instance, most Baptist churches had a covenant that members signed, and a

statement of faith that members adhered to—can you find these? What legal documents (such as a deed) are available?

- What records does your local church have in the office (or in the attic)? Most churches have some file of previous board minutes, Sunday School records, mission reports, and so on. Track these down for they provide a detailed glimpse of the week-by-week life of your church.

- Contact former pastors for their reflections on the church. These reflections are important considerations from a member of the leadership team, and may provide some helpful interpretations of events and decisions.

- Seek out key members in the church such as charter members, long-term members, deacons, youth workers, Sunday School teachers, and so on. The perspectives of these people will provide another pool of information.

- Check the local paper to see if there are any reports on the church.

- What pictures are available that will tell of the past? Also consider plaques, honour rolls, and other things hanging on the walls as potential sources of information.

The acquisition of sources requires patience and a bit of sleuthing. Ask what is missing in the information provided by your sources, and then get to work trying to find sources that will answer your questions or fill in the gaps.

STAGE THREE: RESEARCHING THE HISTORY

- Make sure you get a timeline of key dates and leaders—this provides a framework and helps people place themselves in the larger history of the church.

- Look out for minefields! What are the issues that you need to be VERY careful about addressing (e.g., church splits, firings of leaders, broken relationships)?

- Make sure you try to get a variety of voices on the controversial issues. You may want to stay away from these events as much as possible, or at least try to present a fair portrayal of the events (which

Appendix B

may mean you provide the different perspectives on the events in question).

- Make good notes, and be able to find your sources if someone asks "why did you say that?" or "where did you get that idea?"
- Clarify confidentiality issues with written and oral sources.
- Including pictures in a book is always appreciated by readers (especially if they find themselves in the book!). If you cannot identify someone, leave the picture(s) in the foyer with a sheet of paper beside it asking for people to identify anything they can (e.g., people, event, location, date).

STAGE FOUR: WRITING THE HISTORY

- Do you want multiple authors, or just one?
- Try to tell as a story, not just dump facts on people.
- Make it as positive as possible (without skewing the facts!).
- Relate the history to the events of the day (e.g. wartime, Depression, changing role of women in society).
- Make a few electronic copies of the text, and store in a variety of locations.

STAGE FIVE: CELEBRATING THE HISTORY

- Send a copy to your denominational archives.
- Send a copy to your denominational head office.
- Send a copy to your local library.
- Send a copy to your county archives.
- Place a few in your church library.
- Make them available for members to purchase.
- Provide one to every new pastor.
- Preserve the records that you found (e.g. place in the archives or in a safe place in the church building).

- Have a book-launching party at the church, and tie it into your anniversary service.
- Require members to read the book as preparation for membership.
- Post your results on the church's website (e.g., blog, photos, summary, etc.).

Appendix C

Baptist Distinctives in Canada Comparison[1]

Canadian Baptists of Ontario and Quebec	Canadian Baptists of Atlantic Canada	Canadian Baptists of Western Canada	Fellowship Baptist	Canadian National Baptist Convention[2]	Baptist General Conference of Canada
Jesus is Lord	The Lordship of Jesus Christ	God, Trinity, Creation, Redemption, and Final Judgement	Bible the Word of God		Bible the Word of God
The Word of God is the Authoritative Rule of Faith and Practice	The Authority of the Scriptures	Inspiration and Authority of the Bible	God, Trinity, Incarnation of Jesus		Trinity
The Priesthood of All Believers	The Priesthood of the Believer	Humanity in God's Image, the Fall	Satan, Humans in God's Image, the Fall		Angels, Creation, Humanity in God's Image, the Fall

1. See also Jones, *What Canadian Baptists Believe*.

2. In 2017, the CNBC adopted the Southern Baptist Convention *Baptist Faith and Message 2000* as its statement. Its twenty-three articles are too numerous to fit into this condensed chart. Please see https://cnbc.ca/articles/proposed-preamble-to-cnbc-confession-of-faith-2019 and http://www.sbc.net/bfm2000/bfm2000.asp.

Baptist Distinctives in Canada Comparison

Canadian Baptists of Ontario and Quebec	Canadian Baptists of Atlantic Canada	Canadian Baptists of Western Canada	Fellowship Baptist	Canadian National Baptist Convention[2]	Baptist General Conference of Canada
A Believers' Church	"direct access to God through Jesus Christ"	Incarnation of Jesus, Salvation through Jesus	Salvation through Jesus		Salvation in Jesus
Mission & Evangelism	Regenerate Church Membership	Work of Holy Spirit in Christian Life	Return of Jesus		Live for Glory of God
Church Autonomy & Association	Baptism	New Testament Church	Church of Immersed Believers		Two Ordinances
Freedom & Equality	Local Church Autonomy	Return of Jesus	Two Ordinances		Religious Freedom
	The Separation of Church and State		Separation of Church and State, Religious Liberty		Church Cooperation Church & State
			Lord's Day		Return of Jesus
			Role of Civil Government		

185

Appendix D

Photographs

Edward Manning
Acadia Photograph Collection D1900.039.424
Acadia University Archives

Photographs

Joseph Crandall
Acadia Photograph Collection D1900.039.769
Acadia University Archives

Henriette Feller
Canadian Baptist Archives

Appendix D

Robert E. Fyfe
Canadian Baptist Archives

Alexander "Pioneer" McDonald
Canadian Baptist Archives

Photographs

William McMaster
Canadian Baptist Archives

McMaster University (in Toronto)
Canadian Baptist Archives

Appendix D

Women's Baptist Home Mission Board of Ontario (West), 1902
Canadian Baptist Archives

Jennie Johnson
Canadian Baptist Archives

Photographs

Brandon College
Canadian Baptist Archives

Baptist Home Mission Board, 1906
Baptist Convention of Ontario and Quebec
Canadian Baptist Archives

Appendix D

William White
Acadia Photograph Collection
Acadia University Archives

Watson Kirkconnell
Acadia Photograph Collection 1259
Acadia University Archives

Photographs

Muriel Carder
Canadian Baptist Archives

John Diefenbaker
Canadian Baptist Archives

Appendix D

Jarold K. Zeman
Acadia Divinity College 2009.072.ADC
Acadia University Archives

Tribute to the Unknown Baptist Pastor
McMaster Divinity College

Photographs

Tribute to the Unknown Baptist Pastor
McMaster Divinity College

Bibliography

PRIMARY SOURCES

Periodicals

Atlantic Baptist, 1970, 1974, 1987, 2005
British Colonist, 1875, 1877
Canadian Baptist Magazine and Missionary Register, 1837–1839
Canadian Baptist, 1913
Christian Century, 1944
Christian Missionary Link, 1919
Christian Week, 1991
Gospel Witness, 1922, 1926–1927, 1931
Home Mission Monthly, 1896
Fellowship Baptist, 1953
Maritime Baptist, 1918
Massachusetts Missionary Magazine, 1803–1805
Northwest Baptist, 1891
Watchman Examiner, 1920
Western Baptist, 1917

Confessions, Statements, and Catechisms

"A Brief Confession of Declaration of Faith" (1660). In *Baptist Confessions of Faith*, edited by W. L. Lumpkin, 220–34. Valley Forge: Judson, 1959.
"Association of Baptist Churches of Nova Scotia" (1800), as printed in I. E. Bill, *Fifty Years with the Baptist Ministers and Churches of the Maritime Provinces of Canada*, 36–37. Saint John, NB, 1880.
A Catechism for Girls and Boys (1798).

Bibliography

"Basic Imperatives" (1959), as printed in Margaret E. Thompson, *The Baptist Story in Western Canada*. Calgary: Baptist Union of Western Canada, 1974.

Canadian Baptist Youth & Family Forum. *Imaginative Hope: Reaching and Engaging the Next Generation with the Gospel*. Canadian Baptist Youth & Family Ministry Team, 2016.

Fellowship of Evangelical Baptist Churches. *Affirmation of Faith* (1953), available online: www.fellowship.ca/WhatWeBelieve.

Helwys, Thomas. "A Declaration of Faith of English People Remaining at Amsterdam in Holland" (1611). In *The Life and Writings of Thomas Helwys*, edited by Joe Early, Jr., 68–73. Macon: Mercer University Press, 2009.

Keach, Benjamin. *The Baptist Catechism* (1677).

"Organizing Covenant of the Founders of the First Baptist Church in Swansea, Massachusetts" (1663). Online: http://www.firstbaptistinswansea.org/our-covenant/

Philadelphia Confession, Chapter 25, Of the Civil Magistrate.

Smyth, John. "A Short Confession of Faith" (1609). In *Baptist Confessions of Faith*, edited by W. L. Lumpkin, 97–101. Valley Forge: Judson, 1959.

"Somerset Confession" (1656). In *Baptist Confessions of Faith*, edited by W. L. Lumpkin, 200–215. Valley Forge: Judson, 1959.

"The Amherst Statement" (2003), in *2004 Year Book of the Convention of Atlantic Baptist Churches*, edited by Harry Gardner, B-29–B-30. Saint John, NB: Convention of Atlantic Baptist Churches, 2004.

The Baptist Faith and Message. Southern Baptist Convention, 2000. Online: https://www.fbcneosho.com/welcome/ewExternalFiles/The-Baptist-Faith-and-Message.pdf

"The Faith and Practice of Thirty Congregations, Gathered According to the Primitive Pattern" (1651). In *Baptist Confessions of Faith*, edited by W. L. Lumpkin, 171–187. Valley Forge: Judson, 1959.

"The First London Baptist Confession of Faith" (1644, updated 1646). In *Baptist Confessions of Faith*, edited by W. L. Lumpkin, 144–70. Valley Forge: Judson, 1959.

"The Orthodox Creed" (1679). In *Baptist Confessions of Faith*, edited by W. L. Lumpkin, 295–333. Valley Forge: Judson, 1959.

"The Schleitheim Confession of Faith," Translated by John Christian Wenger. In *The Mennonite Quarterly Review* 19.4 (1945) 247–53.

"The Second London Confession of Faith" (1677/1689). In *Baptist Confessions of Faith*, edited by W. L. Lumpkin, 235–294. Valley Forge: Judson, 1959.

United Baptist Convention of the Maritime Provinces Basis of Union (Doctrinal Statement and Church Polity), (1906).

Other

A Manual for Worship and Service Mississauga: All Canada Baptist Publications, 1998.

Alline, Henry. *The Journal of Henry Alline*, edited by James Beverley and Barry M. Moody. Baptist Heritage in Atlantic Canada Series 4. Hantsport, NS: Lancelot, 1982.

———. "Sermon Preached to, and at the Request, of a Religious Society of Young Men, 19th November, 1782." In *The Sermons of Henry Alline*, edited by G. A. Rawlyk,

Bibliography

43–75. Baptist Heritage in Atlantic Canada Series 7. Hantsport, NS: Lancelot, 1986.

Baptist Federation of Canada. *Proceedings and Minutes of the Assembly of the Baptist Federation of Canada, 1962*. Brantford, ON: Baptist Federation of Canada, 1962.

Baptist World Alliance. *2019-2020 BWA Ministry Update*. Falls Church, VA: Baptist World Alliance, 2020.

Beals, F. H., ed. *The United Baptist Year Book of the Maritime Provinces, 1920–1921*. Truro, NS: News Publishing Co, 1921.

Bennett, W. Arnold. "Facts Concerning Brandon College." Vancouver: W. Arnold Bennett, 1922.

Bunyan, John. *Differences in Judgment about Water Baptism, No Bar to Communion: or, To Communicate with Saints, as Saints, Proved Lawful*. London: John Wilkins, 1673.

Canadian Baptists of Atlantic Canada. "Frequently Asked Questions re: Proposed Name Change." February 2016. Online: www.baptist-atlantic.ca.

———. "Rationale and Notice of Motion Re: Change of Name from the Convention of Atlantic Baptist Churches to Canadian Baptists of Atlantic Canada." February 2016. Online: www.baptist-atlantic.ca.

Carey Theological College. "Grenz Returns to Carey," n.d. [2003?], Online: http://www.stanleyjgrenz.com/articles/Return.htm.

Common Expressions: A Canadian Baptist Manual for Worship and Service. Mississauga: Canadian Baptist Ministries, 2020.

Gregory, L. A. ed., *Year Book 1960-1961 of the Baptist Convention of Ontario and Quebec*. Toronto: Baptist Convention of Ontario and Quebec, 1961.

Government of Canada. *2011 National Household Survey*, n.d. Online: www12.statcan.gc.ca.

———. *The Fourth Census of Canada, 1901*. Ottawa: Government of Canada, 1901.

Harlow, Malcolm, et al. "The Wentworth Statement," signed 15 November 1971.

Hobson, Keith R., ed. *Year Book of the United Baptist Convention of the Atlantic Provinces, 1971*. Saint John, NB: Lingley, 1971.

Interested Laymen. *A Further Message to B.C. Baptists*. Vancouver: Interested Laymen, 1921.

———. *The Dangerous Peril of Religious Education*. Vancouver: Interested Laymen, 1921.

Kiffin, William. *A Sober Discourse of Right to Church-Communion*. London: George Larkin, 1681.

———. "Kiffin Manuscript." n.d.

Lactantius. *Divine Institutes*.

MacBain, W. H. "Inaugural Address," 23 October 1953. Printed in *A Glorious Fellowship of Churches: Celebrating the History of the Fellowship of Evangelical Baptist Churches in Canada, 1953–2003*, edited by Michael A. G. Haykin and Robert B. Lockey, 143. Guelph: The Fellowship of Evangelical Baptist Churches in Canada, 2003.

McDormand, Thomas B. *A Diversified Ministry*. Hantsport, NS: Lancelot, 1987.

Mullins, E. Y. *Axioms of Religion: A New Interpretation of the Baptist Faith*. New York & Philadelphia: American Baptist Publication Society, 1908.

Smith, Terry. "An Apology in the Making: Resetting the Relationship." 21 October 2016. Online: cbmin.org.

Statistics Canada, 2001 Census: Analysis Series Religions in Canada.

Bibliography

———. 2011 National Household Survey.

———. *Immigration and Diversity: Population Projections for Canada and its Regions, 2011 to 2036*.

The Baptist Register for Ontario and Quebec, 1870, Toronto, ON: Baptist Publishing Company, 1870.

The Baptist Register for Ontario and Quebec, 1876, Toronto, ON: Baptist Publishing Company, 1876.

"The Church Articles," Minutes of the Nova Scotia and New Brunswick Baptist Association, 27–29 June 1808, printed in *Baptist Life and Thought: A Source Book*, revised edition, edited by William H. Brackney, 489–91. Valley Forge, PA: Judson, 1998.

Wesley, John. *The Letters of Rev. John Wesley*, edited by John Telford. London: Epworth, 1931.

SECONDARY

Adams, Doug. "The Call to Arms: The Reverend Thomas Todhunter Shields, World War One, and the Shaping of a Militant Fundamentalism." In *Baptists and War, 1640s–1990s*, edited by Gordon L. Heath and Michael A. G. Haykin, 115–47. Canadian Baptist Historical Society Series 2. Eugene, OR: Pickwick, 2015.

———. "Fighting Fire with Fire: T. T. Shields and His Confrontations with Premier Mitchell Hepburn and Prime Minister Mackenzie King, 1934–1948." In *Baptists and Public Life in Canada*, edited by Gordon L. Heath and Paul. R. Wilson, 53–104. Eugene, OR: Pickwick, 2012.

Aldwinckle, Russell F. *Of Water and the Spirit*. Brantford, ON: Baptist Federation of Canada, 1964.

Allen, William Lloyd. "Mining Baptist History and Traditions for Spirituality: Paradigm Sifting for Ores of a Different Color." *Perspectives in Religious Studies* 25.1 (1998) 43–61.

Arnett, Randy. *Pentecostalization: The Evolution of Baptists in Africa*. Eldon: Randy Arnett, 2017.

Atkinson, Terry. "Brunswick Street Baptist Church." In *Maritime Baptist Old First Churches: Narratives and Prospects*, edited by William H. Brackney with Evan Colford, 119–35. Wolfville, NS: ACBAS and the Editorial Committee of the Canadian Baptists of Atlantic Canada Historical Committee, 2017.

Bainton, Roland H. *The Travail of Religious Liberty: Nine Biographical Studies*. London: Lutterworth, 1953.

Barnes, Esther. *Our Heritage Becomes Our Challenge: A Scrapbook History of the Baptist Women's Movement in Ontario and Quebec*. Etobicoke, ON: Canadian Baptist Women of Ontario and Quebec, 2013.

Barry, John M. *Roger Williams and the Creation of the American Soul: Church, State, and the Birth of Liberty*. New York: Viking, 2012.

Beardsall, Sandra. "'One Here Will Constant Be': The Christian Witness of T.C. 'Tommy' Douglas." In *Baptists and Public Life in Canada*, edited by Gordon L. Heath and Paul S. Wilson, 143–66. Canadian Baptist Historical Society Series 1. Eugene, OR: Pickwick, 2012.

Beasley-Murray, G. R. *Baptism in the New Testament*. Grand Rapids: Eerdmans, 1962.

Bibliography

Bebbington, David W. *Baptists Through the Centuries: A History of a Global People.* Waco: Baylor University Press, 2010.

———. *Evangelicalism in Modern Britain: A History from the 1730s to the 1980s.* London and Boston: Unwin Hyman, 1989.

———. *The Nonconformist Conscience: Chapel and Politics, 1870-1914.* London: George Allen and Unwin, 1982.

Bell, D. G. "Allowed Irregularities: Women Preachers in the Early 19th-Century Maritimes." *Acadiensis* 30.2 (2001) 3-39.

Bell, D. G., ed. *New Light Baptist Journals of James Manning and James Innis.* Baptist Heritage in Atlantic Canada Series 6. Hantsport, NS: Lancelot, 1985.

———. "Yankee Preachers and the Struggle for the New Brunswick Christian Conference." In *Revivals, Baptists, & George Rawlyk*, edited by Daniel C. Goodwin, 93-112. Baptist Heritage in Atlantic Canada Series 17. Wolfville, NS: Acadia Divinity College, 2000.

Belyea, Gordon, et al., eds., *Baptism Is . . . The Immersionist Perspective.* Brampton: Kainos Enterprises, 2016.

Bentall, Shirley. *From Sea to Sea: The Canadian Baptist Federation, 1944-1994.* Mississauga: Canadian Baptist Federation, 1994.

Bertley, Leo W. *Canada and Its People of African Descent.* Pierrefonds: Bilongo, 1977.

Beverley, James A. "National Survey of Baptist Ministers." In *Baptists in Canada: Search for Identity Amidst Diversity*, edited by Jarold K. Zeman, 267-76. Burlington, ON: Welch, 1980.

Beverley, James and Barry Moody, eds. *The Journal of Henry Alline.* Baptist Heritage in Atlantic Canada Series 4. Hantsport, NS: Lancelot, 1982.

Bibby, Reginald W. "Post-Christendom in Canada? Not So Fast." *Post-Christendom Studies* 1 (2016) 125-41.

Bill, I. E. *Fifty Years with the Baptist Ministers and Churches of the Maritime Provinces of Canada.* Saint John, NB: Barnes and Company, 1880.

Birch, Ian. *To Follow the Lambe Wheresoever he Goeth: The Ecclesial Polity of the English Calvinistic Baptists 1640-1660.* Monographs in Baptist History 5. Eugene, OR: Pickwick, 2017.

Blackaby, G. Richard. "The Establishment of the Convention of Southern Baptists." In *Memory and Hope: Strands of Canadian Baptist History*, edited by David T. Priestley, 99-110. Editions SR 19. Waterloo: Wilfrid Laurier University Press, 1996.

Bokenkotter, Thomas S. *A Concise History of the Catholic Church.* Garden City: Doubleday, 1977.

Bollen, J. D. *Australian Baptists: A Religious Minority.* London: Baptist Historical Society, 1975.

Bonham, John S. H. "Harvesting on the Prairies: FEBCAST/FEBMID." In *A Glorious Fellowship of Churches: Celebrating the History of the Fellowship of Evangelical Baptist Churches in Canada, 1953-2003*, edited by Michael A. G. Haykin and Robert B. Lockey, 175-204. Guelph: The Fellowship of Evangelical Baptist Churches in Canada, 2003.

Borrie, W.D. "'British' Immigration to Australia." In *Australia and Britain: Studies in a Changing Relationship*, edited by A. F Madden and W. H. Morris-Jones, 101-16. Sydney: Sydney University Press, 1908.

Bibliography

Bourdeaux, M. *Religious Ferment in Russia: Protestant Opposition to Soviet Religious Policy.* London: MacMillan, 1968.

Bourinot, John G. *Builders of Nova Scotia: A Historical Review.* Toronto: Copp-Clark, 1900.

Bowler, Sharon M., ed. *Canadian Baptist Women.* Canadian Baptist Historical Society 3. Eugene, OR: Pickwick, 2016.

———. "Madame Mary Lore: A Lower Canada Baptist Beginning." In *Canadian Baptist Women*, edited by Sharon M. Bowler, 41–67. Canadian Baptist Historical Society Series 3. Eugene: Pickwick, 2016.

Brackney, William H. "A Good Knight in a New Crusade: Archibald Reekie and the Origins of Canadian Baptist Witness in Bolivia." In *Bridging Cultures and Hemispheres: The Legacy of Archibald Reekie and Canadian Baptists in Bolivia*, edited by William H. Brackney, 1–35. Macon: Smyth and Helwys, 1997.

———. *A Capsule History of Baptist Principles.* Atlanta: Baptist History and Heritage Society, 2009.

———. *The Baptists.* Denominations in America 2. New York: Greenwood, 1988.

———. *Baptists in North America.* Oxford: Blackwell, 2006.

———. *Congregation and Campus: North American Baptists in Higher Education.* The Jim N. Griffith Series in Baptist Studies. Macon, GA: Mercer University Press, 2008

———. *A Genetic History of Baptist Thought.* Macon, GA: Mercer University Press, 2004.

———. *Historical Dictionary of the Baptists.* Historical Dictionaries of Religions, Philosophies and Movements 25. Lanham, MD: Scarecrow, 1999.

———. *Voluntarism: The Dynamic Principle of the Free Church.* Wolfville, NS: Acadia Divinity College, 1992.

———. *Walter Rauschenbusch: Published Works and Selected Writings.* 3 vols. Macon: Mercer University Press, 2019.

Brackney, William H., ed. *Baptist Life and Thought: A Source Book.* Rev. ed. Valley Forge, PA: Judson, 1998.

———. *Bridging Cultures and Hemispheres: The Legacy of Archibald Reekie and Canadian Baptists in Bolivia.* Macon: Smyth & Helwys, 1997.

Brackney, William H. with Evan Colford, eds. *Maritime Baptist Old First Churches: Narratives and Prospects.* Wolfville, NS: ACBAS and The Editorial Committee of the Canadian Baptists of Atlantic Canada Historical Committee, 2017.

Bray, Gerald. "English Protestantism to the Present Day." In *The Blackwell Companion to Protestantism*, edited by Alister E. McGrath and Darren C. Marks, 96–108. Malden, MA: Blackwell, 2004.

Bridge, C., and K. Fedorowich. "Mapping the British World." *Journal of Imperial and Commonwealth History* 31.2 (2003) 1–15.

Briggs, John. "The English Baptists." In *Eerdmans' Handbook to the History of Christianity*, edited by Tim Dowley, 395. Grand Rapids: Eerdmans, 1977.

Bush, L. Russ, and Tom Nettles. *Baptists and the Bible: The Baptist Doctrines of Biblical Inspiration and Religious Authority in Historical Perspective.* Chicago: Moody, 1885.

Choudhury, Kamal Narayan. *Christianity in the North-East India: The Baptist Missionaries.* Kolkata: Punthi Pustak, 2014.

Bibliography

Christie, Nancy, and Michael Gauvreau. *Christian Churches and their Peoples, 1840–1965: A Social History of Religion in Canada*. Toronto: University of Toronto Press, 2010.

Chute, Anthony L., Nathan A. Finn, and Michael A. G. Haykin, *The Baptist Story: From English Sect to Global Movement*. Nashville: B&H, 2015.

Clarke, Brian, and Stuart Macdonald. *Leaving Christianity: Changing Allegiances in Canada since 1945*. Montreal and Kingston: McGill-Queen's University Press, 2017.

Clifford, J. Ayson. *A Handful of Grain: The Centenary History of the Baptist Union of New Zealand, Volume 2: 1882–1914*. Wellington: New Zealand Baptist Historical Society, 1982.

Coffey, John. "Church and State, 1550–1750: The Emergence of Dissent." In *The T&T Clark Companion to Nonconformity*, edited by Robert Pope, 47–74. London: T. & T. Clark, 2016.

Coops, P. Lorraine. "'Shelter from the Storm': The Enduring Evangelical Impulse of Baptists in Canada, 1880s to 1990s." In *Aspects of the Canadian Evangelical Experience*, edited by George Rawlyk, 208–22. Montreal: McGill-Queen's University Press, 1997.

———. "That Still Small Voice: The Allinite Legacy and Maritime Baptist Women." In *Revivals, Baptists, & George Rawlyk*, edited by Daniel C. Goodwin, 113–32. Baptist Heritage in Atlantic Canada Series 17. Wolfville, NS: Acadia Divinity College, 2000.

Corrada, Sharyl, and Toivo Pilli, eds. *Eastern European Baptist History: New Perspectives*. Prague: IBTS, 2007.

Cragg, Gerald R. *Freedom and Authority: A Study of English Thought in the Seventeenth Century*. Philadelphia: Westminster, 1975.

Crocker, Chris W. "A Worthy Cause: The Lord's Day in the Baptist Press Amongst Nineteenth-Century Upper Canadian Regular Baptists." MA thesis, McMaster Divinity College, 2013.

Cross, Anthony R. "Baptism Among Baptists." In *Baptism: Historical, Theological, and Pastoral Perspectives*, edited by Gordon L. Heath and James D. Dvorak, 136–55. Eugene, OR: Pickwick, 2011.

———. *Baptism and the Baptists: Theology and Practice in Twentieth-Century Britain*. Studies in Baptist History and Thought 3. Carlisle: Paternoster, 2000.

———. "Baptists, Peace, and War: The Seventeenth-Century British Foundations." In *Baptists and War: Essays on Baptists and Military Conflict, 1640s–1990s*, edited by Gordon L. Heath and Michael A. G. Haykin, 1–31. Eugene, OR: Pickwick, 2015.

———. "'Christ Jesus . . . exalted . . . farre aboue all principalities and powers': Baptist Attitudes to Monarchy, Country, and Magistracy, 1609–1644." In *Freedom from the Powers: Perspectives from Baptist History*, edited by Anthony R. Cross and John H. Y. Briggs, 3–22. Didcot: Baptist Historical Society, 2014.

———. "The Myth of English Baptist Anti-Sacramentalism." In *Recycling the Past or Researching History?: Studies in Baptist Historiography and Myths*, edited by Philip E. Thompson and Anthony R. Cross, 128–62. Studies in Baptist History and Thought 11. Carlisle: Paternoster.

Cross, Anthony R., and Nicholas J. Wood, eds. *Exploring Baptist Origins*. Oxford: Regent's Park College, 2010

Bibliography

Currie, Robert, et al. *Church and Churchgoers: Patterns of Church Growth in the British Isles since 1700*. Oxford: Clarendon, 1977.

Cuthbertson, Brian C., ed. *The Journal of John Payzant (1749-1834)*. Baptist Heritage in Atlantic Canada Series 3. Hantsport, NS: Lancelot, 1981.

Daniel, Orville E. *Moving with the Times: The Story of Baptist Outreach from Canada into Asia, South America, and Africa, during One Hundred Years, 1874-1974*. Toronto: CBOMB, 1973.

Davis, Kenneth R. "The Struggle for a United Evangelical Baptist Fellowship, 1953-1965." In *Baptists in Canada: Search for Identity Amidst Diversity*, edited by Jarold K. Zeman, 237-65. Burlington, ON: Welch, 1980.

Dekar, Paul R. and Murray J. S. Ford, eds. *Celebrating the Canadian Baptist Heritage: Three Hundred Years of God's Providence*. Hamilton: McMaster Divinity College, 1984.

Deweese, Charles W. "Church Covenants and Church Discipline among Baptists in the Maritime Provinces." In *Repent and Believe: The Baptist Experience in Maritime Canada*, edited by Barry M. Moody, 27-45. Baptist Heritage in Atlantic Canada Series 2. Hantsport, NS: Lancelot, 1980.

Donaldson, David. "Who Killed Norman Dabbs?" *Historical Papers 2005: Canadian Society of Church History*, 57-68.

Durnbaugh, Donald F. *The Believers' Church: The History and Character of Radical Protestantism*. New York: MacMillan, 1968.

Elliott, David. "Canadian Baptists and Native Ministry in the Nineteenth Century." *Historical Papers of the Canadian Society of Church History* (2000) 145-64.

Ellis, Walter E. "What the Times Demand: Brandon College and Baptist Higher Education in Western Canada." In *Canadian Baptists and Christian Higher Education*, edited by G. A. Rawlyk, 63-88. Montreal and Kingston: McGill-Queen's University Press, 1988.

Estep, William. *The Anabaptist Story: An Introduction to Sixteenth-Century Anabaptism*. 3rd ed. Grand Rapids: Eerdmans, 1995.

———. *Revolution Within the Revolution: The First Amendment in Historical Context, 1612-1789*. Grand Rapids: Eerdmans, 1990.

Feltmate, Darrell. "'The Help Should be Greatest Where the Need is Most': The Social Gospel Platform of the United Baptist Convention of the Maritime Provinces." MDiv Thesis, Acadia University, 1993.

Fiddes, Paul S. *Tracks and Traces: Baptist Identity in Church and Theology*. Studies in Baptist History and Thought 13. Carlisle, UK: Paternoster, 2003.

Fiddes, Paul S., ed. *Under the Rule of Christ: Dimensions of Baptist Spirituality*. Oxford: Regent's Park College, 2008.

Fitch, E. R. *The Baptists of Canada: A History of their Progress and Achievements*. Toronto: Baptist Young People's Union of Ontario and Quebec, 1911.

Flatt, Kevin. "Theological Innovation from Spiritual Experience: Henry Alline's Anti-Calvinism in Late Eighteenth-Century Nova Scotia and New England." *Journal of Religious History* 33.3 (2009) 285-300.

Ford, Murray J. S., ed. *Canadian Baptist History and Polity: The McMaster Conference*. Hamilton, ON: McMaster Divinity College, 1983.

Fowler, Stanley K. *More than a Symbol: The British Baptist Recovery of Baptismal Sacramentalism*. Studies in Baptist History and Thought 2. Eugene, OR: Wipf and Stock, 2002.

Bibliography

———. *Rethinking Baptism: Some Baptist Reflections*. Eugene, OR: Wipf and Stock, 2015.

Frykenberg, Robert Eric. "Naga Baptists: A Brief Narrative of Their Genesis." In *Baptist Identities: International Studies from the Seventeenth to the Twentieth Centuries*, edited by Ian Randall et al., 213–40. Carlisle: Paternoster, 2006.

Funk, Abe. *Our Story: Baptist General Conference of Canada*. Edmonton: Baptist General Conference of Canada, 2009.

Gammel, William. *A History of American Baptist Missions in Asia, Africa, Europe and North America: Under the Care of the American Baptist Missionary Union*. Boston: Gould & Lincoln, 1854.

Gardner, Robert G. *Baptists of Early America: A Statistical History, 1639–1790*. Atlanta: Georgia Baptist Historical Society, 1983.

Gaustad, Edwin S. *Liberty of Conscience: Roger Williams in America*. Grand Rapids: Eerdmans, 1991.

———. *Roger Williams: Prophet of Liberty*. Oxford: Oxford University Press, 2001.

George, Timothy. *Theology of the Reformers*. Nashville: Broadman & Holman, 2013.

George, Timothy, and David S. Dockery, eds. *Baptist Theologians*. Nashville: Broadman, 1990.

Gibson, M. Allen. *Along the King's Highway*. Lunenburg, NS: Home Mission Board of the United Baptist Convention of the Atlantic Provinces, 1964.

Gibson, Theo T. *Robert Alexander Fyfe: His Contemporaries and his Influence*. Burlington: Welch, 1988.

Gill, Athol. "Human Rights: A Down-Under Perspective." In *Faith, Life and Witness: The Papers of the Study and Research Division of the Baptist World Alliance, 1986–1990*, edited by William H. Brackney and Rudy J. Burke, 243–57. Birmingham: Samford University Press, 1990.

Goertz, Donald. "Alexander Grant: Pastor, Evangelist, Visionary." In *Costly Vision: The Baptist Pilgrimage in Canada*, edited by Jarold K. Zeman, 1–22. Burlington, ON: Welch, 1988.

Goodwin, Daniel C. "'The Footprints of Zion's King': Baptists in Canada to 1880." In *Aspects of the Canadian Evangelical Experience*, edited by George Rawlyk, 191–207. Montreal and Kingston: McGill-Queen's University Press, 1997.

———. *Into Deep Waters: Evangelical Spirituality and Maritime Calvinistic Baptist Ministers, 1790–1855*. Montreal and Kingston: McGill-Queen's University Press, 2010.

———. "The Baptismal Controversy and the Great Awakening in Nova Scotia, 1811–1848." In *A Fragile Stability: Definition and Redefinition of Maritime Baptist Identity*, edited by David T. Priestley, 3–20. Baptist Heritage in Atlantic Canada 15. Hantsport, NS: Lancelot, 1994.

———. "The Meaning of 'Baptist Union' in Maritime Canada, 1846–1906." In *Baptist Identities: International Studies from the Seventeenth to the Twentieth Centuries*, edited by Ian M. Randall, Toivo Pilli, and Anthony R. Cross, 153–74. Studies in Baptist History and Thought. Eugene, OR: Wipf and Stock, 2006.

Gordon, Grant. *From Slavery to Freedom: The Life of David George, Pioneer Black Baptist Minister*. Baptist Heritage in Atlantic Canada Series 14. Hantsport, NS: Lancelot, 1992.

Grace, II, W. Madison. "Early English Baptists' View of the Lord's Supper." *Southwestern Journal of Theology* 57.2 (2015) 159–79.

Bibliography

Grant, John Webster. *A Profusion of Spires: Religion in Nineteenth-Century Ontario.* Ontario Historical Society Series. Toronto: University of Toronto Press, 1988.

———. *The Church in the Canadian Era.* 3rd ed. Vancouver: Regent College Publishing, 1998.

Greene, Theodore P., ed. *Roger Williams and the Massachusetts Magistrates.* Boston: D. C. Heath and Company, 1964.

Grenz, Stanley. *The Baptist Congregation: A Guide to Baptist Belief and Practice.* Valley Forge: Judson, 1985.

———. "Maintaining the Balanced Life: The Baptist Vision of Spirituality." *Perspectives in Religious Studies* 18.1 (1991) 59–68

Griffin-Allwood, Philip, et al., *Baptists in Canada, 1760-1990: A Bibliography of Selected Printed Resources in English.* Baptist Heritage in Atlantic Canada 10. Hantsport, NS: Lancelot, 1989.

Griffin-Allwood, Philip. "Mère Henriette Feller (1800–1868) of La Grande Ligne and Ordered Ministry in Canada." *Historical Papers of the Canadian Society of Church History* (2011) 87–98.

———. "'The Sucksess of the Baptist Denomination In New Brunswick': The Structure of Baptist Triumphalism in 'The Memoirs of the Rev. Jarvis Ring, Baptist Minister." *Historical Papers of the Canadian Society of Church History* (1992) 39–56

Hale, Frederick. "The Baptist Union of Southern Africa and Apartheid." *Journal of Church and State* 48 (2006) 753–77.

Hammett, John S. *Biblical Foundations for Baptist Churches: A Contemporary Ecclesiology.* 2nd ed. Grand Rapids: Kregel, 2019.

Harmon, Steven R. *Baptist Identity and the Ecumenical Future: Story, Tradition, and the Recovery of Community.* Waco: Baylor University Press, 2016.

Harris, J. E. *The Baptist Union of Western Canada: A Centennial History, 1873-1973.* Saint John, NB: Lingley Printing, n.d.

Hayden, Roger. *English Baptist History and Heritage.* Didcot: Baptist Union, 2005.

Haykin, Michael A. G., and Robert B. Lockey, eds. *A Glorious Fellowship of Churches: Celebrating the History of the Fellowship of Evangelical Baptist Churches in Canada, 1953-2003.* Guelph, ON: Fellowship of Evangelical Baptist Churches in Canada, 2003.

Heath, Gordon L., and Michael A. G. Haykin, eds. *Baptists and War, Essays on Baptists and Military Conflict, 1640s–1990s.* Canadian Baptist Historical Society Series 2. Eugene, OR: Pickwick, 2015.

Heath, Gordon L., and Paul R. Wilson, eds. *Baptists and Public Life in Canada.* Canadian Baptist Historical Society 1. Eugene, OR: Pickwick, 2012.

Heath, Gordon L. *A War with a Silver Lining: Canadian Protestant Churches and the South African War, 1899-1902.* Montreal: McGill-Queen's University Press, 2009.

———. *The British Nation is Our Nation: The BACSANZ Baptist Press and the South African War, 1899-1902.* Milton Keynes: Paternoster, 2017.

———. "Dissenting Traditions and Politics in the Anglophone World." In *The Oxford History of Protestant Dissenting Traditions: Volume V; The Twentieth Century: Themes and Variations in a Global Context,* edited by Mark P. Hutchinson, 61–90. Oxford: Oxford University Press, 2018.

———. "Engaging War and Empire: 400 Years of Baptist Attitudes and Actions." In *'Step Into Your Place': The First World War and Baptist Life & Thought,* edited by Larry Kreitzer, 158–88. Oxford: Regent's Park College, 2014.

Bibliography

———. "Ontario Baptists and the War of 1812." *Ontario History* 103.2 (2011) 169–91.
———. "'The Great Association Above': Maritime Baptists and the War of 1812." *Pacific Journal of Baptist Research* 7.2 (2011) 1–22.
———. "Watson Kirkconnell's Covert War against Communism." In *North American Churches and the Cold War*, edited by Paul Mojzes, 64–79. Grand Rapids: Eerdmans, 2018.
Heritage Horizons, "McDermot Ave. Baptist Church, Winnipeg, Manitoba, Canada," Fall 2014, 2.
Hiemstra, Rick, et al. *Renegotiating Faith: The Delay in Young Adult Identity Formation and What It Means for the Church in Canada*. Toronto, ON: The Evangelical Fellowship of Canada, 2018.
Hill, Christopher. *The World Turned Upside Down: Radical Ideas During the English Revolution*. London: Temple Hill, 1972.
Himbury, David Mervyn. *British Baptists: A Short History*. London: Carey Kingsgate, 1962.
Hinson, E. Glenn. "Baptist Approaches to Spirituality." *Baptist Heritage and History* 37.2 (2002) 6–31.
Hitchens, Christopher. *God Is Not Great: How Religion Poisons Everything*. Toronto: McClelland & Stewart, 2007.
Houston, C. J., and W. J. Smith. *The Sash Canada Wore: A Historical Geography of the Orange Order in Canada*. Toronto: University of Toronto Press, 1980.
Hudson-Reed, Sydney. ed. *Together for a Century: The History of the Baptist Union of South Africa, 1877–1977*. Pietermaritzburg: South African Baptist Historical Society, 1977.
Hughes, Philip J. *The Baptists in Australia*. Canberra: Australian Government Publishing Service, 1996.
Hyatt, Irwin T., Jr. *Our Ordered Lives Confess: Three Nineteenth-Century American Missionaries in East Shantung*. Cambridge: Harvard University Press, 1976.
Inglis, K. S. "The Imperial Connection: Telegraphic Communication between England and Australia, 1872–1902." In *Australia and Britain: Studies in a Changing Relationship*, edited by A. F. Madden and W. H. Morris-Jones, 21–38. Sydney: Sydney University Press, 1980.
Ivison, Stuart, and Fred Rosser. *The Baptists in Upper and Lower Canada before 1820*. Toronto: University of Toronto Press, 1956.
Jenkins, Philip. *The Next Christendom*. Oxford: Oxford University Press, 2002.
Jeter, Jeremiah B. *Baptist Principles Reset: Consisting of Articles on Distinctive Baptist Principles*. Richmond: Religious Herald Company, 1902.
Johnson, Keith L. *Theology as Discipleship*. Downers Grove, IL: IVP, 2015.
Johnson, Robert E. *A Global Introduction to Baptist Churches*. Cambridge: Cambridge University Press, 2010.
Jones, Callum. "The Canadian Baptists of Western Canada: Baptist Identity and Ecumenical Relationships, 1907–1986." PhD diss., Middlesex University, 2013.
———. "Western Canadian Baptists and the Southern Baptist 'Invasion' of the 1950s." *Baptist Quarterly* 45.7 (2014) 413–29.
Jones, Keith G. and Ian M. Randall, eds. *Counter-Cultural Communities: Baptistic Life in Twentieth-Century Europe*. Milton Keynes: Paternoster, 2008.
Jones, William H. *What Canadian Baptists Believe*. Etobicoke, ON: ChiRho, 1980.

Bibliography

Jordan, W. K. *The Development of Religious Toleration in England*. 4 vols. Cambridge: Harvard University Press, 1932–1940.

Keefe, Ernie, and Betty Keefe with Ginette Cotnoir. "Fellowship Baptist Churches in French Canada." In *A Glorious Fellowship of Churches: Celebrating the History of the Fellowship of Evangelical Baptist Churches in Canada, 1953-2003*, edited by Michael A. G. Haykin and Robert B. Lockey, 61–114. Guelph: The Fellowship of Evangelical Baptist Churches in Canada, 2003.

Kidd, Thomas S., and Barry Hankins. *Baptists in America: A History*. Oxford: Oxford University Press, 2015.

Klaassen, Walter. *Anabaptism: Neither Catholic nor Protestant*. Kitchener, ON: Pandora Press, 2001.

Kreitzer, Larry J. *Thomas Helwys and His World (Part 1)*. Oxford: Regent's Park College, 2019.

Lane, Hannah M. "Women and Public Prayer in the Mid Nineteenth-Century 'Calvinistic' Baptist Press of New Brunswick and Nova Scotia." In *Canadian Baptist Women*, edited by Sharon M. Bowler, 3–19. McMaster General Series 8. Canadian Baptist Historical Society Series 3. Eugene, OR: Pickwick, 2016.

Lee, Jason K. *The Theology of John Smyth: Puritan, Separatist, Baptist, Mennonite*. Macon, GA: Mercer University Press, 2003.

Leonard, Bill J. *Baptist Ways: A History*. Valley Forge: Judson, 2003.

———. *The Challenge of Being Baptist: Owning a Scandalous Past and an Uncertain Future*. Waco: Baylor, 2010.

Levy, George E., ed. *The Diary of Joseph Dimock*. Baptist Heritage in Atlantic Canada 1. Hantsport, NS: Lancelot, 1979.

Link, Edward B. "North American (German) Baptists." In *Baptists in Canada: Search for Identity Amidst Diversity*, edited by Jarold K. Zeman, 87–104. Burlington, ON: Welch, 1980.

Lockey, Robert B. "Fishing for Men: Fellowship Atlantic." In *A Glorious Fellowship of Churches: Celebrating the History of the Fellowship of Evangelical Baptist Churches in Canada, 1953-2003*, edited by Michael A. G. Haykin and Robert B. Lockey, 33–60. Guelph: The Fellowship of Evangelical Baptist Churches in Canada, 2003.

Lockey, Robert B. and Michael A. G. Haykin. "Polemic, Polity, and Piety: Some Themes in the Story of FEBCentral." In *A Glorious Fellowship of Churches: Celebrating the History of the Fellowship of Evangelical Baptist Churches in Canada, 1953-2003*, edited by Michael A. G. Haykin and Robert B. Lockey, 145–73. Guelph: The Fellowship of Evangelical Baptist Churches in Canada, 2003.

Lohens, Peter. "First Cornwallis Baptist Church." In *Maritime Baptist Old First Churches: Narratives and Prospects*, edited by William H. Brackney with Evan Colford, 137–63. Wolfville, NS: ACBAS and the Editorial Committee of the Canadian Baptists of Atlantic Canada Historical Committee, 2017.

Lovesey, Dorothy May. *To be a Pilgrim: A Biography of Silas Tertius Rand, 1810-1889, Nineteenth Century Protestant Missionary to the Micmac*. Baptist Heritage in Atlantic Canada 13. Hantsport, NS: Lancelot, 1992.

Manley, Ken R. *From Woolloomooloo to 'Eternity,' Vol. 1: Growing an Australian Church, 1831-1914*. Milton Keynes: Paternoster, 2006.

———. *From Woolloomooloo to 'Eternity,' Vol. 2: A National Church in a Global Community, 1914-2005*. Milton Keynes: Paternoster, 2006.

Bibliography

Manley, Ken R., and Michael Petras. *The First Australian Baptists*. Eastwood, NSW: Baptist Historical Society of NSW, 1981.
Maring, Norman H. and Winthrop S. Hudson. *A Baptist Manual of Polity and Practice*. Revised ed. Valley Forge: Judson, 1991.
Marsden, George M. *Fundamentalism and American Culture: The Shaping of Twentieth-Century Evangelicalism, 1870–1925*. New York: Oxford University Press, 1980.
———. *Religion and American Culture: A Brief History*. Grand Rapids: Eerdmans, 2018.
———. *Understanding Fundamentalism and Evangelicalism*. Grand Rapids: Eerdmans, 1991.
McBeth, H. Leon. *A Sourcebook for Baptist Heritage*. Nashville: Broadman, 1990.
———. *The Baptist Heritage*. Nashville: Broadman, 1987.
McCormick, Roland K. *Faith, Freedom & Democracy: The Baptists in Atlantic Canada*. Tantallon, NS: Four East, 1993.
McKay, R. R. "The Story of our Convention." In *Our Baptist Fellowship: Our History, Our Faith and Polity, Our Life and Work*, edited by J. Gordon Jones, 30–43. N.p.: Baptist Convention of Ontario and Quebec, 1939.
McClendon, James William Jr. *Doctrine: Systematic Theology, Volume II*. Nashville: Abingdon, 1994.
———. *Ethics: Systematic Theology, Vol. 1*, revised edition. Waco: Baylor University Press, 2012.
McLeod, Hugh. "Protestantism and British National Identity, 1815–1945." In *Nation and Religion*, edited by P. van der Veer and H. Lehmann, 44–70. Princeton: Princeton University Press, 1990.
McLeod, Tommy. "McKee of Brandon College." *Manitoba History* 40 (2000–2001) n.p. Online: http://www.mhs.mb.ca/docs/mb_history/40/mckeebrandoncollege.shtml.
———. "'To Bestir Themselves:' Canadian Baptists and the Origins of Brandon College." *Manitoba History* 56 (2007) 22–31.
Mitchell, Craig. "National Law and Religious Liberty." In *First Freedom: The Baptist Perspective on Religious Liberty*, edited by Thomas White et al., 111–24. Nashville: B&H Academic, 2007.
Mol, Hans. *Faith and Fragility: Religion and Identity in Canada*. Burlington: Trinity Press, 1985.
Moody, Barry M. "The Maritime Baptists and Higher Education in the Nineteenth Century." In *Repent and Believe: The Baptist Experience in Maritime Canada*, edited by Barry M. Moody, 88–102. Baptist Heritage in Atlantic Canada Series 2. Hantsport, NS: Lancelot, 1980.
Moriah, Lionel Maurice. "Christian Discipline: Legalism or Covenant Responsibility." DMin Thesis, Acadia University, 1997.
———. *The Thirteenth Discipline: Formative and Reformative Discipline in Congregational Life*. Eugene, OR: Wipf and Stock, 2011.
Morrison, Barry D. "Tradition and Traditionalism in Baptist life and Thought: The Case of the Lord's Supper." In *Memory and Hope: Strands of Canadian Baptist History*, edited by David T. Priestley, 39–51. Waterloo, ON: Wilfrid Laurier University Press, 1996.
———. "What it Means to be a Baptist in the 1990s." In *In Search of the Canadian Baptist Identity: Essays Celebrating the 150th Anniversary of First Baptist Church*

Bibliography

Kingston, Ontario, 1840–1990, edited by G. A. Rawlyk, 29–45. Kingston, ON: Alex Zander Press, 1991.

Mouw, Richard J. "Reflections on My Encounter with the Anabaptist-Mennonite Tradition." *Mennonite Quarterly Review* 74 (2000) 571–76.

Mullen, Vesta Dunlop. *"I Believe in the Communion of Saints": Ordained Ministers of the Reformed Baptist Church, 1888–1966*. Old Shoals, IN: Old Paths Tract Society, 2006.

Murray, James S., ed. *"Through Him who Strengthens Me": Selected Shorter Writings and Sermons of Stuart Eldon Murray*. Baptist Heritage in Atlantic Canada 11. Hantsport, NS: Lancelot, 1989.

Murray, Taylor. "Against 'Historical Amnesia': A Bibliography of Baptists in Canada, 1990–2017." *Journal of Baptist Studies* 9 (2018) 77–113.

———. "Exodus to Exile: Independent Baptists in Nova Scotia, 1934–1939." *American Baptist Quarterly* 37.3 (2017) 282–303.

———. "From Exodus to Exile: The Early Fundamentalist Movement Among Maritime Baptists, 1930–1939." MA thesis, Acadia University, 2016.

Music, David W. and Paul A. Richardson, *"I Will Sing the Wondrous Story": A History of Baptist Hymnody in North America*. Macon, GA: Mercer University Press, 2008.

Ngursangzeli, Marina and Michael Biehl, eds. *Witnessing to Christ in North East India*. Edinburgh: Regnum, 1916.

Niebuhr, Richard H. *The Social Sources of Denominationalism*. New York: Meridian Books, 1960.

Noll, Mark A. *A History of Christianity in the United States and Canada*. Grand Rapids: Eerdmans, 1992.

———. *American Evangelical Christianity: An Introduction*. Oxford: Blackwell, 2001.

———. *The Rise of Evangelicalism: The Age of Edwards, Whitefield, and the Wesleys*. Downers Grove: IVP, 2003.

———. *Turning Points: Decisive Moments in the History of Christianity*. 2nd edition. Grand Rapids: Baker Academic, 2000.

Noll, Mark A., and Carolyn Nystrom. *Is the Reformation Over?: An Evangelical Assessment of Contemporary Roman Catholicism*. Grand Rapids: Baker, 2008.

Norman, R. Stanton. *The Baptist Way: Distinctives of a Baptist Church*. Nashville: B&H Academic, 2005.

Oliver, Pearleen. *A Brief History of the Colored Baptists of Nova Scotia, 1782–1953*. Halifax: African United Baptist Association of Nova Scotia, 1953.

Outler, Albert C. "The Wesleyan Quadrilateral in Wesley." *Wesleyan Theological Journal* 20.1 (1985) 7–18.

Parker, Calvin. *The Southern Baptist Mission in Japan, 1889–1989*. Lanham: University Press of America, 1991.

Parker, G. Keith. *Baptists in Europe: History and Confessions of Faith*. Nashville: Broadman, 1982.

Payne, Ernest A. *The Baptist Union: A Short History*. London: Carey Kingsgate, 1959.

Penner, James, et al. *Hemorrhaging Faith: Why and When Canadian Young Adults are Leaving, Staying and Returning to Church*. Toronto: EFC Youth and Young Adult Ministry Roundtable, 2012.

Perkin, James R. C. "The Baptists." In *What do Churches Really Believe!*, edited by David Morrison, 30–49. Dialogue: Christianity in Canada Series 2. Charlottetown, PEI: Strathmor, 1994.

Bibliography

Pierard, Richard V., ed. *Baptists Together In Christ 1905–2005: A Hundred-Year History of the Baptist World Alliance*. Falls Church: Baptist World Alliance, 2005.

Pinnock, Clark H. *Most Moved Mover: A Theology of God's Openness*. Carlisle: Paternoster, 2001.

———. "Systematic Theology." In *The Openness of God: A Biblical Challenge to the Traditional Understanding of God*, by Clark H. Pinnock et al., 101–25. Downers Grove, IL: IVP, 1994.

———. "The Modernist Impulse at McMaster University, 1887–1927." In *Baptists in Canada: Search for Identity Amidst Diversity*, edited by Jarold K. Zeman, 193–207. Burlington, ON: Welch, 1980.

———. *The Scripture Principle*. New York: Harper and Row, 1984.

Pitts, Bill. "Arguing Regenerate Church Membership: Baptist Identity in its First Decade, 1610–1620." *Baptist History and Heritage* 44.1 (2009) 20–39.

Pope, Robert., ed. *T & T Clark Companion to Nonconformity*. London: Bloomsbury, 2013.

Priestley, David T. "Canadian Baptist Historiography." In *Faith, Life, and Witness: The Papers of the Study and Research Division of the Baptist World Alliance, 1986–1990*, edited by William H. Brackney and Ruby J. Burke, 76–92. Birmingham: Samford University Press, 1990.

———. "Ethnicity and Piety Among Alberta's 'German' Baptists." *Historical Papers of the Canadian Society of Church History* (1994) 143–64.

Priestley, David T., ed. *Memory and Hope: Strands of Canadian Baptist History*. Editions SR 19. Waterloo, ON: Wilfrid Laurier University Press, 1996.

Project Ploughshares. "Canadian Churches say 'No' to Iraq War." Online: https://ploughshares.ca/pl_publications/canadian-churches-say-no-to-iraq-war/

Prokhorov, Constantine. *Russian Baptists and Orthodoxy, 1960–1990: A Comparative Study of Theology, Liturgy, and Traditions*. Carlisle: Langman, 2013.

Randall, Ian M. *Baptists and the Orthodox Church: On the Way to Understanding*. Prague: IBTS, 2003.

———. *Communities of Conviction: Baptist Beginnings in Europe*. Schwarzenfeld: Neufeld Verlag, 2009.

Rawlyk, G. A. "A. L. McCrimmon, H. P. Whidden, T. T. Shields, Christian Higher Education, and McMaster University." In *Canadian Baptists and Christian Higher Education*, edited by G. A. Rawlyk, 31–62. Montreal and Kingston: McGill-Queen's University Press, 1988.

———. "Baptist Distinctives: Are There Any Left?" In *In Search of the Canadian Baptist Identity: Essays Celebrating the 150th Anniversary of First Baptist Church Kingston, Ontario, 1840–1990*, edited by G. A. Rawlyk, 1–10. Kingston, ON: Alex Zander press, 1991.

———. "The Champions of the Oppressed?": Canadian Baptists and Social, Political and Economic Realities." In *Church and Canadian Culture*, edited by Robert E. VanderVennen, 105–23. Lanham, MD: University Press of America, 1991.

———. *Champions of the Truth: Fundamentalism, Modernism, and the Maritime Baptists*. Montreal: McGill-Queen's University Press, 1990.

———. "The Holiness Movement and Canadian Maritime Baptists." In *Amazing Grace: Evangelicalism in Australia, Britain, Canada, and the United States*, edited by George A. Rawlyk and Mark A. Noll, 293–316. Montreal & Kingston: McGill-Queen's University Press, 1994.

Bibliography

———. "J. M. Cramp and W. C. Keirstead: The Response of Two Late Nineteenth-Century Baptist Sermons to Science." In *Profiles of Science and Society in the Maritimes Prior to 1914*, edited by Paul A. Bogaard, 119–134. Fredericton: Acadiensis, 1990.

———. *Is Jesus your Personal Saviour? In Search of Canadian Evangelicalism in the 1990s*. Montreal and Kingston: McGill-Queen's University Press, 1996.

———. *Ravished by the Spirit: Religious Revivals, Baptists, and Henry Alline*. Kingston and Montreal: McGill-Queen's University Press, 1984.

———. *Wrapped up in God: A Study of Several Canadian Revivals and Revivalists*. Burlington, ON: Welch, 1988.

Rawlyk, G. A., ed. *New Light Letters and Songs, 1778–1793*. Baptist Heritage in Atlantic Canada Series 5. Hantsport, NS: Lancelot, 1983.

———. *The Sermons of Henry Alline*. Baptist Heritage in Atlantic Canada Series 7. Hantsport, NS: Lancelot, 1986.

Reid-Maroney, Nina. *The Reverend Jennie Johnson and African Canadian History, 1868–1967*. Rochester, NY: University of Rochester Press, 2013.

Reilly, Brent. "Baptists and Organized Opposition to Roman Catholicism 1941–1962." In *Costly Vision: The Baptist Pilgrimage in Canada*, edited by Jarold K. Zeman, 181–98. Burlington: Welch, 1988.

Reimer, Sam, and Michael Wilkinson. *A Culture of Faith: Evangelical Congregations in Canada*. Montreal and Kingston: McGill-Queen's University Press, 2015.

Renfree, Harry A. *Heritage and Horizon: The Baptist Story in Canada*. Mississauga, ON: Canadian Baptist Federation, 1988.

Richards, John Byron. "Baptists in British Columbia: A Struggle to Maintain 'Sectarianism.'" MA thesis, University of British Columbia, 1964.

Robertson, Allen B., and Carolene E. B. Robertson, eds. *Memoir of Mrs. Eliza Ann Chipman, wife of the Rev. William Chipman, of Pleasant Valley, Cornwallis*. Hantsport, NS: Lancelot, 1989.

Ross, H. Miriam. "Sharing a Vision: Maritime Baptist Women Educate for Mission, 1870–1920." In Changing Roles of Women within the Christian Church in Canada, edited by Elizabeth Gillian Muir and Marilyn Färdig Whiteley, 77–98. Toronto: University of Toronto Press, 1995.

Rudy, Adam D. "'The Ecumenical Movement, is it of God?': Central Canadian Baptist Identity and Ecumenism in the 1960s." MA thesis, McMaster Divinity College, 2017.

Runciman, Steven. *The Great Church in Captivity*. Cambridge: Cambridge University Press, 1968.

Stanley, Brian. "Baptists, Antislavery and the Legacy of Imperialism." *Baptist Quarterly* 42 (2007) 284–95.

Stanley, Brian. *The History of the Baptist Missionary Society, 1792–1992*. Edinburgh: T. & T. Clark, 1992.

Saunders, Edward M. *History of the Baptists of the Maritime Provinces*. Halifax, NS: John Burgoyne, 1902.

Schaff, Philip., ed. *The Creeds of Christendom*. 3 vols. Reprint, Grand Rapids: Baker, 1983.

Scott, J. Brian. "Brandon College and Social Christianity." In *Costly Vision: The Baptist Pilgrimage in Canada*, edited by Jarold K. Zeman, 139–63. Burlington, ON: Welch, 1988.

Bibliography

———. "D. R. Sharpe and A. A. Shaw: Progressive Social Christianity in Western Canada." In *Memory and Hope: Strands of Canadian Baptist History*, edited by David T. Priestley, 197–208. Waterloo: Wilfrid Laurier University Press, 1996.

Sealey, Donna Byard. *Colored Zion: The History of Zion United Baptist Church & The Black Community of Truro, Nova Scotia*. Dartmouth: Donna Byard Sealey, 2000.

Sharpe, D. R. *Walter Rauschenbusch*. New York: MacMillan, 1942.

Smale, Robert Richard. "For Whose Kingdom? Canadian Baptists and the Evangelization of Immigrants and Refugees, 1880–1945." EdD diss., University of Toronto, 2001.

Soper, J. Christopher, et al. *The Challenge of Pluralism: Church and State in Six Democracies*. Lanham: Rowman & Littlefield, 2017.

Stewart, Gordon. "Moulton, Ebenezer." In *Dictionary of Canadian Biography*, vol. 4, University of Toronto/Université Laval, 1979, n.p. Online: http://www.biographi.ca/en/bio/moulton_ebenezer_4E.html.

Strickland, Arthur B. *Roger Williams: Prophet and Pioneer of Soul Liberty*. Boston: Judson Press, 1919.

Studebaker, Steven. "Theology: A Question of Discipleship." *McMaster Journal of Theology and Ministry* 8 (2007) 9–22.

Sutherland, Martin, and Laurie Guy. *An Unfolding Story: A History of Carey Baptist College*. Auckland: Archer, 2014.

Sutherland, Martin. *Conflict and Connection: Baptist Identity in New Zealand*. Auckland: Archer, 2011.

Sutton, Matthew Avery. *Jerry Falwell and the Rise of the Religious Right: A Brief History with Documents*. Boston: Bedford, 2013.

Thiessen, Joel. *The Meaning of Sunday: The Practice of Belief in a Secular Age*. Montreal: McGill-Queen's University Press, 2015.

Thompson, Eugene M., et al. "The Status of Transcongregational Polity." In *Canadian Baptist History and Polity: The McMaster Conference*, edited by Murray J. S. Ford, 93–107. Hamilton, ON: McMaster Divinity College, 1983.

Thompson, Margaret E. *The Baptist Story in Western Canada*. Calgary: Baptist Union of Western Canada, 1974.

Thomson, W. Nelson. "Witness in French Canada." In *Baptists in Canada: Search for Identity Amidst Diversity*, edited by Jarold K. Zeman, 45–65. Burlington, ON: Welch, 1980.

Trites, A. A. "An Assessment of the Baptist/Reformed Dialogue." *Reformed World* 38.7 (1985) 385–95.

———. "New Brunswick Baptist Seminary, 1836–1895." In *Repent and Believe: The Baptist Experience in Maritime Canada*, edited by Barry M. Moody, 103–23. Hantsport, NS: Lancelot, 1980.

Underhill, Edward Dean., ed. *Tracts on Liberty of Conscience and Persecution 1614–1661, with an Historical Introduction*. New York: Burt Franklin, 1846.

Underwood, A.C. *A History of English Baptists*. London: Baptist Union of Great Britain and Ireland, 1947.

Vickruck, Vernon. "Middle Sackville Baptist Church (NB)." In *Maritime Baptist Old First Churches: Narratives and Prospects*, edited by William H. Brackney with Evan L. Colford, 27–39. Wolfville, NS: Acadia Centre for Baptist and Anabaptist Studies and the Editorial Committee of the CBAC Historical Committee, 2017.

Walker, James W. St. G. *Racial Discrimination in Canada: The Black Experience*. Ottawa: Canadian Historical Association, 1985.

Bibliography

Watt, J. H. *The Fellowship Story: Our First 25 Years*. N.p.: Fellowship of Evangelical Baptist Churches, 1978.

Watt, James T. "Anti-Catholic Nativism in Canada: The Protestant Protective Association." *Canadian Historical Review* 48 1 (1967) 45–58.

Watts, Michael. *The Dissenters: From the Reformation to the French Revolution*. Oxford: Clarendon, 1978.

Weber, Samuel F. "A Catholic Looks at Baptist Spirituality." *Baptist History and Heritage* 37.2 (2002) 61–72.

Weber, Timothy P. "Premillenialism and the Branches of Evangelicalism." In *The Variety of American Evangelicalism*, edited by Donald W. Dayton and Robert K. Johnston, 5–21. Eugene, or: Wipf and Stock, 1991.

Wells, J. E. *Life and Labors of Rev. R. A. Fyfe*. Toronto: W. J. Gage and Company, n.d.

White, Barrie. "Early Baptist Arguments for Religious Freedom: Their Overlooked Agenda." *Baptist History and Heritage* 24 (1989) 3–10.

White, James Emery. *The Rise of the Nones: Understanding and Reaching the Religiously Unaffiliated*. Grand Rapids: Baker, 2014.

Whiteley, Marilyn Färdig. "Crossing Boundaries: The Mission of Isabel Crawford." In *Canadian Baptist Women*, edited by Sharon M. Bowler, 113–31. Canadian Baptist Historical Society Series 3. Eugene: Pickwick, 2016.

Whitley, W. T. *A History of British Baptists*. London: The Kingsgate Press, 1992.

———. "Leonard Busher, Dutchman." *Transactions of the Baptist Historical Society* 1.2 (1909).

Winks, Robin W. *The Blacks in Canada: A History*. New Haven: Yale University Press, 1971.

———. *More than I Asked For: The Life of Isabel Crawford*. Eugene, OR: Pickwick, 2015.

———. "Prairie College, Rapid City, Manitoba: The Failed Dream of John Crawford." *Historical Papers of the Canadian Society of Church History* (2013) 82–97.

Wilson, Paul R. "A Mission Transformed: Fellowship Baptist Outreach in Quebec, 1953–1986." In *Baptists and Mission: Papers from the Fourth International Conference on Baptist Studies*, edited by Ian M. Randall and Anthony R. Cross, 189–204. Studies in Baptist History and Thought 29. Milton Keynes: Paternoster, 2007.

———. "Torn Asunder: T. T. Shields, W. Gordon Brown, and the Schisms at Toronto Baptist Seminary and within the Union of Regular Baptist Churches of Ontario and Quebec." *McMaster Journal of Theology and Ministry* 19 (2017–2018) 34–80.

Wilson Robert S., and Léon Thériault, eds. *Moncton's Religious Heritage: Historical Sketches of Moncton's Religious Congregations*. Moncton: Moncton 100, 1990.

Wilson, Robert S. "Atlantic Baptists Confront the Turbulent Sixties." In *A Fragile Stability: Definition and Redefinition of Maritime Baptist Identity*, edited by David Priestley, 149–69. Baptist Heritage in Atlantic Canada Series 15. Hantsport, NS: Lancelot, 1994.

———. "Baptist Convention of Ontario and Quebec." In *Religions of the World: A Comprehensive Encyclopedia of Beliefs and Practices*, 2nd ed., Vol. 1, edited by J. Gordon Melton and Martin Baumann, 288–89. Santa Barbara: ABC-CLIO, 2010.

———. "British Influence in the Nineteenth Century." In *Baptists in Canada: Search for Identity Amidst Diversity*, edited by Jarold K. Zeman, 22–44. Burlington: Welsh, 1980.

———. "'Conservative but not Contentious': The Early Years of the United Baptist Bible Training School." In *Revivals, Baptists, & George Rawlyk*, edited by Daniel

C. Goodwin, 133–52. Baptist Heritage in Atlantic Canada Series 17. Wolfville, NS: Acadia Divinity College, 2000.

———. "Patterns of Canadian Baptist Life in the Twentieth Century." *Baptist History and Heritage* 36.1 (2001) 27–60.

———. "Union d'Églises Baptistes Françaises au Canada." In *Religions of the World: A Comprehensive Encyclopedia of Beliefs and Practices*, 2nd ed., Vol. 4, edited by J. Gordon Melton and Martin Baumann, 2950–51. Santa Barbara: ABC-CLIO, 2010.

Wolffe, John. *The Protestant Crusade in Great Britain, 1829–1860*. Oxford: Clarendon Press, 1991.

———. "Anti-Catholicism and the British Empire, 1815–1914." In *Empires of Religion*, edited by Hilary M. Carey, 43–63. New York: Palgrave MacMillan, 2008.

———. "Anti-Catholicism and Evangelical Identity in Britain and the United States." In *Evangelicalism: Comparative Studies in Popular Protestantism in North America, the British Isles and Beyond, 1700–1990*, edited by Mark A. Noll et al., 179–97. New York: Oxford University Press, 1994.

Wright, Nigel G. *Free Church, Free State: The Positive Baptist Vision*. Milton Keynes: Paternoster, 2005.

———. *New Baptists, New Agenda*. Milton Keynes, UK: Paternoster, 2002.

Yarnell III, Malcom B. "Political Theology among the Earliest Baptists: The Foundational Contribution of Leonard Busher, 1614–1646." In *Freedom and the Powers: Perspectives from Baptist History*, edited by Anthony R. Cross and John H. Y. Briggs, 23–34. Didcot: Baptist Historical Society, 2014.

Zeman, Jarold K. *Open Doors: Canadian Baptists 1950–1990: Popular Addresses and Articles by Jarold K. Zeman*. Baptist Heritage in Atlantic Canada Series 12. Hantsport, NS: Lancelot, 1992.

———. "The Courage to be a Minority." In *Open Doors: Canadian Baptists 1960–1990*, 105–111. Hantsport: Lancelot, 1992.

Zeman, Jarold K., ed. *Baptists in Canada: Search for Identity Amidst Diversity*. Burlington, ON: Welch, 1980.

———. *Costly Vision: The Baptist Pilgrimage in Canada*. Burlington, ON: Welch, 1988.

Index of Subjects

A Declaration Concerning the Public Dispute, 104
A Declaration of Faith of English People Remaining at Amsterdam in Holland, 102
A Global Introduction to Baptist Churches, xi
A Short Declaration of the Mystery of Iniquity, 7, 150
A Short History of the Baptists, 2
A Sober Discourse of Right to Church-Communion, 103, 104
Aboriginal peoples, 45
Acadia College (Queen's College; Acadia University), 39, 40, 60, 64, 71, 74, 75, 169
Acadians, 13, 27
Act of Toleration, 133
African Americans, 160
African Baptist, 18
African Baptist Association of Nova Scotia, 35
African Churches, 72
African community, 17
Albigensians, 2
All African Baptist Fellowship (AABF), 19
Allinite Revival(s), 30, 31, 39
American Baptist, 12, 37, 40, 83, 135
American Baptist Missionary Union, 172
American Missionaries, 13, 33, 40
American Revolutionary War, 13
American Settlers, 13
American Tract Society, 51
American War for Independence, 31
Amherstburg First Baptist Church, 41
Amherstburg Regular Missionary Baptist Association, 41
Amillennialism, 65, 80
An Enquiry into the Obligations of Christians to Use Means for Conversion of the Heathens, 21
An Exhortation unto the Learned Divines Assembled at Westminster, 152
An Orthodox Catechism, 89
An Orthodox Creed, 87, 153
Anabaptists, 1, 3–5, 17, 85, 93, 97, 98, 101–3, 149
Anglican Church, 34, 93, 119
Anglican priest, 6
Anglicans, 4, 13, 38, 48, 69, 85, 136, 149, 161
Anglicized, 67
Anglophone, 5, 17, 19, 23, 161
Anglo-Saxon, 36, 67, 79, 169
Anti-Catholicism, 82
Antichrist, 82
Antinomian, 29, 134
Antinomianism, 28, 134
Apostle, 28
Apostle's Creed, 87
Arab Baptist Theological Seminary, 21

Index of Subjects

Arminianism, 16, 22, 30, 38, 80
Associationalism, 134, 139
Athanasius' Creed, 87
Atlantic Baptist, 128, 172
Atlantic Baptist Archives, xi
Atlantic Baptist Fellowship (Canadian Association for Baptist Freedoms), 62
Atlantic District of the Wesleyan Church, 26, 39
Atonement, 8
Australian Baptist, 14
Australian Commonwealth, 15

Baptism, 3, 32, 46, 62, 86, 88, 96, 98, 102, 103, 105, 106, 109, 110, 112–17, 119–21, 125–27; Believers Baptism, 35, 90–92, 102–4, 107, 109, 117, 121, 123, 124
Baptist Associations, 34, 35, 145–47, 173
Baptist "Basic Imperatives," 137
Baptist British settlers, 13
Baptist Church(es), 6, 7, 12, 21, 22, 26, 27, 32–34, 69, 87, 104, 130, 134, 138, 145–47, 152, 166
Baptist Community, 21, 33, 36, 124, 166
Baptist Congregation, 18, 23, 29, 33–35, 38, 41, 49, 71, 97, 103, 105, 108, 110, 111, 115, 117, 127, 130–40, 142–57, 166, 168, 174
Baptist Convention of Manitoba, 53
Baptist Convention of Nova Scotia, New Brunswick, and Prince Edward Island (also see Baptist Convention of The Maritime Provinces and Maritime Baptist Convention; and United Baptist Convention), 35
Baptist Convention of Ontario and Quebec (BCOQ; also see Canadian Baptists of Ontario and Quebec), 13, 53, 55, 58, 60, 61, 63, 64, 66, 70, 72, 73, 78
Baptist Convention of The Maritime Provinces and Maritime Baptist Convention (also see Baptist Convention of Nova Scotia, New Brunswick, and Prince Edward Island; and United Baptist Convention), 35
Baptist Denominations, 26, 92
Baptist Distinctives, 81, 94, 98, 100
Baptist DNA, 95, 157, 160, 167, 174
Baptist Ecclesiology, 100, 101, 104, 133
Baptist Family in Canada, xi
Baptist Federation of Canada (Federation Baptist; Canadian Baptist Federation; also see Canadian Baptist Ministries—CBM), 13, 60, 61, 63, 64, 68–73, 76, 143, 168
Baptist General Conference of America (Swedish Baptist Conference of America), 67
Baptist General Conference of Canada, 26, 68
Baptist Identity, 30, 92, 94–96, 171
Baptist in New Zealand, 16
Baptist in Nigeria, 163
Baptist in Quebec, 163
Baptist in The Maritime Provinces, 108, 135
Baptist Leaders, 38
Baptist Leadership Training School, 75
Baptist Life and Thought, x
Baptist Ministers, 21
Baptist Ministerial Association of Greater Vancouver, 59
Baptist Ministry, 34, 45, 46
Baptist Missionaries, 22, 37
Baptist Missionary Convention of Upper Canada, 41
Baptist Missionary Magazine of Nova Scotia and New Brunswick, 35
Baptist Missionary Society (BMS), 21
Baptist Missions, 46
Baptist Movement, 10
Baptist Pastor, 27, 73
Baptist Polity, 26
Baptist Preacher, 37, 72, 82, 113
Baptist Seminary, 74
Baptist Spirituality, 98

Index of Subjects

Baptist Theology (Theologian), 90, 92–94, 115
Baptist Times and Freeman, 23
Baptist Union, 13, 16, 137
Baptist Union of Australia, 14
Baptist Union of New Zealand, 15
Baptist Union of Scotland, 9
Baptist Union of Western Canada (BUWC; also see Canadian Baptists of Western Canada), 13, 54, 55, 59, 61, 66, 73, 75, 78
Baptist Union's Moscow Theological Seminary, 83
Baptist Vision, 91, 92, 96, 101, 130, 150, 175, 176
Baptist Women's Home and Foreign Missionary Society, 48
Baptist Women's Missionary Society of Ontario and Quebec, 43
Baptist World Alliance (BWA), 18–20, 23, 24, 154, 157, 163
Baptists of Canada, x
Baptists Through the Centuries: A History of a Global People, xi
Baptizing, 95; unbaptized, 123; re-baptize, 126 (also see Baptism)
Basis of Union, 137
Beaverhouse First Nation, 64
Believers' Church, 76, 81, 100, 102, 115
Benalto Baptist Church, 59
Black Baptist, 41
Black congregations, 35
Black River Baptist Association, 32
Bloudy Tenent of Persecution for Cause of Conscience Discussed, 11, 152
Bloudy Tenent Washed and Made White in the Bloud of the Lamb, 11, 152
Bloudy Tenent yet more Bloudy, 11, 152
Blunt-Blacklocke Baptisms, 117
Boer Territory, 16
Bolivian Baptist Convention, 20
Bolivian Baptist Union, 20
Book of Acts, 87, 132
Boxer Rebellion, 22
Brandon Academy, 51

Brandon College, 51, 59, 60, 64, 75
Brazilian Baptist, 20
Brethren, 86
Bridgeport Baptist Church, 51
British Baptists, 10
British Columbia Baptist Convention, 50
British Colombia Missionary Council, 59
British Empire, 9, 16, 82, 160, 173
British Territory, 13
Brown University, 58

Calvary Baptist Church, 49
Calvinism, 16, 22, 28, 30
Calvinists, Calvinistic, 3, 8, 30, 34, 48, 80, 85, 93, 118
Cambridge, 8
Cambridge University, 6, 11
Canada Baptist Foreign Missionary Society, 42
Canada Baptist Missionary Conference, 53
Canada Baptist Missionary Convention East, 42
Canada Baptist Missionary Society, 41
Canada Baptist Union, 41
Canada's (first) Bill of Rights, 164
Canadian Baptist(s), viii, 20, 21, 26, 57, 63, 69, 71, 72, 77–80, 84, 114, 120, 124, 125, 136
Canadian Baptist Archives, xi
Canadian Baptist College, 41, 44, 124
Canadian Baptist Federation (also see Canadian Baptist Ministries), xi, 62, 68, 69
Canadian Baptist Foreign Mission Board (Canadian Baptist Overseas Missions Board; also see Canadian Baptist Ministries), 60, 61
Canadian Baptist Foreign Missionary Society of Ontario and Quebec, 53
Canadian Baptist Historical Society, x
Canadian Baptist History, 58
Canadian Baptist Identity, 124

Index of Subjects

Canadian Baptist International Ministries, 76
Canadian Baptist International Mission, 61
Canadian Baptist Ministries (CBM; Federation Baptist; Canadian Baptist Federation; also see Baptist Federation of Canadian), xi, 13, 25, 61–64, 68–73, 76, 78, 95, 143, 163, 168
Canadian Baptist Missionary Society, 46
Canadian Baptist of Atlantic Canada, 26, 78
Canadian Baptist of Ontario and Quebec (CBOQ; also see Baptist Convention of Ontario and Quebec), 26, 78, 79, 95, 166
Canadian Baptist of Western Canada (also see Baptist Union of Western Canada), 26, 78
Canadian Baptist polity, 34
Canadian Baptist Seminary, 68
Canadian Baptist Theologian, 112
Canadian Baptist Tradition, 26
Canadian Baptist Youth & Family Team, 168
Canadian Christian community, 145
Canadian Confederation, 165
Canadian Council of Churches, 61–63, 146
Canadian Literary Institute, 44, 50
Canadian National Baptist Convention (also see Canadian Southern Baptist Convention), 26, 68
Canadian Pacific Railway, 40
Canadian Southern Baptist Conference (Canadian Convention of Southern Baptists, Canadian National Baptist Convention), 68
Canadian Southern Baptist Seminary and College, 69
Canterbury Baptist Association, 15
Cape Colony, 16
Carey Theological College (Carey Hall), 75
Catechism, 89, 128

Catholics, Catholicism, 20, 83, 87, 88, 167
Central Baptist in Victoria, 59
Central Canadian Baptists, 56
Certain Queries or Points now in Controversy Examined, 103
Chinese Baptists, 22
Christ (Jesus), 8, 81, 84, 86, 87, 96, 97, 101, 102, 104, 106, 111, 113, 115–117, 119, 121– 23, 125, 127, 131–33, 137, 138, 142, 144, 145, 147, 151–53, 159, 170, 176
Christ's College, 6
Christendom, 86, 117
Christian(s) Christianity, vii, ix, xi, 2, 3, 10, 15, 19, 21, 33, 75, 85–89, 97, 98, 100, 106, 113, 117–20, 123, 125–27, 130, 136, 142, 145, 148, 151–57, 161, 165, 169
Christian Churches, 87
Christian discipleship, 91, 136
Christian Messenger, 35
Christian Missionary Alliance, 86
Christian Sabbath, 55
Christian Restorationism, 86
Church Coercion, 96
Church Governance and Issues of Authority, 96, 97
Church Membership, 96
Church of England, 1, 3–11, 45, 86, 95, 115, 130, 149, 150, 151, 154
Church of Scotland, 131
Church Ordinances, 96, 125
Church Privileges, 123
Civil War, 8, 22
Clergy Reserves, 45
Cold War, 164
Commission of the Churches of Switzerland Associated for Evangelism, 45
Communion, 35, 41, 47, 81, 84, 88, 97, 100, 112, 113, 120–25, 127, 128
Communist, 22, 80
Concerned Pastors Group, 62
Confederation, 43
Confessions of Faith (Statements of Faith), 89, 96, 107

Index of Subjects

Congregationalist, 27, 53, 83, 85, 134
Conservative Baptist Association of Canada (Association of Regular Baptist Churches), 65
Conservative Baptists, 94, 169
Constitutional Act of 1791, 31, 45
Consubstantiation, 122
Continental Baptists, 18
Convention Baptists, 26, 172
Convention of Atlantic Baptist Churches, 78
Convention of Regular Baptist Churches of British Columbia, 59
Corinthians, 121; 1 Corinthians, 133
Covenant, 107
Covenants, 89, 90, 108, 112
Crandall University (United Baptist Bible Training School; Atlantic Baptist College; Atlantic Baptist University), 74–75
Credobaptist (non-credobaptist), 118, 120, 125
Creeds, 97, 131
Cultural Mosaic, 80

Dallas Theological Seminary in Texas, 78
Darwinism, 86
Differences about Water Baptism, No Bar to Communion, 103
Discipleship, 111
Dispensationalism, 65
Divine Assurance, 136
Divine Saviour, 32
Dominion of Canada, 72
Dutch Reformed churches, 16
Duck River Baptists, 94
Dutch settlers, 16

Eastern Orthodoxy, 83, 87
Ecclesiastical, 89, 90
Economic depression, 15
Ecumenical, 61–63, 68, 76, 81, 86, 88, 119, 146, 175
Educational institutions, 22
Edward VI, 5
Emmanuel Baptist Church, 59

English Baptists, vii, 3, 16, 135
English Baptists, 124
English Separatists, 4, 22, 24
Enlightenment, 154, 160
Episcopacy, 88, 95
European Baptists, 12, 17, 18
European Baptists Federation, 18, 21
European Baptists Fellowship (EBF), 18
Evangelical Fellowship of Canada, 63, 76–79, 145, 146
Evangelicals, 20, 56, 58, 62, 63, 73, 80, 82, 86, 93, 99, 167
Evangelism, 61, 66, 86, 99, 100, 162
Evangelistic, 45; evangelize, 176
Excommunicate, 93
Exeter Hall, 23

"Fact Concerning Brandon College," 59
Faith Baptist Church, 77
Federal Council of American Churches of Christ, 56
Feller Institute, 46, 70
Fellowship Baptists, 109, 172
Fellowship Baptist Young People's Association, 65
Fellowship of Evangelical Baptist Churches in Canada, xi, 26, 64, 66, 120, 138
Fellowship of Independent Baptist Churches of Canada, 65, 138
"Female Mite Society," 172
First Baptist Church, 51
First Baptist Church in America, 11
First Baptist Church of Winnipeg, 47, 48, 49
First Baptist Church of Victoria, 49
First Baptist Kamloops, 59
First Great Awakening, 12, 28
First London Confession, 123, 132
First Nation, 64
First Scandinavian Baptist Church of Winnipeg (Grant Memorial Baptist Church), 52
First World War, 67
Foot-Washing Baptists, 94
Foreign mission, 21

Index of Subjects

Foreign Mission Board, 36
Free Baptist, 39, 40, 53, 70
Free Baptist Conference of New Brunswick, 38
Free Baptist Conference of Nova Scotia, 39
Free Christian Baptist Conference, 38, 39
Free Christian Baptists, 38, 137
Free Christian Conference, 38
Free Will Baptist, 38, 39, 94
French and Indian War, 26
French Baptist, 71
French-Catholic, 82
French Nationalism, 71
French-speaking inhabitants of Acadia, 26
Fundamentalism, 22, 56, 60, 62, 66, 86
Fundamentalist, 57, 59, 60, 62, 64, 68, 74, 75, 78, 80, 86, 138
Fundamentalist Baptist Young People's association, 138
Fundamentalist-modernist controversy 58–60, 64, 68
Fyfe's Canadian Literary Institute, 47

General Association of Regular Baptist Churches, 77
General Baptist(s), 6, 7, 8, 9, 94, 104, 122, 123
General Court in Boston, 11
General Six-Principle Baptists, 94
German and Swedish Baptist, 67
German Baptist, 16
German Baptist Church (McDermot Avenue Baptist Church), 51
German settlers, 16
"Glorious Revolution," 4
Great Awakenings, 17, 86
Great Depression, 75

Haldimand Association, 135
Hard Shell Baptist, 94
Heaven and Hell, 87
Heidelberg Catechism, 89
Heimthal Baptist Church (Rabbit Hill Baptist Church), 52

Henry VIII, 5
Hemorrhaging Faith, 167
Heretical, 123, 148, 159
Heritage and Horizon, ix
Heritage College and Seminary, 78
High Church Baptist, 93, 94
Hindu, 170
Historical Black Institution, 72
Holy Scripture (Scripture), 25, 62, 84, 89, 97–99, 103, 110, 122, 131, 139, 144, 147, 150, 169
Holy Spirit, 87, 103, 106, 107, 132, 137, 144, 147, 153; Spirit of God, 102, 116; Spirit, 118, 125, 131, 156, 157
Home Mission Board, 36, 53
Horton Academy, 39
Hospitals, 22
Human rights Day, 157

Idolatries, 122
Immersion, 35, 62, 91, 117–20, 123
Independent Baptists, 69, 94, 142
Independent Congregations, 26
Independent Fellowship, 65, 66
Indigenous, 11, 34, 36, 43, 47, 48, 70, 79, 160, 168, 169
Indigenous Baptist community, 21
Indigenous Community Development, 169
Indigenous peoples, 45
Infant Baptism, 83, 85, 86, 88, 103, 104, 115, 117, 118, 125, 126
Inter-Church Committee on Protestant-Roman Catholic Relations, 61
Interdenominational church, 145

James Street Baptist Church (Hamilton), vii
Jamestown, 10
Jarvis Street Baptist Church (JSBC), 57, 58, 65
Jesus (Christ), vii, 3, 23, 29, 115, 116, 118, 124, 125, 128, 134, 136, 144, 145, 156–58, 160, 168
Jews, 149, 150; Jewish, 170
JLJ Church, 8, 117

Index of Subjects

John the baptizer, 118
Joseph's famous coat, viii

Kingdom of God, 64; Kingdom of our Saviour, 108

L' Eglise Baptiste Francaise, 71
L'Union d'Eglises Baptistes Francophones du Canada, 26, 70, 71
La Faculte de Theologie Evangelique, 71
La Grande Ligne, (also see L'Union d'Eglises Baptistes Francophones du Canada), 70
Lactantius, 159
Lake Baptist Missionary Society, 32
Last Supper, 121
Le Grand Derangement, 26
Liberalism, 22, 56, 57, 93
Local churches, 22
London Baptist Bible College and Seminary, 78
Lord, 97, 98, 113, 132, 147, 150
Lords supper, 123, 124
Lordship of Jesus (Christ), 98, 99, 147, 156; Lord Jesus, 116, 153, 160
Loyalists, 13
Lutheran, 3, 13, 85

Main Street Baptist Church, 77
Manitoba and North-West Convention, 48
Maritime Baptist Convention, 36
Maritime Baptists, 29, 30
Maritime Baptists' Foreign Mission Board, 37
Maritime Baptist missionary, 36
Massachusetts Baptist Missionary Society, 32, 33
Massachusetts Bay Colony, 11, 152
Mayflower, 7
McMaster's Board of Governors, 57
McMaster Divinity College, xii, 73, 74
McMaster University, 44, 51, 58, 60, 66, 73, 75, 84
Medieval world, 5, 23
Melvern Square Independent Baptist Church, 77

Mennonites, 7, 13, 85, 115, 117, 151
Mennonite Church, 7
Methodists, 13, 52, 69, 136, 161, 175
Methodist Revivals, 17
Methodist, 86, 119
Michigan Association of Free Will Baptist, 72
Middle Eastern Baptists, 21
Ministry, 28, 71, 72, 75, 145, 157
Missions (Missionaries), 9, 12, 15, 18, 20, 22, 32, 33, 36, 42–45, 47, 48, 51, 57, 72, 141, 157, 168, 172, 173
Modernism (modernists; also see liberalism), 56–60, 62, 64, 66, 68, 73, 74, 86
Montanists, 2

Napoleonic Wars, 16
National Baptist Everlasting Life and Soul Saving Assembly, 94
Nationalism, 93
Native Americans, 11
Native Baptists, 70
Natural Law, 157
Nelson colony, 15
New Brunswick Baptist Association, 34
New Democratic Party, 63
New Dispensation, 28, 29, 30
New England Baptists, 13
New Hampshire Confession of Faith, 47
New Light(s), x, 13, 28–30, 38, 39, 119, 134
New Testament, 2, 87, 91, 96, 115, 116, 118, 132, 138, 141, 154, 155, 157, 159
New Testament Baptist Church, 87
New Testament Church, 3, 83, 84, 86
New World, 82, 152
New York Baptist Missionary Society, 32
New Zealand Baptist Missionary Society, 15
Nigerian Baptist Convention, 19
Non-Anglophone, 17
Non-antinomian, 29
Nonconformist, 9

Index of Subjects

Non-denominational underground house churches, 22, 26
North American Baptist College, 67
North American Baptist Conference, 67
North American Baptist Divinity School (Edmonton Baptist Seminary), 67
North American Institute for Indigenous Theological Studies (NAIITS), 169
Northern Baptists, 12
Northwest Baptist Bible College (Northwest Baptist Theological College; Northwest Baptist Seminary), 77, 78
Nova Scotia Baptist Association (also see Nova Scotia and New Brunswick Baptist Association), 29, 35
Nova Scotia's Legislative Assembly, 74

Ohsweken Baptist Church (also see Tuscarora Baptist Church), 70
Old Testament, 141, 158, 159
Olivet Baptist Church, 50
Open/closed communion, 22, 53
Orangemen, 82
Ordinances, 125, 127, 128
Orserites, 39
Orthodox(y), 83, 87, 159, 163 orthodoxy (Religious), 151, 156
Oxford, 8

Pacifism, 3
Papal, Papist, Papacy, 6, 83, 84
Parish system, 101, 102
Parliament, 90
Parochial church, 101
Particular Baptists, 8, 9, 94, 103, 104, 117, 118, 123, 132
Particular Baptist Church, 8, 122
Particular Baptist Society for the Propagation of the Gospel Amongst the Heathen (also see Baptist Missionary Society), 9
Pastoral Theology, 58
Peace and Unity of the Church, 103
Pentecostal(s), 19, 69, 85, 87

Philadelphia Association, 12
Philadelphia Confession, 98, 154
Pietist, 17
Planters, 26
Plymouth, 10
Pope, 82, 96, 130
Post-Christendom, 15, 16, 164, 166, 169, 175
Post-Christian, 166
Post-Colonial, 166
Post-Conversion, 29
Post-Denominationalism, 166, 171
Polity, 90, 91
Postmodern perspectivalism, 91
Prairie College, 50
Premillennialist, 65, 78, 80, 93
Presbytery, 97
Presbyterians, 53, 85, 86, 131, 136, 161
Priesthood of all believers, 99
Primitive Baptists, 39, 87
Prince Edward Island Baptist Association, 35
Profession of Faith, 121
Progressivism, 64
Prohibitionary laws, 56
Prophetic, 29
Protestant denomination, 12, 99
Protestant Protective Association, 82
Protestant, Protestantism, 18, 20, 61, 82–84, 86, 88, 130, 148, 161, 166, 172
Protestant Reformation, 5, 122
Protestantism, 3, 5, 99
Proto-Baptists, 2
Providence Baptist Church in Monrovia, 19
Providence Church, 11
Puritanism, 14
Puritans, 6, 10, 149

Quakers, 1, 13, 85, 157
Quebec Act of 1774, 45

Rapid City Academy, 50
Reagent Road Baptist Church of Freetown, Sierra Leone, 18, 19
Red River Association, 48

Index of Subjects

Reform movements, 6
Reformation(s), 3, 4, 82, 86, 95, 101, 102, 122, 148, 155
Reformed Baptists, 39, 72, 85, 86, 131, 149
Reformed missionary, 45
Reformers, 5
Regent College, 75
Regionalism, 60, 93
Regular Baptists, 38–40, 53, 54, 77, 78, 94, 124, 137
Regular Baptist Convention of British Columbia, 68
Regular Baptist Missionary and Education Society of Canada, 58
Regular Baptist Missionary Convention, 53
Regular Baptist Missionary Convention of Canada West, 42
Regular Baptist Missionary Convention of Manitoba and the Northwest, 48
Regular Baptist Missionary Society, 59
Regular Baptist Missionary Union of Canada, 41
Regular (Calvinist) Baptist, 29, 35
Religious Peace; or, A Plea for Liberty of Conscience, 151
Religious freedom, 160
Religious hegemony, 25
Religious liberty, 160, 164
Renegotiating Faith, 167
Residential School System, 79
Revolutionary wars in American and France, 10
Revolutionary War with America, 14
Rhode Island's legal status, 11
Rochester Theological Seminary, 54
Roman Catholic Church, 20, 45, 81, 102, 130
Roman Catholicism, 6, 122
Roman Catholics, 9, 61, 69, 71, 82, 87, 136, 148–150, 155, 160, 172

Sabbath laws, 2
Sacraments, 113, 114, 124
Salvation Army, 69
Sanctification, 39

Schism, 39, 138
Schleitheim Confession, 102
Scottish Baptists, 31
Scottish Presbyterians, 9
Second Great Awakening, 12, 30
Second London Confession, 89, 97, 98, 118, 122
Second Vatican Council, 88
Second World War, 67, 69, 70
Sectarian 2, 8, 15
Secular, 88
Seminaire Baptiste Evangelique Du Quebec, 76
Seminary, 21, 39, 40, 75
Separate Baptists, 94
Separation of church and state, 98, 160, 162; church-state, 156
Separatist(s), 4–7, 11, 24, 104, 115, 147, 150
Separatist movement, 6
Separatist church, 7, 11
Separatist congregation, 6
Seventeenth-century Baptist theology and polity, 4
Seventh Day Baptists, 94
Shaftsbury Baptist Association, 32
Short Confession of Faith, 102
Six Nations Reserve, 34, 43, 70
Six-Principle (Arminian) Baptist church, 27
Social Gospel, 55, 56, 64
Social Justice, 158
Somerset Confession, 118
Soul Competency, 160
Soul Liberty, 160
South African Baptists, 16
South American Baptists, 20
Southern Baptist, 68, 69
Southern Baptist Convention, 12, 68, 158
Southern Baptist Ethics & Religious Liberty Commission, 163
Spanish Inquisition, 84
Spurgeon, Charles Haddon, 9
St. John River Valley, 13
St. Peter's Reserve, 48, 49
Stanley Avenue Baptist Church (Hamilton), vii

Index of Subjects

Swedish Baptist Conference of America (also see Baptist General Conference of America), 52, 67
Swedish Baptist community, 52
Synod, 97, 99

Taylor University College and Seminary, 67
Temperance Movement, 121
Ten Commandments, 11, 156
Test and Corporations Acts, 9
The Baptist Argus, 23
The Baptist Heritage, xi, 92
The Baptist Story: From English Sect to Global Movement, xi
The Canada Baptist Magazine and Missionary Register, 41
The Fundamentals, 57
The Gospel Witness, 58
"The Great Commission," 116
The Holy Exercise of a True Fast, Described Out of God's Word, 149
The Imaginative Hope Report: Revealing the Obstacles and Opportunities to Reaching and Engaging the Next Generation with the Gospel, 168
The London Confession, 8, 164
The Orthodox Creed, 122
The Pilgrim's Progress, 103, 123
The Toleration Act, 8
The Trail of Blood, 2
Thirteen Colonies, 6, 13
Thirteen Southern British Colonies, 27
Three-Self Patriotic Movement (TSPM), 22
Thurlow association, 135
Toronto Association as a Mission Field, 136
Toronto Baptist College (also see McMaster University), 44
Toronto Baptist Seminary, 58, 65, 76
Transcongregational, 147
Transdenominational Evangelical Seminary, 75
Transdenominational groups, 145
Transubstantiation, 82, 122

"Triennial Project," 69
Trinity, 87
Truth and Reconciliation Commission of Canada, 168
Tuscarora Baptist Church (Ohsweken Baptist Church), 34, 70
Two Seed in the Spirit Predestinarians Baptist, 94
"Two Kingdoms," 149
Tyndale University, 57

Underground Railroad, 41
Union Baptist Seminary, 40
Union of Baptists in Latin American, 20
Union of Regular Baptists, 64, 65
Union of Regular Baptist Churches of Ontario and Quebec, 58, 138
United American Free Will Baptists, 94
United Baptist, 53, 55, 56, 60–63, 70, 71, 73, 74, 77, 78
United Baptist Bible Training School (UBBTS; also see Crandall University), 74, 75
United Baptist Convention, 77
United Baptist Convention of the Atlantic Provinces, 70
United Baptist Convention of the Maritime Provinces, 13, 53
United Church of Canada, 53, 61, 69
United Empire Loyalists, 13, 26, 31
United Nations, 64
Universal Declaration of Human Rights, 157
University of British Columbia, 75
University of Chicago, 60
University of Manitoba, 51, 75
Upper Canada Baptist Mission Society, 41

Via Media, 4
Victorian gender roles, 37
Virgin birth, 87

Waldensians, 2
War of 1812, 40

Index of Subjects

Washington-Oregon convention of the Southern Baptist convention, 77
"Wentworth Statement," 62, 63
Wesleyan Church, 39
Western Christendom, 5
Westerners, 22
Wilberforce University, 72
Women in ministry, 22, 171
Women's Baptist Foreign Mission Society of Eastern Canada, 42
Women's Baptist Foreign Missionary Society of Ontario (West), 43
Woman's Baptist Missionary Union, 37
Women's Mission Aid Societies, 37
Women's Missionary Society, 64, 138
Woodstock Baptist Association of Vermont, 32
Word of God, 89, 122, 153, 176
Wowsers, 15

Index of Names

Aberhart, William "Bible Bill," 59
Alline, Henry, 13, 27–30
Andrews, Elisha, 32
Ansley, Thomas, 29
Apostle Paul, 37
Aquinas, 157
Augustine, 157

Baldwin, Thomas, 46, 47
Bates McLaurin, John and Mary, 42
Bellous, Ken, 64
Benedict, Mae, 73
Bennett, W. Arnold, 59
Bergh, Martin, 52
Binga, Anthony, 41
Blunt, Richard, 117
Bond, Mary Narraway, 38
Booker, Lucy, 48
Brackney, William H., 74
Brown, John Newton, 107
Browne, Robert, 104
Bunyan, John, 103, 123
Burke, J., 43
Burpee, Richard and Laleah, 36
Busher, Leonard, 151

Calvin, John, 3, 102, 149
Carey, Lott, 19
Carey, William, 100
Carter, Muriel Spurgeon, 73
Cartwright, Thomas, 149
Case, Shirley Jackson, 60

Chipman Handley, Thomas 29
Christ (Jesus), 8, 81, 84, 86, 87, 96,
    97, 101, 102, 104, 106, 111, 113,
    115–117, 119, 121– 123, 125,
    127, 131–33, 137, 138, 142, 144,
    145, 147, 151–153, 159, 170, 176
Clarke, John, 12
Claus, Seth, 43
Clyde, Alexander, 49
Collier, Thomas, 103
Cornell, Joseph, 33
Cotton, John, 11, 152
Coxe, Benjamin, 104
Crandall, Joseph, 29, 75
Crawford, Alexander, 31
Crawford, John, 50
Crawford, Jonathan, 43
Crawford, Isabel, 43
Crawley, A. R. R., 36

Daggett, J. B., 60
Davidson, Thomas, 46, 47
DeWolfe, Minnie B., 37, 172
Diefenbaker, John, 164
Dimock, Joseph, 29, 37
Dolamore, Decimus, 15
Douglas, Thomas Clement "Tommy,"
    63

Edwards, Jonathan, 9
Elgee, William, 73
Elizabeth, 5

Index of Names

Eschelmann, J. B., 51
Everett, Mary, 72

Faunce, William H. P., 58, 60
Feller, Henrietta, 45, 46
Fowler, Stanley K., 78
Frith, Mary Jane, 43
Fyfe, Robert Alexander, 44

George, David, 19, 29, 35
Grant, John Webster, 36, 61
Grantham, Thomas, 23
Grenz, Stanley J., 75

Hadassah, Ella, 72
Haldane, James, 40
Haldane, Robert, 40
Halykin, Michael A. G., 78
Harding, Harris, 29, 30
Harding, Theodore Seth, 29
Harris, Elmore, 57
Hebberd, John, 32
Helwys, Thomas 5, 7, 115, 116, 121, 150, 151

Inglis, Charles, 119

Jacob, Henry, 8
Jefferson, Thomas, 160
Jessey, Henry, 8
John the baptizer, 118
Johnson, Francis, 6
Johnson, Jennie, 72

Kendrick, Ariel, 32
King James I, 7
Kiffin, William, 103, 104, 117, 123
Kirkconnell, Watson ("Father of Canadian Multiculturalism"), 64, 163
Knollys, Hanserd, 104
Knox, John, 3

Lactantius, 159
Lanctin, Henri, 71
Lathrop, John, 8
Leland, John, 154
Longfish, Joseph, 43

Lore, Mary, 45
Luther, Martin, 3, 5, 102, 149

MacBain, W. H., 66
Maclaren, Alexander, 23
Manning, Edward, 29
Manning, James, 29
Marshall, L. H., 58
Mary, 5
Mason, Nathan, 27
McCoy, Tim, 79
McDonald, Alexander (Pioneer McDonald), 47, 48, 52, 75
McDonald, Lucinda, 48
McKee, S. J., 50
McMaster, William (Senator), 44
McNeill, Harris, 59
Mikolaski, Samuel J., 75
Miner, John, 34
Moore, Josephine, 73
Moulton, Ebenezer, 27
Mueller, F. A, 52
Murton (or Morton), John, 7, 151

Newton Prestridge, John, 23
Norris, Hannah Maria (Hannah Maria Armstrong), 37

Olivier, Henri, 45
Oncken, Johann Gerhard, 18
Orser, George Whitefield, 39

Payzant, John, 29
Pinnock, Clark H., 73
Pipe, Norman W., 66
Preston, Richard, 35
Prince, William Henry, 48

Queen Elizabeth, 4
Queen Mary (Bloody), 84

Rand, Silas Tertius, 36
Rauschenbusch, August, 51, 54
Rauschenbusch, Walter, 54, 55
Rawlyk, George, 31, 41, 56, 93, 125
Reekie, Archibald, 42
Rippon, John, 23
Roussy, Louis, 45, 46

Index of Names

Rowell, James B., 59

Sanders, Ella Kinney, 72
Scylla and Charybdis, 91
Servetus, Michael, 149
Shakespeare, John Howard, 23
Sharpe, D. R., 55
Shields, T. T., 57, 58, 60, 65, 66, 82
Sidey, J. J., 60
Spurgeon, Charles Haddon, 9
Stackhouse, W. T., 53
Stewart, Alexander, 43
Stobo, E. J., 57

Taylor, J. Hudson, 67
Tertullian, 159
Timothy, 141
Timpany, Americus and Jane, 42
Tupper, Charles, 37

Wesley, John and Charles, 8, 9, 28, 175
Whitefield, George, 9, 28, 82
Williams, Roger, 10, 152, 153, 156, 157, 160
Zeman, Jarold, 76
Zwingli, Ulrich, 3, 102

www.ingramcontent.com/pod-product-compliance
Lightning Source LLC
Chambersburg PA
CBHW051638230426
43669CB00013B/2347